READING WITH FEELING

SEMEIA STUDIES

Steed V. Davidson, General Editor

Editorial Board:
Eric D. Barreto
L. Juliana M. Claassens
Jin Young Choi
Katie B. Edwards
Jacqueline Hidalgo
Monica Jyotsna Melanchthon
Shively T. J. Smith

Number 95

READING WITH FEELING

Affect Theory and the Bible

Edited by
Fiona C. Black and Jennifer L. Koosed

SBL PRESS

Atlanta

Copyright © 2019 by Society of Biblical Literature

All rights reserved. No part of this work may be reproduced or transmitted in any form or by any means, electronic or mechanical, including photocopying and recording, or by means of any information storage or retrieval system, except as may be expressly permitted by the 1976 Copyright Act or in writing from the publisher. Requests for permission should be addressed in writing to the Rights and Permissions Office, SBL Press, 825 Houston Mill Road, Atlanta, GA 30329 USA.

Library of Congress Cataloging-in-Publication Data

Names: Black, Fiona C., editor. | Koosed, Jennifer L., editor.
Title: Reading with feeling : affect theory and the Bible / edited by Fiona C. Black and Jennifer L. Koosed.
Description: Atlanta : SBL Press, 2019. | Series: Semeia studies; 95 | Includes bibliographical references and index.
Identifiers: LCCN 2019036261 (print) | LCCN 2019036262 (ebook) | ISBN 9781628372601 (paperback) | ISBN 9780884144168 (hardcover) | ISBN 9780884144175 (ebook)
Subjects: LCSH: Bible—Criticism, interpretation, etc. | Emotions.
Classification: LCC BS511.3 .R436 2019 (print) | LCC BS511.3 (ebook) | DDC 220.601/9—dc23
LC record available at https://lccn.loc.gov/2019036261
LC ebook record available at https://lccn.loc.gov/2019036262

Printed on acid-free paper.

Contents

Abbreviations vii

Introduction: Some Ways to Read with Feeling
   Fiona C. Black and Jennifer L. Koosed 1

Affect and Animality in 2 Samuel 12
   Ken Stone 13

Echoes of How: Archiving Trauma in Jewish Liturgy
   Jennifer L. Koosed 37

The Affective Potential of the Lament Psalms of the
Individual
   Amy C. Cottrill 55

Public Suffering? Affect and the Lament Psalms as Forms
of Private-Political Depression
   Fiona C. Black 71

Prophecy and the Problem of Happiness: The Case of Jonah
   Rhiannon Graybill 95

The Disgusting Apostle and a Queer Affect between Epistles
and Audiences
   Joseph A. Marchal 113

"Not Grudgingly, nor under Compulsion": Love, Labor, Service,
and Slavery in Pauline Rhetoric
   Robert Paul Seesengood 141

"Though We May Seem to Have Failed": Paul and Failure in
   Steve Ross's *Blinded*
   Jay Twomey 157

Responses

Palpable Traumas, Tactile Texts, and the Powerful Reach of
   Scripture
   Erin Runions 175

The Rage for Method and the Joy of Anachronism: When
   Biblical Scholars Do Affect Theory
   Stephen D. Moore..187

Contributors..213
Ancient Sources Index..217
Modern Authors Index...222

Abbreviations

ABRL	Anchor Bible Reference Library
BA	*Biblical Archaeologist*
BAR	*Biblical Archaeology Review*
BCT	*Bible and Critical Theory*
BibInt	*Biblical Interpretation*
BSac	*Biblioteca Sacra*
BZ	*Biblische Zeitschrift*
BBR	*Bulletin for Biblical Research*
CBQ	*Catholic Biblical Quarterly*
ECL	Early Christianity and Its Literature
HAR	*Hebrew Annual Review*
HTR	*Harvard Theological Review*
Int	*Interpretation*
JBL	*Journal of Biblical Literature*
JFSR	*Journal of Feminist Studies in Religion*
JSOT	*Journal for the Study of the Old Testament*
JSOTSup	Journal for the Study of the Old Testament Supplement Series
JSP	*Journal for the Study of Pseudepigrapha*
LHBOTS	Library of Hebrew Bible/Old Testament Studies
Neot	*Neotestamentica*
NICNT	New International Commentary on the New Testament
New Lit. Hist.	New Literary History
RBS	Resources for Biblical Study
SemeiaSt	Semeia Studies
SymS	Symposium Series
USQR	*Union Seminary Quarterly Review*
VT	*Vetus Testamentum*
WUNT	Wissenschaftliche Untersuchungen zum Neuen Testament

Introduction: Some Ways to Read with Feeling

Fiona C. Black and Jennifer L. Koosed

This volume appears as part of what might now be described as a small but determined trickle of affect-critical readings in biblical studies. To date, there have been a few edited collections, a good handful of articles, and a few monographs devoted to engagements of the biblical text with affect theory. Yet, for many in biblical studies, it may not be entirely clear what all the fuss is about. What is the cause of those packed American Academy of Religion sessions sponsored by the Religion, Affect, and Emotion unit? Why have there been the excited conversations in receptions and hallways during the Annual Meeting, to which Jennifer Koosed and Stephen Moore refer (Koosed and Moore 2014b, 382)? Or, why have scholars from all over the world descended upon Lancaster, Pennsylvania, where trickles have been turned into streams at the Capacious Conference, a meeting focused on a wide range of affect-inspired inquiries, hosted by Millersville University? Affect-critical readings continue to grow in biblical studies, fed by the tributaries of other disciplines. *Reading with Feeling* seeks to provide an entry point to those who want to test the waters: What is affect theory, and how can it be used in biblical criticism?

Affect theory is a critically informed analysis of emotions and bodily sensations, one that resists any neatly bifurcated analysis of emotions as either interior states or as social-political conditions. Instead, affect theory refuses both essentialism and the linguistic turn that dominated so much of scholarship in the late twentieth century. Different disciplines bring different insights and emphases to affect theory, but religious studies has proven a particularly rich arena for the exploration of affects. Religions are not just sets of doctrine or theological tenets, intellectually affirmed. Religions move people in their bodies, sometimes alongside but sometimes counter to rational thought. Bodies touch, feel, sense, come together, and move apart as affects circulate. Affect theory gives us the conceptual tools to explore these movements, intensities, sensations.

Teresa Brennan (2004, 1) begins her book *The Transmission of Affect* in this way: "Is there anyone who has not, at least once, walked into a room and 'felt the atmosphere'?" In many ways, that is an ideal place to start: affects are tangible, palpable. They have shape, are transmissible, and leave traces. Brennan notes that affects are "material, physiological things," often understood interchangeably with emotions (but not feelings).[1] She adds, "affects have an energetic dimension. This is why they can enhance or deplete. They enhance when they are projected outward, when one is relieved of them.... Frequently, affects deplete when they are introjected, when one carries the affective burden of another" (6). Greg Seigworth and Melissa Gregg explain these material, energetic things as "forces or intensities." They elaborate: "affect is found in those intensities that pass body to body (human, nonhuman, part-body and otherwise), in those resonances that circulate about, between, and sometimes stick to bodies and worlds, *and* in the very passages or variations between these intensities and resonances themselves" (Seigworth and Gregg 2010, 1). Kathleen Stewart (2007, 3) further adds that affects are effectively viewed in the ordinary, the everyday, as "a kind of contact zone where the overdeterminations of circulations, events, conditions, technologies, and flows of power literally take place." They are the "things that happen," the "stuff that seemingly intimate lives are made of" (2). Finally, Sara Ahmed (2004, 4) wishes to draw our attention to how affects work to shape the surfaces of bodies (individual and collective), drawing the inevitable political consequences of such shaping to the fore.

These introductory snippets from representative voices in the field of affect theory show how the scholarship that engages affect theory attempts to articulate lived experience, as well as to appreciate how this experience leaves traces in the world. So, for instance, when Ahmed studies affects such as fear (2004) or happiness (2010a; 2010b), she painstakingly recounts and reflects on the somatic responses to and public interventions in such emotions. For example, fear lodges in the body and is felt through shud-

---

1. Brennan distinguishes *feelings* from *affects* by defining feeling as a "unified interpretation" of sensory information, i.e., "sensations that have found the right match in words" (5). This distinction proves helpful in her charting of the movement of affect. Different theorists configure the relationship between affect, feeling, and emotion differently.

ders and shivers. This fear opens up pathways that connect disparate times, places, and objects, creating webs of associations. Such relationships, created by and sustained by fear, can have consequences in the social and political world (Ahmed 2004). Happiness, on the other hand, is "sticky," it can be transmitted between subjects and objects for social effects, desired by some but oppressive to others (Ahmed 2010a; 2010b). Ultimately, like many, Ahmed understands emotion as emerging at the nexus of somatic, social, and political forces. She is interested in recording the workings of an affective archive (defined differently from Cvetkovich 2003; Ahmed 2004, 14), which she sees as a recounting of "how words for feeling, and objects of feeling, circulate and generate effects: how they move, stick and slide. We move, stick and slide with them" (2015, 15). As do the histories of the term *affect theory*. There have been a number of trajectories proposed to account for how affect theory came to be and to track its presence, such as Brennan's (2004, 4) three-way taxonomy for affect: ancient, Darwinian, and modern. However, the most common understanding posits a dual trajectory, whose "watershed moment" came in 1995 with the publication of two seminal essays: one by Eve Kosofsky Sedgwick and Adam Frank (1995) and the other by Brian Massumi (1995) (see Seigworth and Gregg 2010, 5; see also Kotrosits 2016, 7–11; Koosed and Moore 2014b, 383–85; Schaefer 2015, 23–34). Sedgwick and Frank picked up and redeployed the work of Silvan Tomkins, a psychobiologist who coined the term *affect* as it relates to biological systems of stimulus-response. Massumi picked up and redeployed the work of Gilles Deleuze, a French philosopher who (often in conjunction with Félix Guattari) was steeped in poststructuralist thinking but already resisting its focus on language alone.

For those interested in the biological or neurological bases of behavior, the Tomkins path perceives affects as the biological system that underlies emotion. These innate protocols are hardwired into our biology; when triggered, they bring matters to our attention and prompt us to act. One might see this clearly in Tomkins's well-known work on shame, and in Sedgwick and Frank's (1995) foundational essay on the same. Despite what may look like some kind of essentialism or biologism, Tomkins undermines the purported relationship between external stimulus and internal response. For Tomkins, the subject receives a stimulus which triggers neural firing, the density of which determines which affective system is activated. While Tomkins might seem to be touting a biological determinism, as he continues to describe the process and the outcome, it becomes clear that the simple on/off switch of the neuron does not result in any predictable affective arousal; "neural firing is virtually never a direct translation of some external event" into an internal state. In fact, in the words of Sedgwick and Frank (1995, 10–11), "it already itself reflects the complex, interleaving of endogenous and exogenous, perceptual, proprioceptive and interpretive—causes, effects, feedbacks, motives, long-term states such as moods and theories, along with distinct transitory physical or verbal events." In other words, despite what at first glance appears to be a thoroughgoing biologism in Tomkins's work, he resists any notion of one-to-one correspondences and a core self. Rather, firing neurons trigger arousals in different and irregular ways; identity is open, contingent, and subject to change. The basis of behavioral psychology, the clear link between stimulus and response, the clear distinction between external and internal, is vitiated in Tomkins's theory of affect. Affect theory therefore is not determinative but provides a way to think about the role of the body, particularly the role of drives that exceed cognition, in individual behavior and social interactions.

Deleuze, on the other path, is certainly interested in bodies, but he is not proposing anything as concrete as a theory of neurological systems. Affects for him are not primarily on/off switches, even those that fire in unpredictable ways; rather, as he writes with Guattari (Deleuze and Guattari 1987, 256), "affects are becomings." Affects are what preexist all perception, cognition, and language; they preexist even the bodily sensations that we experience as emotions. As Felicity Colman (2010, 11) summarizes, for Deleuze, affect is "a transitory thought or thing that occurs prior to an idea or perception. Affect is the change, or variation, that occurs when bodies collide, or come into contact." More than Tomkins, Deleuze analyzes the ways in which affect moves through communities and culture, shaping history and memory, establishing systems of knowledge and power (Colman 2010, 12). Perhaps, more comfortable with an embodiment that does not actually probe the body, many affect theorists are inclined to draw more on Deleuze than on Tomkins in their work.[2] However, as with everything in affect, any neat tracing of trajectories ultimately fails. Maia Kotrosits is particularly pointed in her critique of the two-source hypothesis (2016, 7–9; more on Kotrosits's understanding below), and Seigworth and Gregg (2010, 6–8) enumerate eight more

---

2. Donovan O. Schaefer (2010, 36–59), however, grounds his theory of affect and religion in Tomkins's understanding of bodily processes (what he calls "phenomenological affect theory").

approaches to affect. Tomkins and Deleuze could not be more divergent in terms of training, research, and interest. This brief tracing of the two trajectories they initiate illustrates how affect moves and sticks and slides in unpredictable ways, making a fulsome mapping of its scholarly history a challenge.

Many biblical scholars who use affect theory tend to follow the Deleuzian path, since it lends itself well to the facilitation of inquiry into the bodily, cultural, and political markers of emotion and sensation. The entry of affect-critical readings into the discipline has not, however, been entirely comfortable. The challenge of bringing affect theory to biblical studies moves beyond the typical conservatisms of our discipline. With its focus on feelings, emotions, pre-cognition, bodily intensities, and movements, affect theory seems the antithesis of what constitutes the matter and substance of "good critical biblical scholarship." French philosophers are not often invoked in discussions of the Documentary Hypothesis, in debates about the united monarchy, or in readings of the Petrine epistles. Even for biblical scholars generally open to theoretical engagements borrowed from philosophy and literary theory, affect's origins in psychology and its apparent biologism are suspicious. Discussing resistance to Tomkins in particular, Sedgwick and Frank (1995, 2) write: "You don't have to be long out of theory kindergarten to make mincemeat of, let's say, a psychology that depends on the separate existence of eight (only sometimes it's nine) distinct affects hardwired into the human biological system." What is affect theory, then, to biblical studies?

Just as a general history of affect theory is difficult to trace, so might would-be plotters of affect theory in biblical studies find it slippery and evasive. As Koosed and Moore (2014b, 387) note in their own introduction, "affect theory does not yield a 'method' in the standard biblical-scholarly sense of the term. There is not even a 'single, generalizable theory of affect,' as Seigworth and Gregg observe." Theories of affect are as "diverse and singularly delineated as their own highly particular encounters with bodies, affects, worlds." Erin Runions's article "From Disgust to Humor: Rahab's Queer Affect" (2008) is the first to bring affect theory into conversation with a biblical passage. Her article explores disgust and humor as they play off against each other in Joshua to destabilize colonial impulses, a pattern Runions thinks is reflected in contemporary US politics. Kotrosits (2016, 3) names Runions as the first biblical scholar to engage affect theory but also draws our attention to other important points in this history, such as Virginia Burrus's work on shame (2007), which has been formative, although not explicit in its use of affect theory, and Colleen Shantz's contributions (e.g., 2009), which use cognitive science and emotion in readings of New Testament texts. Kotrosits, in fact, offers a (corrective) lineage for affect theory in biblical studies, one that traces the work of many women scholars in the field as they talk to each other in coffee shops, attend each other's papers at conferences, and, of course, read each other's work. Affect compels our encounters; relationships shape our thinking; the personal drives our passions.

In addition to articles and introductions, several monographs have been published that explicitly use affect theory as their major theoretical framework (Kotrosits and Taussig 2013; Kotrosits 2015; Moore 2014 and 2017). Other works have also engaged affect theory in a much broader mode. The proceedings from the conference *Sexual Disorientations, Queer Temporalities, Affects, Theologies* (Drew University, Transdisciplinary Theological Colloquium) contains essays on biblical studies, theology, religion, and affect theory (Brintnall, Marchal, and Moore 2018). A second volume of essays from Drew, also the proceedings from a colloquium in 2016 on *Religion, Emotion, Sensation: Affect Theories and Theologies* has just appeared (Bray and Moore 2019). In addition, we hasten to add, there is a small but active corner of the field that has been working on feeling and sensation for some time. Some of these works are informed by theories and methods that also feed into affect theory. To cite our own scholarship, Fiona C. Black (1999; 2006; 2009) has been writing about affective texts and interpretation with respect to enamored readers of the Song of Songs in order to trace textual and interpretive *feeling*. Koosed (2006) has explored bodily organs in Qoheleth, noting the ways in which the skin of the texts themselves touch readers. For much of his lengthy career, Francis Landy (1983; 2015) has written about emotion and sensation in connection with imagery and the poetic persona. Leading up to his fascination with affect, Moore (1996; 2002) had been messing about with what revolts and disgusts and attracts in New Testament texts and the Song of Songs in a queer-critical mode for quite some time. There is also a lot of inquiry into emotion in biblical texts that is not affect-theoretical, but nevertheless is contributing in interesting and strong ways to our collective thinking about the subject (for example, the Society of Biblical Literature/European Association of Biblical Studies section on the Bible and Emotion; and Spencer 2017). Given this backstory, it is clear that affect-critical reading is not a sudden irruption ex nihilo; one wonders instead if it is less of a new thing in biblical studies than an intensity of interests in poetics, cultural-critical approaches, reception, and queer readings, explored in a new critical vein.

Excitement about the explanatory power of affect is rapidly growing in religious studies; this excitement has infected a growing number of biblical scholars who seek to read texts and understand histories with attention to affect. Our volume is a collection of essays that include both Hebrew Bible and New Testament texts and contexts; the authors engage a variety of different affect theorists and provide multiple entry points into this body of work. In this way, it is much like *Affect Theory and the Bible* (Koosed and Moore 2014a) but extended and in conversation with more recent works that have engaged affect. Ken Stone, for example, begins the volume with an essay grounded in Schaefer's (2015) innovative work on affect theory, animality, and religion. Schaefer argues for the centrality of bodies in any understanding or definition of religion. Religion is not just about language—doctrine, sermon, text—but also about communities, objects, and other bodies. By focusing on bodily sensations, religion becomes not something that separates and divides humans from other animals, but something that binds all of our animal bodies together. Once Stone establishes a shared affective economy between people and (especially) their companion species, he brings those insights to a reading of 2 Sam 12—the parable of the ewe lamb used by Nathan to confront David over the Bathsheba-Uriah affair. Stone's reading highlights the "circulation of women and animals as sticky affective objects" and hence uncovers a gendered power dynamic at work in the story and in how we read it.

The next three essays explore trauma as it manifests in the literature of lament; affect theory and trauma theory enrich each other. Jennifer L. Koosed's essay addresses the way in which phrases from Lamentations are found in Jewish prayers. Using Ann Cvetkovich's (2003) assessment of trauma, which cautions against a strictly medicalized understanding and instead recognizes how trauma creates new genres and cultures, Koosed argues that the Jewish prayer book is an "archive of feeling," transmitting and transforming the experience of war, loss, and exile. She considers Jewish prayer as an act of collective recovery, through the making of community that transcends time and space as well as the bringing of the physical, emotional, and intellectual together as the body prays. Fiona C. Black and Amy C. Cottrill read select psalms of lament, with Black stretching the limits of the genre to include psalms that struggle against traditional classifications. Cottrill's intention is to weigh the effectiveness of affect theory for the psalms. In so doing, she focuses explicitly on the body, the one who inhabits the "I" of the individual lament. Affect moves through bodies—in this way, it is not just about how someone feels but it is also about the social and political consequences of those circulating affects. Cottrill's political analysis is aided by Massumi's (2017) affect theory; Denise Riley (2005) and Sarah McNamer (2007; 2010) help her turn theory into a method for reading texts. Thus armed, she explores the "volatile, unstable, and multivalent experience" of praying Ps 109.

Black, with Cvetkovich (2012), asks about depression as a public feeling rather than an interior state and then integrates the lament psalms into a history of depression, with fear, pain, and (lack of) happiness being the three affects on which she chiefly focuses. Ahmed (2004; 2010a) and Riley (2005) are incorporated along the way as Black analyzes how lament psalms describe both physical and emotional wounds. These wounds are localized in individual bodies, but the community body is also subject to the pain of, and reflects, dislocation and colonialization. Affect theory provides a way to chart pain's movement (and all of the concomitant feelings that accompany it) in individual and communal bodies and assess the ways in which this pain enters the political sphere.

Rhiannon Graybill shifts the volume from trauma to unhappiness in her reading of the book of Jonah. Ahmed's *The Promise of Happiness* (2010b) provides Graybill her theoretical frame as she explores how unhappiness circulates among bodies—human, animal, plant, object—in the final chapter of Jonah. In this reading, Jonah emerges as a "melancholic migrant" and an "affect alien"—one who refuses to feel the happiness he should. As such, he troubles the affective politics of prophecy and challenges readers to do the same.

The three essays that address the New Testament all focus on the Pauline corpus. Joseph A. Marchal, Robert Paul Seesengood, and Jay Twomey all note that the Pauline corpus is an affective bounty. Not only do Paul and his imitators write letters laden with emotion, but also readers have a variety of emotional responses to his person and to his texts. For example, as Marchal notes, many readers of Paul feel disgusted by him. Even more, Paul's letters deploy the figure of disgust as part of his rhetorical strategy. The works of Ahmed (2004), Eugenie Brinkema (2014), and Sianne Ngai (2007) help Marchal take up disgust, how it both repulses and attracts, how it sticks to certain bodies (especially those deemed sexually perverse or ethnically-religiously deviant), how it creates and transgresses boundaries.

Seesengood, on the other hand, talks about love—the way in which service is constructed in the Pauline letters as a labor of love and how emotions become an essential part of economic exchange. Not only is this true for Paul, but it is enjoined on slaves as well. The labor of slaves is coerced but so is their affective orientation—they should embrace the virtues of work, they should *want* to work, or at least make it seem as if they do. Seesengood uses Ahmed (2010b) as well as current research on capitalism's service economy to further illuminate the entanglement of work, love, economics, obligation, and freedom in Paul's world and in our own.

The volume ends by pursuing failure. Twomey examines the figure of the failed Paul not just as a rhetorical strategy in his own letters but also how this figure manifests in other arenas, especially in the graphic novels of Steve Ross. Ahmed (2010b) and Cvetkovich (2012) prove again rich resources for thinking through biblical and contemporary texts, as do Lauren Berlant (2011) and Judith Halberstam (2011). Paul's visions of the end become sites of failure as he predicts an apocalypse that never comes; followers of Paul fail to achieve the better lives they were promised; some end their lives in meaningless suicides. In this, there is not just a critique of a certain kind of Christian optimism, but also of a related US fantasy of global power.

How are feelings represented in texts? How are the experiences of the body (happiness, depression, pain, trauma, disgust, etc.) produced by and made meaningful through culture? Affect is not just about individual and interior emotional states but always also about how emotion is a socially produced sensation; affects circulate body to body, produced by and producing certain political and cultural phenomena. As these essays demonstrate, affect readings intersect with feminist and queer theory, trauma theory, animal studies, cultural criticism, and reception history. If you are looking for a hermeneutical method that can be employed as a tool for extracting meaning on an inert (and even unsuspecting) text, then affect theory will disappoint. If instead you are open to encounters that move, stick, and slide, probing the meanings that manifest in the spaces between the words, tracing the circulation of power—in this case, the power of biblical texts—then this is the volume for you. Indeed, affect-theoretical readings lend themselves well in biblical studies to highly nuanced, interdisciplinary interpretations and for good reason: this is affect theory's own heritage. Open the book, touch its pages, fold them with your fingertips. Move your eyes across the words or let their sounds shake the bones within your ears, vibrate its membrane stretched tight. In any way you do it, read the essays we have assembled for you. Read them with feeling.

Bibliography

Ahmed, Sara. 2004. *The Cultural Politics of Emotion*. New York: Routledge.
———. 2010a. "Happy Objects." Pages 29–51 in *The Affect Theory Reader*. Edited by Melissa Gregg and Gregory J. Seigworth. Durham, NC: Duke University Press.
———. 2010b. *The Promise of Happiness*. Durham, NC: Duke University Press.
Berlant, Lauren. 2011. *Cruel Optimism*. Durham, NC: Duke University Press.
Black, Fiona C. 1999. "What Is My Beloved? On Erotic Reading and the Song of Songs." Pages 35–52 in *The Labour of Reading: Desire, Alienation and Biblical Interpretation*. Edited by Fiona C. Black, Roland Boer, and Erin Runions. SemeiaSt 36. Atlanta: Scholars Press.
———. 2006. "Writing Lies: Autobiography, Textuality, and the Song of Songs." Pages 161–83 in *The Recycled Bible: Autobiography, Culture, and the Space Between*. Edited by Fiona C. Black. SemeiaSt 51. Atlanta: Society of Biblical Literature.
———. 2009. *Artifice of Love: The Grotesque Body in the Song of Songs*. New York: T&T Clark.
Bray, Karen, and Stephen D. Moore. 2019. *Religion, Emotion, Sensation: Affect Theories and Theologies*. New York: Fordham University Press.
Brennan, Teresa. 2004. *The Transmission of Affect*. Ithaca, NY: Cornell University Press.
Brinkema, Eugenie. 2014. *The Forms of the Affects*. Durham, NC: Duke University Press.
Brintnall, Kent, Joseph A. Marchal, and Stephen D. Moore, eds. 2018. *Sexual Disorientations, Queer Temporalities, Affects, Theologies*. New York: Fordham University Press.
Burrus, Virginia. 2007. *Saving Shame: Martyrs, Saints, and Other Abject Subjects*. Philadelphia: University of Pennsylvania Press.
Colman, Felicity J. 2010. "Affect." Pages 11–14 in *The Deleuze Dictionary*. Edited by Adrian Parr. rev. ed. Edinburgh: Edinburgh University Press.
Cvetkovich, Ann. 2003. *An Archive of Feelings: Trauma, Sexuality and Lesbian Public Cultures*. Durham, NC: Duke University Press.
———. 2012. *Depression: A Public Feeling*. Durham, NC: Duke University Press.
Deleuze, Gilles, and Félix Guattari. 1987. *A Thousand Plateaus: Capitalism and Schizophrenia*. Minneapolis: University of Minnesota Press.

Halberstam, Judith. 2011. *The Queer Art of Failure.* Durham, NC: Duke University Press.
Koosed, Jennifer. 2006. *Permutations of Qohelet: Reading the Body in the Book.* New York: T&T Clark.
Koosed, Jennifer L., and Stephen D. Moore, eds. 2014a. *Affect Theory and the Bible. BibInt* 22.4–5.
———. 2014b. "Introduction: From Affect to Exegesis." *BibInt* 22.4–5:381–87.
Kostrosits, Maia, and Hal Taussig. 2013. *Re-reading the Gospel of Mark Amidst Pain and Trauma.* New York: Palgrave Macmillan.
Kotrosits, Maia. 2015. *Rethinking Early Christian Identity: Affect, Violence, and Belonging.* Minneapolis: Fortress.
———. 2016. *How Things Feel: Affect Theory, Biblical Studies, and the (Im) Personal.* Leiden: Brill.
Landy, Francis. 1983. *Paradoxes of Paradise: Identity and Difference in the Song of Songs.* Sheffield: Almond Press.
———. 2015. "Between the Words I Write." Pages 361–75 in *History, Memory, Hebrew Scriptures: A Festschrift for Ehud Ben Zvi.* Edited by Ian Wilson and Diana Edelman. Winona Lake, IN: Eisenbrauns.
Massumi, Brian. 1995. "The Autonomy of Affect." *Cultural Critique* 31:83–109.
———. 2017. *Politics of Affect.* Cambridge: Polity Press.
McNamer, Sarah. 2007. "Feeling." Pages 241–57 in *Oxford Twenty-First Century Approaches to Literature: Middle English.* Edited by Paul Strohm. Oxford: Oxford University Press.
———. 2010. *Affective Meditation and the Invention of Medieval Compassion.* Philadelphia: University of Pennsylvania Press.
Moore, Stephen D. 1996. *God's Gym: Divine Male Bodies of the Bible.* New York: Routledge.
———. 2002. *God's Beauty Parlor: And Other Queer Spaces in and around the Bible.* Palo Alto, CA: Stanford University Press.
———. 2014. *Untold Tales from the Book of Revelation: Sex and Gender, Empire and Ecology.* RBS 79. Atlanta: SBL Press.
———. 2017. *Gospel Jesuses and Other Nonhumans: Biblical Criticism Post-poststructuralism.* SemeiaSt 89. Atlanta: SBL Press.
Ngai, Sianne. 2007. *Ugly Feelings.* Cambridge: Harvard University Press.
Riley, Denise 2005. *Impersonal Passion: Language as Affect.* Durham, NC: Duke University Press.

Runions, Erin. 2008. "From Disgust to Humour: Rahab's Queer Affect." *Postscripts* 4:41–69.

Schaefer, Donovan O. 2015. *Religious Affects: Animality, Evolution and Power.* Durham, NC: Duke University Press.

Sedgwick, Eve Kosofsky, and Adam Frank. 1995. "Shame in the Cybernetic Fold: Reading Silvan Tomkins." Pages 1–28 in *Shame and Its Sisters: A Silvan Tomkins Reader.* Edited by Eve Kosofsky Sedgwick and Adam Frank. Durham, NC: Duke University Press.

Seigworth, Gregory J., and Melissa Gregg. 2010. "An Inventory of Shimmers." Pages 1–25 in *The Affect Theory Reader.* Edited by Melissa Gregg and Gregory J. Seigworth. Durham, NC: Duke University Press.

Shantz, Colleen. 2009. *Paul in Ecstasy: The Neurobiology of the Apostle's Life and Thought.* Cambridge: Cambridge University Press.

Stewart, Kathleen. 2007. *Ordinary Affects.* Durham, NC: Duke University Press.

Spencer, F. Scott, ed. 2017. *Mixed Feelings and Vexed Passions: Exploring Emotions in Biblical Literature.* RBS 90. Atlanta: SBL Press.

Affect and Animality in 2 Samuel 12

Ken Stone

In his remarkable book *Religious Affects*, Donovan Schaefer makes a compelling case for the significance of affect theories for the disciplines of religious studies. Building in part on materialist theories of religion that highlight bodily practices more than symbols and texts (e.g., Vásquez 2011), Schaefer (2015, 10) suggests that religious studies has fallen prey to a "linguistic fallacy" that overemphasizes "language as the medium of power and the primary analytic focus of religious studies." This linguistic fallacy leads to a "myth that where bodies go is fundamentally determined by language" (117). Without denying the importance of worldview analysis, ideology critique, or social-linguistic construction, Schaefer (2015, 3) argues that religions should also be understood in terms of "the way things feel, the things we want, the way our bodies are guided through thickly textured, magnetized worlds … the way our bodies flow into relationships—loving or hostile—with other bodies" and with "clustered material forms, aspects of our embodied life, such as other bodies, food, community, labor, movement, music, sex, natural landscapes, architecture, and objects." Affects are not simply personal feelings, on the one hand, or means for accomplishing supposedly more important ideological, political, or religious ends, on the other hand. They are forces of their own, which move through and among us. They are channels for power, which "makes bodies move" (35), and they are "queer little gods" (a phrase that Schaefer borrows from, e.g., Sedgwick 2011, 42–68; Sedgwick and Snediker 2008), which "choreograph our bodies in relation to power" through multiple spaces and practices, including those we associate with religion (35).

Schaefer's project of expanding "what gets called religion" (207) is not only built upon theories of affect, it also entails significant engagement with the growing interdisciplinary literature in animal studies. Indeed,

Schaefer opens and closes his book by recalling famous descriptions from Jane Goodall of a "dance" (Goodall 1999, 189) or "ritual" (Goodall 1990, 202) that she watched chimpanzees perform when they arrived at an African waterfall or at the beginning of a rainstorm. These performances led Goodall to speculate that such emotional reactions to natural forces, reactions that she later came to associate with "primate spirituality" (Goodall 2005), might undergird the early emergence of religion among humans. Human religion too, after all, is a kind of primate spirituality. Schaefer, in turn, rearticulates these types of suggestions from Goodall and others (e.g., Guthrie 2002; Harrod 2014) with his affective approach to religion. If our understanding of religion is no longer grounded narrowly in language, social construction, and ideology, there is less justification for considering religion a uniquely human phenomenon. Schaefer proposes in fact that "a turn to affect can help us better understand human religion as animal." Religion may be "something that puts us in continuity with other animal bodies rather than something that sets us apart" (Schafer 2015, 3; cf. Schafer 2012). Here, Schaefer is encouraging his readers to rethink our definitions of religion in light of one of the most significant contributions of contemporary animal studies: the blurring or dissolution of boundaries between humans and other animals (cf. Calarco 2015; Gross 2015). There are, to be sure, many different types and expressions of religions, just as there are many types of animal bodies and bodily affects. But "animal religion," Schaefer (2015, 199) suggests, whether found among humans, chimpanzees, or other animals, is "an affective economy" that "emerges out of an embodied, affective response to the things of power in the world, a dance of emotions, sensations, bodies, compulsions, and memories."

I do not evaluate Schaefer's theory of religion; I rather explore the usefulness of that theory's conjunction between affect and animality for the interpretation of religious texts. There is, to be sure, some irony in using theoretical work to read literary texts when that work suggests that we have placed too much emphasis on language and symbols. Nevertheless, relationships between affect and animality have recently been taken up to interpret other bodies of literature (e.g., Chez 2017). Thus, I suggest that recognition of such relationships may also shed light on a particular textual scene that is sometimes described by scholars in terms of its emotional dynamics. By taking yet another look at 2 Sam 12, a text that has long affected me as a reader of biblical texts (see, e.g., Stone 1996, 93–106; 2005, 73–77), I therefore merge two currents in biblical scholarship that might otherwise be understood as having little to do with one another (but see Koosed 2014b for an earlier example). First, and most obviously, like other essays in this volume and several additional contributions elsewhere (e.g., Runions 2011a; 2011b; Koosed and Moore 2014; Kotrosits 2015; 2016), I find myself enlivened by the possibility that affect and affect theories might allow us to see biblical literature in new ways. Here my views on affect are influenced not only by Schaefer, but also by Sara Ahmed, from whom Schaefer borrows the phrase "affective economies" (e.g., Ahmed 2004c, 42–61; 2004a) and who, like Schaefer, explores the political dimensions of such economies. Concurrently, I take seriously the relevance for biblical interpretation of contemporary animal studies (see also Stone 2017; 2016a; 2016b; Koosed 2014a; Moore 2014). By attaching these ways of reading to one another rather than keeping them apart, I anticipate that new light can be shed on one of the Bible's most frequently read narrative texts.

Emotions and Bodies in 2 Samuel 12

In 2 Sam 11, David has sexual relations with Bathsheba, the wife of Uriah. To cover his transgression after Bathsheba becomes pregnant and Uriah refrains from having intercourse with her, David arranges for Uriah to be killed. Bathsheba laments for Uriah (11:26); but when her mourning is complete, David brings Bathsheba to his house, where she bears a son (11:27). YHWH, however, is displeased with David's actions and sends the prophet Nathan to confront him, which Nathan does at the beginning of chapter 12. Although the story is well-known, this confrontation and portions of its aftermath are important enough for my argument to quote here:

> [Nathan] went in before [David] and said to him, "There were two men in one city, one rich and one poor. The rich man had very many flocks and cattle, but the poor man had only one small ewe lamb that he bought. He took care of it and it grew up with him and his children. Together with him it would eat from his morsel of bread and drink from his cup and lie on his bosom. It was like a daughter to him. A traveler came to the rich man, but he was unwilling to take anything from his own flocks or cattle to prepare something for the man on a journey who came to him. So he took the lamb of the poor man and he prepared it for the man who came to him." Now David became enraged at the man, and he said to Nathan, "As YHWH lives, the man who did this is a son of death! The lamb he took, he should pay for four times, because he did this thing and did not show any pity!" But Nathan said to David, "You are the man!

> Thus says YHWH the god of Israel, 'I anointed you as king over Israel and I rescued you from the hand of Saul. I gave to you the house of your master and the women of your master into your bosom, and I gave you the house of Israel and Judah. And if that were too little, I would have given you that much more. Why did you treat with contempt the word of YHWH, to do what is evil in his eyes? Uriah the Hittite you struck down with the sword, and his woman you took for your woman, and killed him with the sword of the Ammonites. And now the sword will never depart from your house, because you treated me with contempt and took the woman of Uriah the Hittite to be your woman.' Thus says YHWH, 'Now look, I'm going to raise up for you trouble from your house, and I will take your women before your eyes and give them to your enemy, and he will lie with your women in the sight of this very sun. For you did it in secret, but I will do this thing before all Israel and before the sun.'" (12:1–12)[1]

At this point David acknowledges his transgression. Nathan tells him, however, that God will not kill David but will kill his son. When the child is subsequently born and then becomes sick,

> David pleaded with God for the boy. David fasted, and he went in and stayed all night and lay on the ground. The elders of his house stood over him to get him to rise from the ground. But he was unwilling, and he did not eat food with them. (12:16–17)

In light of David's actions, these elders are understandably concerned when the child does die. After all, if David was so upset while his son was still alive, how distraught might he become when he learns that the boy is dead? They worry that surely he will "do something bad" (12:18). As it turns out, however, David doesn't respond this way at all. To the contrary, upon learning of his son's death,

> David got up from the ground, and washed, and anointed himself, and changed his clothes. He went to the house of YHWH and worshiped. Then he went to his own house. When he asked, they put food in front of him and he ate. (12:20)

When his servants ask why he is reacting so differently now than he did while his son was alive, David observes that, while the boy was alive, there

---

1. Except where otherwise noted, translations from Hebrew to English are my own.

was still a chance God would save him. He thought that perhaps "YHWH will show favor to me" (12:22). Now that the child is dead, however, fasting will not bring him back. David then goes to comfort Bathsheba. After he has sexual intercourse with her, she gives birth to another son, Solomon, whom God loved (12:24).

Here we have a story suffused with feelings. Quite apart from the contemporary surge of theoretical interest in affect, readers have recognized the importance in 2 Sam 12 of what Jeremy Schipper (2007, 386), for example, refers to as David's "emotional display." Stuart Lasine (1984), too, frames the story in terms of what he calls "David's topsy-turvy emotions." Lasine's discussion of those emotions is particularly interesting in this context because, in addition to placing more emphasis on David's emotions than most studies of the story, Lasine acknowledges at least implicitly the importance of interpreting affect in relation to animality when reading 2 Sam 12, an acknowledgment I return to in a moment. Yet Lasine's "analysis of David's emotions" (102), which represents David's narrative in part as a "psychological portrait" (120) of a king characterized by "emotionalism" (108), "emotional imbalance" (109–10), and "continued emotional instability" (114), also replicates a widespread understanding of emotions as psychological phenomena existing inside individuals who may express them externally. And Lasine is not alone among scholars in bringing this understanding of emotion to bear on David's story. Shimon Bar-Efrat (1989, 58), for example, in his study of characterization in biblical narrative, includes the reference to David's anger in 2 Sam 12:5 on a short list of passages that are said to shed light on David's inner states.

Rather than reconstruct such inner states here, I reconsider 2 Sam 12 in terms of what we might call, borrowing from Sara Ahmed, "the sociality of emotions." In *The Cultural Politics of Emotion*, Ahmed (2004c, 8), like other affect theorists, rejects the psychologizing notion of what she calls "emotion as interiority." This understanding of emotion rests upon an "'inside out' model," according to which "I have feelings, which then move outwards towards objects and others." Both Lasine and Bar-Efrat appear to presuppose some version of this view of emotions in their interpretation of David's story, and it seems likely that other readers do as well. Ahmed, however, rejects this individualistic understanding of interior emotion. Yet she also takes some distance from sociological (e.g., Durkheimian) or anthropological versions of "an 'outside in' model," according to which "emotions are assumed to *come from without and move inward*" (9, emphasis original; cf. Ahmed 2004b, 28). In this model, emotions are still understood as "something that 'we have'" (2004c, 10), even though we obtain them from a sociological outside.

Rather than conceptualizing emotions as moving inside out or outside in, or belonging to individuals, Ahmed prefers to emphasize the "circulation" of "objects of emotion." Emotions, which "are after all moving," move about in part because their objects move about: "Such objects become sticky, or saturated with affects, as sites of personal and social tension." As objects and emotions move around, moreover, they provide sites for "attachment." Their movement "connects bodies to other bodies: attachment takes place through movement, through being moved by the proximity of others." But this "circulation of objects of emotion involves the transformation of others into objects of feeling" (11). As the word *transformation* indicates, we should not think of the movement of objects as a circulation of essentialized, substantive, unchanging entities. Rather, attachment and emotion in Ahmed's view "create the very surfaces and boundaries that allow all kinds of objects to be delineated. The objects of emotion take shape as effects of circulation" (10). "Emotions are relational," then, involving subjects, objects, and contacts with objects (8). If our encounter with an object generates feeling or emotion, that is partly because it has made an impression on us. Such an impression may involve feeling, perception, cognition, or belief; but it also depends upon the object. As Ahmed notes, "*We need to remember the 'press' in an impression. It allows us to associate the experience of having an emotion with the very affect of one surface upon another, an affect that leaves its mark or trace*" (2004c, 6, emphasis original; cf. Ahmed 2004b, 29–30). Affect involves the various ways in which our bodies are touched by other objects, including other bodies.

And here, significantly, Ahmed gives an animal illustration. Drawing on an example from the literature of psychology, Ahmed discusses the fear that may appear when a child encounters a bear, perhaps causing the child to run. The scene is not uncomplicated (as Ahmed acknowledges), since we are unsure what influences may have led to the particular image of bears that the child has, or even whether every child will be afraid of the bear at all. Cultural influence does play a role here. But to the extent that fear moves the child, the emotionality of the scene is relational: "It is not that the bear is fearsome 'on its own,' as it were. It is fearsome *to* someone or somebody. So fear is not in the child, let alone in the bear, but is a matter of how child and bear come into contact" (2004c, 7, emphasis original). The child encounters the bear, and the bear "leaves an impression" (8). A feeling moves the child in the context of encounter, and the child's body moves as well. With this reflection on the press of two animal bodies, then, Ahmed, like Schaefer, brings together affect and animality.

Two animal bodies also press, of course, in 2 Sam 12. The ewe lamb in Nathan's parable does not only live with the poor man and his children. She does not simply "eat from his morsel of bread and drink from his cup." She also "lies on his bosom" (12:3). We might translate this, with Kyle McCarter (1984, 292), as "lie in his embrace"; but in either case, we are referring to contact between bodies. To be sure, other bodies are pressed in this story as well. By the time Nathan comes to David at the beginning of 2 Sam 12, David has had sexual relations with Bathsheba. After she has mourned for Uriah, David brings her to his house, and once their son dies, David comforts Bathsheba and has sexual relations with her again. A kind of parallel is set up, then, between the lamb who lies on the poor man's bosom in Nathan's story and the woman who lies with the king in the narrative of 2 Samuel.

Language about lying on a bosom is used multiple times in the Hebrew Bible to represent several types of close physical relations between humans, including sexual relations (e.g., Abraham and Hagar in Gen 16:5). Because Nathan's story is told in the context of David's sexual intercourse with Bathsheba, and because Nathan subsequently uses the same language about "bosom" or "embrace" to describe the way in which God had previously given the women of other men to David (12:8), we may be tempted to focus solely on the sexual dimensions of the language when interpreting the parable. The sexual connotations are certainly present in the story, and the language about eating and drinking contributes to them (cf. Fewell and Gunn 1993, 159–60; Stone 2005, 93–95). Given the conjunction in 2 Sam 12 between David's sexual acquisition of Bathsheba and the rich man's acquisition of the lamb for food, moreover, we might characterize this story in terms of Derrida's language about "carnivorous virility" and "carnophallogocentrism" (Derrida 1995, 280). Derrida uses these terms to call attention to a symbolic schema in Western culture that links the subordination of women, for example as objects of sex, to the subordination of animals, for example as objects of carnivorous eating. The roles that both sex and eating play in 2 Sam 12 indicate that the text's representation of animality relies upon just such a schema to associate Nathan's parable, where sex is not mentioned explicitly, with David's sexual actions. But the language used to refer to the lamb lying "on his bosom" or "in his embrace" can also be used, for example, for maternal relations. Thus Naomi takes the son of Ruth and puts him "on her bosom" when she become his nurse (Ruth 4:16). The woman who accidentally kills her infant son in 1 Kgs 3 takes the son of the woman who lives with her and puts him to her own bosom while placing her own dead son at the bosom of the other mother (3:20). When Elijah revives the son of a widow, he takes that son from his mother's bosom before crying out to God and stretching himself over the boy (1 Kgs 17:19). The infants who die for lack of food and drink in Lam 2 do so while lying at the bosom of their mothers (2:12). In all of these contexts, maternal relationships are emphasized. The maternal care associated with these relationships can also be applied by extension to male characters, as when Moses asks rhetorically whether he gave birth to Israel that he would have to carry them on his bosom like a nurse (Num 11:12). So, too, Nathan is using the language of lying on one's bosom to characterize the poor man in terms of parental care and affection, as is made clear by Nathan's subsequent statement that the lamb "was to him like a daughter" (2 Sam 12:3). Such language puts the lamb in a context of kinship as much as a sexual context. As George Coats (1981, 372) notes, the description of the lamb depicts her as "an active member of the poor man's family and a passive victim of the rich man's hospitality." She is an "animal who lives in a human world, does human things, and functions in the family as a human member" (376). By representing the lamb in such a fashion, Nathan's story tends to cross, and so to undermine, the boundary between humans and other animals. The emphasis falls upon the press of bodies, in both a parental sense and a sexual sense, more than the species of those bodies.

Now if it is the case that, as Gregory Seigworth and Melissa Gregg (2010, 1) put it, "affect is found in those intensities that pass body to body (human, nonhuman, part-body, and otherwise)," we should not be surprised to find some textual acknowledgment of emotion or feeling in this story about a human body and a lamb's body lying together. But such acknowledgment emerges at an unexpected site. The narration of the story by Nathan generates rage or "kindled anger" on the part of David (2 Sam 12:5). As noted earlier, David's strong reaction to Nathan's story affects commentators in turn. Schipper (2007, 389), for example, refers to David's "emotionally charged condemnation" of the rich man while asking whether David "overinterprets" Nathan's story. Lasine, going further, suggests that what he calls David's "intense emotional reaction" is most appropriate to the genre of melodrama. Noting that David approaches Nathan's story as a "righteously indignant judge," Lasine (1984, 101–2) argues that David responds with an "unrealistically harsh judgment." In Lasine's view, however, David's "vehement emotional response" is proportionate to the nature of Nathan's story. For the "melodramatic nature" of Nathan's "totally unrealistic" tale is apparent from its "excessive," "indulgent" and "unrealistic sentimentality" (103–5). And what specific features of Nathan's story cause Lasine to refer to its "unrealistic sentimentality"? Lasine (103) criticizes readers who are, in his view, misled by the story's "mawkish tone and unnatural relationships." The phrase *unnatural relationships* clearly refers to the poor man and his lamb. The transgression of the species line, in a context of kinship and bodily contact, provokes a kind of normalizing, humanistic reaction. Lasine connects the story's "unrealistic sentimentality" to its representation of "the lamb in human terms." This representation of the lamb leads Lasine (105) to conclude that the story "provides an imaginary escape from the real world." "Because the tale is blatantly unrealistic," Lasine (105–6) tells us, it would be "inappropriate … to use 2 Sam 12:3 as evidence of ancient Israelite attitudes toward pets" or of "social customs."

As we have already seen, Lasine (114) himself is more interested in David's "fluctuating emotions," here and in the larger narrative about David, than he is in either the poor man's lamb or biblical representations of animals. In his view, "by telling David this sentimental story, Nathan evokes a melodramatic response which … unmasks the king's emotional imbalance …" (109–10). At the least, this interpretation acknowledges the role of affect in David's story. It also connects that affect to the presence in the story of an animal. But might animal studies allow us to reread this connection in ways that do not require us to link David's affect to emotional imbalance?

From Modern Pets to Israelite Companion Species

Lasine's choice of the word *pets*, noted above, as well as an earlier reference in his discussion to a "pet lamb" (103), may facilitate his characterization of the story of the poor man and the ewe lamb as an unnatural relationship. Humans have lived alongside domesticated animals for centuries; and the association between beloved animals with whom "intense emotional attachments" are formed, on the one hand, and children, on the other hand, occurs cross-culturally, even among hunter-gatherer populations (Serpell and Paul 2011, 298). Nevertheless, the use of the word *pet* can lead to connotations that are more common in modern consumer capitalism, particularly today, when the pet industry has grown to unprecedented size. And these connotations are not all positive. James Serpell points out that, even with the increased popularity of pets, pet owners are sometimes viewed with suspicion by those who "regard people's relationships with their animal companions as absurd, sentimental, and somewhat pathetic." Numerous popular stereotypes circulate about pet owners, including "the belief, or at least suspicion, that pets are no more than substitutes for so-called 'normal' human relationships" (Serpell 1996, 24–25; cf. Rudy 2011; 2012).

Thus, rather than speaking about Nathan's story in language that risks reducing it to a "sentimental" tale depicting a man's "unnatural" relationship with his pet lamb, as Lasine does, it may be preferable to follow the lead of feminist biologist and cultural theorist Donna Haraway and utilize the conceptual framework of "companion species." As explicated by Haraway, companion species include, but are not identical to, "companion animals," those individual animals (such as pets) with whom many humans live and form affective bonds. The notion of companion species is used in a more comprehensive sense to analyze what Haraway (2008, 73; cf. Haraway 2003; 2016) calls "co-constitutive human relationships with other critters." Human nature and human cultures do not preexist such relationships. Individually and collectively, humans "become who they are" with other living and non-living entities in particular "situated histories, situated naturecultures" (2008, 25). As the neologism *naturecultures* indicates, Haraway's understanding of companion species calls into question dichotomizing oppositions between *culture* and *nature*, as well as associated oppositions between *human* and *animal*, or even *living* and *nonliving*. Against tendencies to understand human existence independently of other beings and circumstances, Haraway argues that we are always "entangled" with other "critters" in specific "contact zones." Haraway takes the phrase *contact zone* from canine agility training, but she notes that it occurs also in postcolonial studies, acknowledging thereby that power relations and histories of conflict structure companion species contact zones. Starting from specific examples of species interaction (this training dog with this woman, these herding dogs with these sheep, these sheep with this scientist) in particular contact zones, she explores these interactions in ways that make animals active participants worthy of attention rather than simply objects or background. While Haraway is especially interested in interactions between humans and dogs, she also gives attention to other companion species, including other domesticated animals such as sheep, and to the histories of labor, economy, technology, geography, migration, colonialism, ethnic relations, gender relations, and so forth that shape the contact zones in which humans and our companion species coevolve.

Now it is not difficult to recognize that sheep, as well as goats, could be considered examples of companion species in Haraway's sense for the writers of biblical literature. Their presence testifies to the origin of that literature in the situated naturecultures of the ancient Levant, where, as histories of domestication and archaeological evidence have shown, the herding of goats and sheep (often referred to collectively, in biblical terminology, as a "flock") was crucial for human livelihood both before and during the times in which the Bible was written (Clutton-Brock 1987, 52–61; 2007; 2012, 47–69; Hesse 1995; Zeder 1996; Borowski 1998, 39–71; King and Stager 2001, 112–22; Hesse and Wapnish 2002; MacDonald 2008; Sasson 2010; Boer 2015). Given how intertwined the narrated lives of Israelite ancestors such as Jacob are with their animals (see Stone 2016b; 2017), it is unsurprising that biblical writers found in relationships with goats and sheep a rich resource for political and religious imagery. Like other ancient texts, biblical literature utilizes the language of shepherding and flocks to refer to both human leaders and God, on the one hand, and the people they lead or care for, on the other hand. Significantly, David himself has been characterized as a shepherd in 1 Samuel (e.g., 1 Sam 16:11, 19; 17:15, 20, 28, 34–37), a fact I return to below.

The use of a category such as companion species to read 2 Sam 12 serves as a check against glossing over the lamb as merely an insignificant element of the story. At the same time, it avoids focusing too narrowly on the sentimental relationship between an individual human character and an individual animal character in isolation from the larger context in which that relationship takes place. By considering humans and sheep as companion species, as that phrase is elaborated by Haraway, we can read 2 Sam 12 while asking about the roles and interactions of humans and sheep in the specific natureculture of ancient Israel. Our interpretation of the story is enriched by attention to the particular embodied relationships involved in the use of a lamb as a character in the story, a character chosen to symbolize yet another character, a woman, in the larger narrative in which Nathan's tale is embedded.

Consider, for example, the fact that, according to Nathan's story, the poor man is raising the ewe lamb in his house. No doubt this seems extraordinary to many modern readers, who seldom see sheep and certainly do not live with them. Grasping for a cultural framework with which to understand this representation, such readers understandably gravitate toward the category of *pet*. But in fact, living in the same structure with sheep may have been more common for ancient Israelites than modern readers realize. Archaeologists and historians suggest that Israelite houses were sometimes constructed to allow livestock to live inside the same structure as their human owners (Borowski 1998, 45; King and Stager 2001, 34). No doubt most animals lived outside or in separate structures; and archaeological excavations have also uncovered what appear to be walled pens of stone that contained animals. Larger flocks were certainly kept somewhere other than the house, and particular types of animal husbandry could involve pasturing at some distance (Borowski 1998, 40–45). But a household with fewer animals, which is explicitly the case for the poor man in Nathan's story, might well keep those animals in the same structure in which the family lived. Indeed, 1 Sam 28:24 indicates that the woman consulted by Saul in Endor had a calf already in the house. Although Nathan's story depicts a special closeness between the poor man and his ewe lamb, the physical proximity between human and lamb in the story may well have seemed less unusual to an audience immersed in the material naturecultures of ancient Israel and Judah than it seems to us. Such an audience would have known that humans and sheep, as companion species, sometimes shared the same physical space.

Our interpretation of the affective relations between characters needs to take those naturecultures into account as well. Recall that, in Ahmed's example of the child and the bear, the fear that is generated depends not only on the presence of two bodies, that of the child and that of the bear, but also on "past histories of contact" between humans and bears that shape the child's "impression of bears": "Another child, another bear, and we might even have a different story" (Ahmed 2004c, 7–8). So too, the physical proximity of the bodies of humans and sheep in the naturecultures of Israel and Judah, though not automatically leading to affective relations, certainly made such relations possible. This is true on a general level but also at the level of the individual: those persons who spend more time around sheep are more likely to develop affective relations with them than persons who spend less time around sheep. Past histories of contact lay the groundwork for impressions in the present, so it may be important to recall that David is not simply a shepherd in the sense that, in the ancient world, any king might be represented as a symbolic shepherd. Inside the narrative traditions about him, David's past histories include a history of actual shepherding (1 Sam 16:11, 19; 17:15, 20, 28). Indeed, he appeals to this history when explaining to Saul that, since he was able to kill lions and bears while protecting his father's flock, he would also be able to kill the beastly, uncircumcised Philistine, Goliath (1 Sam 17:34–37). Thus Nathan's parable, though sometimes thought to have originated independently from the narrative context of the books of Samuel (e.g., Gunkel 1987, 34–35), appears well chosen for a rhetorical confrontation with David specifically: Who is more likely than a shepherd to understand and react emotionally to the affective relations that can flow between humans and sheep?

That such affective relations did sometimes develop in the ancient world may be suggested by the discovery of a lamb buried with a human at Catalhöyük in Neolithic Anatolia (Russell and Düring 2006). Because this burial is unusual in the ancient archaeological record, interpretations of it are even more tentative than, say, still-contested interpretations of the more common burials of dogs, some of which are much closer geographically and/or temporally to Israel (see, e.g., Davis and Valla 1978; Stager 1991; Wapnish and Hesse 1993; Tchernov and Valla 1997; Halpern 2000; Morey 2010). Nevertheless, the burial of the lamb alongside a human, and under a house where other humans were buried, can be taken as evidence of, in the words of archaeologists Nerissa Russell and Bleda Düring (2006, 81–82; cf. Russell 2007), "a particularly intense relationship": "The personal ties between the dead man and this particular lamb were so strong that it was felt necessary to include it" in the man's grave.

Haraway's work on companion species indicates, moreover, that our interpretations of relations between humans and other animals need to give attention to the particular characteristics of the animal species in question. In the case of sheep, this requires us to consider characteristics that make sheep amenable to domestication. Like most domesticated mammals, sheep are highly social animals. They do not mind being "bunched up together in compact groups" and "even flourish better when crowded together" (Clutton-Brock 1987, 55). Sheep are inclined, then, to situations in which their bodies press against other bodies. Yet they also form close individual relationships or "long-lasting bonds" (Rowell 1991; cf. Rowell and Rowell 1993). Although traditionally dismissed as dumb or stupid animals, sheep in fact "possess highly acute forms of spatial, social and emotional intelligence, and they are far from being faceless, insensitive or unthinking toward each other. On the contrary, each flock involves a network of carefully worked-out relationships that take into account both individuals and the collective, and are based on meticulously remembered past experiences" (Armstrong 2016, 52). In certain respects sheep "epitomise domestication as subordination" (Franklin 2007, 89), and their sense of hierarchy "predisposes them to leadership by a herdsman" (Clutton-Brock 1987, 55). But this characteristic also allows shepherds to "develop especially close relationships with one or a few animals" (Russell and Düring 2006, 81). A former shepherd may know this, of course—and so too, we may imagine, a storyteller who imagines the type of parable that will generate an emotional response from a shepherd who has become a king.

Affective Economies of Women and Sheep

More than only the physical proximity of humans and sheep, and the particular characteristics of sheep, facilitate an emotional response to the ewe lamb's story. As we have seen, Ahmed associates the movement of affect with the circulation of objects, which become "sticky" sites for attachment. In order to understand David's reaction, then, we have to ask: What affective objects are circulating in 2 Sam 12? Here we must note that the story concerns not only the circulation of flocks and cattle (12:2, 4), but also women (12:8–11).

Although some readers of 2 Sam 12 understand the lamb in Nathan's story to refer to Uriah (e.g., Wesselius 1990, 347), other readers associate her rather with Bathsheba (e.g., Koenig 2011, 63–66; Boer 1997, 103; Schwartz 1991, 47). Indeed, the fact that the lamb is described as being "like a daughter" (Hebrew *bat*) to the poor man (12:3) allows us to link the lamb to "*bat-sheva*, the *bat* of Eliam" (11:3). Though we may hear a forewarning in Nathan's oracle about the fate of David's own daughter (*bat*) Tamar in chapter 13, the oracle also links Bathsheba and the lamb to women belonging to other men ("your master's wives," 12:8) whom God has previously given to David, and to women belonging to David that God will soon give to other men (12:8–11). I have argued elsewhere (Stone 1996; 2005, 82–84) that this passing around of women in the books of Samuel can usefully be interpreted in terms of the "political economy" of sex, gender, and kinship famously glossed by anthropologist Gayle Rubin as "the traffic in women." Rubin's feminist explication of "the traffic in women," however, also includes animals among the objects that circulate in such economies (e.g., Rubin 2011, 43–44) and even refers at one point to Abraham's "wives, children, herds, and dependents" (41) in order to illustrate the patriarchal social structures that are often associated with these economies. While we can see evidence for this economy in numerous biblical passages, Gen 34 is one of the more interesting texts for my purposes. In Gen 34 the men of Shechem, while pondering the offer of Jacob's sons to form an alliance by exchanging daughters (34:16–17), note that such an exchange of daughters would also involve the acquisition of livestock, animals, and other objects (34:21–23). That men might wish to acquire animals, slaves, and other objects alongside women is also made clear in the tenth commandment, which uses masculine linguistic forms to warn a male audience that "you will not covet the house of your neighbor. You will not covet the woman of your neighbor, or his male slave, or his female slave, or his ox, or his donkey, or anything that belongs to your neighbor" (Exod 20:17; cf. Deut 5:21). Leaving aside the undefined "anything" (Hebrew *kol*, "all") at the end of this list, what the rest of these classes have in common, of course, is that they are all living subordinates, subject to the male heads of households addressed by this stipulation.

Might we consider this political economy of gender, kinship, slavery, and animality to be an affective economy as well? In *The Promise of Happiness*, Ahmed associates her theory of affect and "the coming and going of objects" (2010, 23) with, among other things, family forms. Ahmed is focused primarily on the affective dimensions of modern forms of family ("happy families," 45–49), the norms that structure them, and the subjects who find themselves estranged from such norms. There seems little reason to refrain, however, from interpreting other forms of kinship in terms of the circulation of affect as well. The question that must be asked, rather, is whether such an affective interpretation sheds light on the texts we are attempting to read.

In the case of biblical literature, affective relations do appear in the context of the traffic in women and animals. The dialogue noted above between the sons of Jacob and the men of Shechem is preceded by an observation that the *nephesh* of Shechem, the son of Hamor, was "drawn" to Dinah after their sexual encounter "and he loved the girl and spoke to the girl's heart" (Gen 34:3). For this reason, Shechem asks his father to "get for me this young woman as a wife" (34:4). The scene is a troubling one, since Shechem's initial encounter with Dinah is plausibly understood as a rape. Although Lyn Bechtel (1994) suggests that the nature of the encounter is more ambiguous than the English word *rape* implies, 34:2 does describe Shechem's actions using verbs that are also applied to Abner's rape of Tamar in 2 Sam 13:14, indicating that Shechem actively shames or humiliates Dinah sexually. For our purposes here, any tension between this initial power-laden encounter and Shechem's subsequent feeling for Dinah need not be explained away. As both Ahmed and Schaefer recognize, affective relations are also conduits for power.

Affect, animality, and the traffic in women appear earlier in Jacob's story as well. Genesis 29:11, for example, describes an emotional meeting between Jacob and Rachel after Rachel brings "the flock of her father" (29:9) to the well where Jacob is speaking with other shepherds. The meeting includes bodily contact between Jacob and Rachel, in the form of a kiss. Following another emotional meeting with his uncle Laban, including another kiss (29:13–14), "Jacob worked for Rachel seven years, but they were in his eyes like a few days because of his love for her" (29:20). Although Jacob has sexual relations with both Leah and Rachel, we are told that Jacob "loved Rachel more than Leah" (29:30) and even that Leah is "hated" (29:31). Here again we have a story suffused with feelings.

Genesis 29 is also a story full of animals and offspring, human and otherwise. Jacob reminds Laban in 30:25–30 that the work Jacob has done to acquire Laban's daughters, Leah and Rachel, includes tending Laban's livestock, which flourish under Jacob's care. He continues working for Laban as part of a deal that allows Jacob to keep "all the sheep that are speckled or spotted and all the sheep that are black among the lambs and all the spotted or speckled among the goats" (30:32). Though Laban attempts to hide such animals, the text describes in detail how Jacob, through a kind of magic, manipulates the breeding of goats and sheep to increase the number of animals received as wages (30:37–42). By the end of chapter 30, Jacob, who has already fathered eleven sons and a daughter with his two wives and their two female slaves, has not only amassed "great flocks" of sheep and goats, but also "female slaves and male slaves and camels and donkeys" (30:43). In chapter 31, Jacob calls Rachel and Leah to join him in a field that holds his flock. There he notes how God increased his livestock by causing speckled animals to be born when Laban pays in speckled animals, and striped animals to be born when Laban pays in striped animals. He then recounts a dream about male goats mounting other goats. God's messenger implies in the dream that God caused striped, speckled, and spotted male goats to breed, to Jacob's benefit. Later in the chapter, Jacob gives a speech about the twenty years he spent tending Laban's flocks and assuming the costs when sheep or goats were taken by wild animals. As Jacob notes, "I served you fourteen years for your two daughters and six years for your flock" (31:41). In the next chapter, Jacob attempts to defuse Esau's anger with a gift of "two hundred female goats and twenty male goats, two hundred ewes and twenty rams, thirty nursing camels and their offspring, forty cows and ten bulls, twenty she-asses and ten he-asses" (32:14–15). When he eventually meets Esau, however, Esau "embraced him and fell on his neck and kissed him, and they wept" (33:4). Once again, emotion and physical contact appear to be intertwined, and take place in the presence of domesticated animals. The offspring of these animals, moreover, are occasionally associated with Jacob's human offspring. After Jacob persuades his brother to accept the gifts of animals, for example, he also notes that he needs to travel more slowly than Esau so as not to overtax either his many children or his own remaining "flocks and herds, which are nursing" (33:13), in other words, which have many young of their own. Young animals and young children are both objects of care and concern.

What we find in these and other texts is thus both a political economy and an affective economy, in which women, children, slaves, and livestock circulate among men. To return to Ahmed's (2004c, 11) language, these circulating bodies become "sticky" "objects," which are "saturated with affects." Affective relations develop between the men who are subjects of circulation and the objects they are circulating (e.g., Jacob with Rachel, Shechem with Dinah). But since, as Rubin (2011, 44) notes, women serve as a "conduit of a relationship rather than a partner of it," affective relations also develop among the men themselves who are subjects of circulation (e.g., Jacob with Laban, Jacob with Esau). In Jacob's story, the traffic in women and the traffic in animals are, together, not only part of a symbolic and political economy, as Rubin emphasizes. The relations created by the circulation of women and animals also create and sustain an affective economy, to return to the phrase used by both Ahmed and Schaefer.

In the story of David, of course, the affective relationships at play include the relationship between David and God. God, after all, has previously given the women of David's enemies to David, as well as the house of Israel and Judah (2 Sam 12:8); and it is God who takes David's women and give them to other men (12:11). God also has the power to take David's children, as both Nathan and David himself make clear (12:14–23). David's emotional response to his son's illness, in fact, which scares his servants after the boy dies, appears to be aimed at God rather than the child ("YHWH will show favor to me," 12:22). This understanding of God's role as the giver and taker of children is at least broadly consistent with those passages that ascribe to God the generation of both human offspring and animal offspring, as well as the successful growth of crops. As Moses argues in Deut 7:14, if the Israelites obey the stipulations of God's covenant, "there will not be sterility or barrenness among you or among your animals." But God as giver/taker is also consistent with passages indicating that the Israelites owe God their firstborn children and animals (e.g., Exod 22:29–30 [Heb. 22:28–29]), even if according to some texts they can substitute an animal for the firstborn child or for a donkey (Exod 13:2, 12–13; 34:19–20). Such passages open the door for child sacrifice, which, though broadly condemned in the Hebrew Bible, appears to have been accepted among some of the Israelites, possibly including those who gave us the stipulation in Exod 22 that does not include an option for redeeming the child with an animal (cf. Levenson 1995; Stavrakopoulou 2004; Stone 2016a; 2017, 87–90). As Jephthah's distraught reaction to his daughter in Judg 11:35 indicates, this sacrificial giving of children could also become an occasion for significant emotion. But if the line between children and animals, including sheep, is blurred in passages on sacrifice, we should not be surprised to find emotion on display, not simply when David is trying to persuade God to save his son, but also when he hears from God's prophet about the slaughter of a female lamb who is treated like a daughter.

Conclusion

I suggest that attention to both affect and animality allows us to make sense of David's reaction to the story of the poor man's lamb in 2 Sam 12. Such a reading seems more felicitous to me than reducing David's reaction to emotional imbalance or dismissing the poor man's relationship to his lamb as a sentimental or even an unnatural relationship. But by linking Nathan's story and oracle, and David's reaction, to the circulation of women and animals as sticky affective objects, my reading also brings affect and animality into alignment with analyses of power and subordination found, for example, in feminist criticism. That Ahmed (2010, 13) associates her work with "feminist cultural studies of emotion and affect," or that Schaefer highlights the relationship between affect and power, is not accidental. To study affect and animality in biblical literature is to take seriously the coexistence there of "dominance and affection," to recall the title of a book by Yi-Fu Tuan. Tuan, it should be noted, also juxtaposes a discussion of "dominance and affection" with one's animals (1984, 69–114) to a discussion of "dominance and affection" with women and children (115–31) and slaves (132–61), all of whom may be considered "immature and naive, animal-like, and sexual" (167). But Tuan also links the dynamics of "dominance and affection" to the Bible's representation of God as a shepherd, including in texts that are associated by tradition with David, such as Ps 93 (92). Thus he brings us back to Schaefer, and to Schaefer's attempt to redefine religion in relation to the "dance" of affect.

The books of Samuel certainly include other texts in which we might link the bodily religious practices of characters to affect, as in David's near-naked dance before the ark (2 Sam 6:14, 16) in a story that also includes animals who are killed (6:13, 17–19) and women who have been given to David (6:20–23); or, even earlier, Saul's ecstatic prophecy under the influence of "the spirit of God" following a search for wandering donkeys (1 Sam 10:10; cf. 19:20–24) as well as his torment under the influence of an "evil spirit of God" (16:14–23; 18:10–11). The books of Samuel and other biblical texts are themselves, also, sticky affective objects. In addition to representing characters being choreographed affectively by queer little gods, such texts circulate among us as readers. They move among us, and they move us, in multiple ways that we cannot always anticipate. Precisely because we feel them, and not simply because we agree or disagree with their theologies or ideologies, these texts continue to influence the economies of power, affect, and animality within which we, like our fellow primates, dance.

Bibliography

Ahmed, Sara. 2004a. "Affective Economies." *Social Text* 79:117–39.

———. 2004b. "Collective Feelings: Or, The Impressions Left by Others." *Theory, Culture and Society* 21.2:25–42.

———. 2004c. *The Cultural Politics of Emotion*. New York: Routledge.

———. 2010. *The Promise of Happiness*. Durham, NC: Duke University Press.

Armstrong, Philip. 2016. *Sheep*. London: Reaktion.

Bar-Efrat, Shimon. 1989. *Narrative Art in the Bible*. Translated by Dorothea Shefer-Vanson. Sheffield: Almond Press.

Bechtel, Lyn. 1994. "What If Dinah Is Not Raped? (Genesis 34)." *JSOT* 62:19–36.

Boer, Roland. 1997. "National Allegory in the Hebrew Bible." *JSOT* 74:95–116.

———. 2015. *The Sacred Economy of Ancient Israel*. Louisville: Westminster John Knox.

Borowski, Oded. 1998. *Every Living Thing: Daily Use of Animals in Ancient Israel*. Walnut Creek, CA: AltaMira.

Calarco, Matthew. 2015. *Thinking through Animals: Identity, Difference, Indistinction*. Stanford, CA: Stanford University Press.

Chez, Keridiana W. 2017. *Victorian Dogs, Victorian Men: Affect and Animals in Nineteenth-Century Literature and Culture*. Columbus: Ohio State University Press.

Clutton-Brock, Juliet. 1987. *A Natural History of Domesticated Animals*. Austin: University of Texas Press.

———. 2007. "How Domestic Animals Have Shaped the Development of Human Societies." Pages 71–96 in *A Cultural History of Animals in Antiquity*. Edited by Linda Kalof. A Cultural History of Animals 1. New York: Berg.

———. 2012. *Animals as Domesticates: A World View through History*. East Lansing: Michigan State University Press.

Coats, George W. 1981. "Parable, Fable, and Anecdote: Storytelling in the Succession Narrative." *Int* 35:368–82.

Davis, Simon J. M., and François R. Valla. 1978. "Evidence for Domestication of the Dog 12,000 Years Ago in the Natufian of Israel." *Nature* 276:610.

Derrida, Jacques. 1995. "'Eating Well,' or the Calculation of the Subject." Pages 255–87 in *Points…: Interviews, 1974–1994*. Edited by Elizabeth Weber. Translated by Peggy Kamuf et al. Stanford, CA: Stanford University Press.

Fewell, Danna Nolan, and David M. Gunn. 1993. *Gender, Power, and Promise: The Subject of the Bible's First Story*. Nashville: Abingdon.

Franklin, Sarah. 2007. *Dolly Mixtures: The Remaking of Genealogy*. Durham, NC: Duke University Press.

Goodall, Jane. 1990. *Through a Window: Thirty Years with the Chimpanzees of Gombe*. London: Weidenfeld & Nicolson.

———. 1999. *Reason for Hope: A Spiritual Journey*. New York: Soko.

———. 2005. "Primate Spirituality." Pages 1303–6 in *The Encyclopedia of Religion and Nature*. Edited by Bron Taylor. New York: Continuum.

Gross, Aaron S. 2015. *The Question of the Animal and Religion: Theoretical Stakes, Practical Implications*. New York: Columbia University Press.

Gunkel, Hermann. 1987. *The Folktale in the Old Testament*. Translated by M. D. Rutter. Sheffield: Almond Press.

Guthrie, Stewart. 2002. "Animal Animism: Evolutionary Roots of Religious Cognition." Pages 38–67 in *Current Approaches to the Cognitive*

Science of Religion. Edited by Ilkka Pyysiäinen and Veikko Anttonen. New York: Continuum.

Halpern, Baruch. 2000. "The Canine Conundrum of Ashkelon: A Classical Connection?" Pages 133–44 in *The Archaeology of Jordan and Beyond: Essays in Honor of James A. Sauer*. Edited by Lawrence E. Stager, Joseph A. Greene, and Michael D. Coogan. Winona Lake, IN: Eisenbrauns.

Haraway, Donna. 2003. *The Companion Species Manifesto: Dogs, People, and Significant Otherness*. Chicago: Prickly Paradigm Press.

———. 2008. *When Species Meet*. Minneapolis: University of Minnesota Press.

———. 2016. *Staying with the Trouble: Making Kin in the Chthulucene*. Durham, NC: Duke University Press.

Harrod, James B. 2014. "The Case for Chimpanzee Religion." *Journal for the Study of Religion, Nature and Culture* 8.1:8–45.

Hesse, Brian. 1995. "Animal Husbandry and Human Diet in the Ancient Near East." Pages 203–22 in vol. 1 of *Civilizations of the Ancient Near East*. Edited by Jack M. Sasson. 4 vols. New York: Simon & Schuster.

Hesse, Brian, and Paula Wapnish. 2002. "An Archaeozoological Perspective on the Cultural Use of Mammals in the Levant." Pages 457–91 in *A History of the Animal World in the Ancient Near East*. Edited by Billie Jean Collins. Leiden: Brill.

King, Philip J., and Lawrence E. Stager. 2001. *Life in Biblical Israel*. Louisville: Westminster John Knox.

Koenig, Sara M. 2011. *Isn't This Bathsheba? A Study in Characterization*. Eugene, OR: Pickwick.

Koosed, Jennifer L., ed. 2014a. *The Bible and Posthumanism*. SemeiaSt 74. Atlanta: SBL Press.

———. 2014b. "Moses: The Face of Fear." *BibInt* 22.4–5:414–29.

Koosed, Jennifer L., and Stephen D. Moore, eds. 2014. *Affect Theory and the Bible*. *BibInt* 22.4–5.

Kotrosits, Maia. 2015. *Rethinking Early Christian Identity: Affect, Violence, and Belonging*. Minneapolis: Fortress.

———. 2016. *How Things Feel: Biblical Studies, Affect Theory, and the (Im)Personal*. Brill Research Perspectives in Biblical Interpretation 1.1. Leiden: Brill.

Lasine, Stuart. 1984. "Melodrama as Parable: The Story of the Poor Man's Ewe-Lamb and the Unmasking of David's Topsy-Turvy Emotions." *HAR* 8:101–24.

Levenson, Jon D. 1995. *The Death and Resurrection of the Beloved Son: The Transformation of Child Sacrifice in Judaism and Christianity*. New Haven: Yale University Press.

MacDonald, Nathan. 2008. *What Did the Israelites Eat?* Grand Rapids: Eerdmans.

McCarter, P. Kyle, Jr. 1984. *II Samuel*. Anchor Bible. Garden City, NY: Doubleday.

Moore, Stephen D., ed. 2014. *Divinanimality: Animal Theory, Creaturely Theology*. New York: Fordham University Press.

Morey, Darcy F. 2010. *Dogs: Domestication and the Development of a Social Bond*. Cambridge: Cambridge University Press.

Rowell, Thelma. 1991. "Til Death Do Us Part: Long-Lasting Bonds between Ewes and Their Daughters." *Animal Behaviour* 42:681–82.

Rowell, T. E., and C. A. Rowell. 1993. "The Social Organization of Feral Ovis Aries Ram Groups in the Pre-rut Period." *Ethology* 95:213–32.

Rubin, Gayle. 2011. "The Traffic in Women: Notes on the 'Political Economy' of Sex." Pages 33–65 in *Deviations: A Gayle Rubin Reader*. Durham, NC: Duke University Press.

Rudy, Kathy. 2011. *Loving Animals: Toward a New Animal Advocacy*. Minneapolis: University of Minnesota Press.

———. 2012. "LGBTQ ... Z?" *Hypatia* 27.3:601–15.

Runions, Erin. 2011a. "From Disgust to Humor: Rahab's Queer Affect." Pages 45–74 in *Bible Trouble: Queer Reading at the Boundaries of Biblical Scholarship*. Edited by Teresa J. Hornsby and Ken Stone. Atlanta: Society of Biblical Literature.

———. 2011b. "Prophetic Affect and the Promise of Change: A Response." Pages 235–42 in *Jeremiah (Dis)Placed: New Directions in Writing/Reading Jeremiah*. Edited by A. R. Pete Diamond and Louis Stulman. London: T&T Clark.

Russell, Nerissa. 2007. "The Domestication of Anthropology." Pages 27–48 in *Where the Wild Things Are Now: Domestication Reconsidered*. Edited by Rebecca Cassidy and Molly Mullin. New York: Berg.

Russell, Nerissa, and Bleda Düring. 2006. "Worthy Is the Lamb: A Double Burial at Neolithic Catalhöyük (Turkey)." *Paléorient* 32.1:73–84.

Sasson, Aharon. 2010. *Animal Husbandry in Ancient Israel: A Zooarchaeological Perspective on Livestock Exploitation, Herd Management and Economic Strategies*. Oakville, CT: Equinox.

Schaefer, Donovan O. 2012. "Do Animals Have Religion? Interdisciplinary Perspectives on Religion and Embodiment." *Anthrozoös* 25.S1:173–89.

———. 2015. *Religious Affects: Animality, Evolution, Power*. Durham, NC: Duke University Press.
Schipper, Jeremy. 2007. "Did David Overinterpret Nathan's Parable in 2 Samuel 12:1–6?" *JBL* 126:383–91.
Schwartz, Regina M. 1991. "Adultery in the House of David: The Metanarrative of Biblical Scholarship and the Narratives of the Bible." *Semeia* 54:35–55.
Sedgwick, Eve Kosofsky. 2011. *The Weather in Proust*. Edited by Jonathan Goldberg. Durham, NC: Duke University Press.
Sedgwick, Eve Kosofsky, and Michael D. Snediker. 2008. "Queer Little Gods: A Conversation." *The Massachusetts Review* 49:194–218.
Seigworth, Gregory J., and Melissa Gregg. 2010. "An Inventory of Shimmers." Pages 1–25 in *The Affect Theory Reader*. Edited by Melissa Gregg and Gregory J. Seigworth. Durham, NC: Duke University Press.
Serpell, James A. 1996. *In the Company of Animals: A Study of Human-Animal Relationships*. 2nd ed. Cambridge: Cambridge University Press.
Serpell, James A., and Elizabeth S. Paul. 2011. "Pets in the Family: An Evolutionary Perspective." Pages 297–309 in *The Oxford Handbook of Evolutionary Family Psychology*. Edited by C. Salmon and T. K. Shackleford. Oxford: Oxford University Press.
Stager, Lawrence E. 1991. "Why Were Hundreds of Dogs Buried at Ashkelon?" *BAR* 17.3:26–42.
Stavrakopoulou, Francesca. 2004. *King Manasseh and Child Sacrifice: Biblical Distortions of Historical Realities*. Berlin: de Gruyter.
Stone, Ken. 1996. *Sex, Honor and Power in the Deuteronomistic History*. Sheffield: Sheffield Academic.
———. 2005. *Practicing Safer Texts: Food, Sex and Bible in Queer Perspective*. London: T&T Clark.
———. 2016a. "Animal Difference, Sexual Difference, and the Daughter of Jephthah." *BibInt* 24:1–16.
———. 2016b. "Animating the Bible's Animals." Pages 444–55 in *The Oxford Handbook of Biblical Narrative*. Edited by Danna Nolan Fewell. Oxford: Oxford University Press.
———. 2017. *Reading the Hebrew Bible with Animal Studies*. Stanford, CA: Stanford University Press.
Tchernov, Eitan, and François R. Valla. 1997. "Two New Dogs, and Other Natufian Dogs, from the Southern Levant." *Journal of Archaeological Science* 24:65–95.

Tuan, Yi-Fu. 1984. *Dominance and Affection: The Making of Pets*. New Haven: Yale University Press.

Vásquez, Manuel A. 2011. *More Than Belief: A Materialist Theory of Religion*. Oxford: Oxford University Press.

Wapnish, Paula, and Brian Hesse. 1993. "Pampered Pooches or Plain Pariahs? The Ashkelon Dog Burials." *BA* 56.2:55–80.

Wesselius, J.W. 1990. "Joab's Death and the Central Theme of the Succession Narrative (2 Samuel IX–1 Kings II)." *VT* 40.3:336–51.

Zeder, Melinda. 1996. "Sheep and Goats." Pages -23–25 in volume vol. 5 of *The Oxford Encyclopedia of Archaeology in the Near East*. Edited by Eric M. Meyers. 5 vols. Oxford: Oxford University Press.

Echoes of How: Archiving Trauma in Jewish Liturgy

Jennifer L. Koosed

In the novel *A Guide for the Perplexed*, Dara Horn imagines the spectacular find of the Cairo Genizah by Solomon Schechter with the aid of Agnes Lewis and Margaret Gibson, widowed twin sisters and adventurers. In one scene, the three are sorting through thousands of parchments in Schechter's home library after bringing them to England from Egypt. Reading could only happen in the daytime because gaslights provided inadequate illumination and were a fire hazard. As the sun sets, Margaret and Agnes stop their work and gently urge Schechter to do the same.

> "We need your eyes," Agnes added. "This archive is only a heap of dust without your eyes."
> "It's actually the opposite of an archive, isn't it?" Margaret said as she sifted through a stack of dark leather scraps.
> "Not quite," huffed Agnes. She pointed to a pile of brown dust on the table where Margaret had been working, the remains of a parchment accidentally crushed. "*That* is the opposite of an archive. And please be a bit more careful, or this entire room will become the opposite of an archive."
> Schechter coughed, coughed again, sputtered. The heaps of dust had affected his health. He wasn't yet fifty, but he already resembled an old man. As he glanced at the dust that had caused his trouble—disintegrated animal matter that coated everything he touched and that floated in the air he breathed—it occurred to him that his body would ultimately become something just like it, that the bodies of every person alive would ultimately become something just like it, that every human being, in the end, becomes the opposite of an archive. (Horn 2013, 314–15)

In this passage, "the opposite of an archive" slides across several significations. First, the idea is attached to the disorganized mass of parchments, first thrown into the genizah as trash, then gathered up and stuffed into bags in the hope of treasure, carted off to another country to be dumped and spread out across Schechter's room. Second, not the whole but only a part—a parchment accidentally crushed—is the opposite of an archive. Wafting through the air, the fragments of that crushed parchment—the dead and disintegrating bodies of animals—touch and enter into the body of Schechter. Through direct physical contact, the third meaning of the opposite of an archive transfers on to Schechter. His body—in some future when it too is dead and disintegrating—is the opposite of an archive. In the end, we will all become the opposite of an archive.

I begin this essay not with the book of Lamentations or the siddur (Jewish prayer book) or with affect theory or an "archive of feeling" (Cvetkovich 2003) or any other archive, but with its opposite. Because it is in this knowledge—the knowledge of the fragility of our ideas, our products, and our bodies—that we write and strive to create archives to begin with. Traumatized animal bodies become books; traumatized animal bodies write books. We hope the archive will live on after us, leaving some trace, some memory that we were actually here. Even archives that are not explicitly linked to trauma, then, are records of them nevertheless. For the final trauma, the one we all participate in, is the trauma of our own death.

Much of the Hebrew Bible is written in response to trauma: the Assyrian onslaught against Israel in the eighth century BCE, the Babylonian destruction of Jerusalem and the subsequent exile at the end of the sixth century BCE, the persecutions under Greek rule in the second century BCE. As David Carr (2014, 4) notes, "The Bible's distinctive themes and emphases can be traced back to century after century of crisis.... Thus suffering, and survival of it, was written into the Bible." The national catastrophe of the Babylonian attack was particularly pivotal for Judean history, theology, and texts. Much of the Scriptures were written and redacted by those who experienced the assault first-hand, remaining alive in its wake and wanting to remember, as well as those who experienced it through the speech and the silences of their parents and grandparents, who needed still to process a trauma that did not personally happen to them. Within this literature of trauma, foremost is the book of Lamentations (whose Hebrew title is, *Eicha* or "How"; for work on Lamentations as trauma literature, see especially Boase 2008; 2014; 2016). As a response to one historically situated trauma, Lamentations then moves forward carrying that trauma into a variety of other contexts. In Jewish ritual, appropriately enough, Lamentations is canted in its entirety on the holiday of Tisha b'Av, the commemoration of the destruction of the First and Second Temples. More subtly, though, fragments of Lamentations break off and embed themselves in other parts of Jewish liturgy, which seemingly have nothing to do with Jerusalem's destruction. In fact, Jewish liturgy proves a remarkably rich repository for the reception and transformation of the trauma of the Babylonian assault.

This essay examines two echoes of Lamentations—one heard in a private morning prayer (*Modeh ani*) and the second in a public prayer recited after the Torah reading (*Etz hayim hi*)—through the work of affect theorist Ann Cvetkovitch. Trauma wounds and disrupts, physically but sometimes more profoundly, emotionally and psychologically. The word *trauma* emerges at the intersections of the psychic and the somatic in a manner parallel to how affect theory resists any mind-body dualism. Affect theory probes the body and all that which resists representation; affect intersects with feminist and queer work, cultural studies, literary theory, philosophy, psychology, psychobiology, and, more to this essay's point, trauma studies.[1] Both are interdisciplinary approaches that exist in the nexus of the natural sciences, the social sciences, and the humanities. Trauma theory in biblical studies particularly draws on psychology, sociology, cultural studies, and literary theory (Frechette and Boase 2016, 4) and thus traverses much of the same territory as affect theory.

Drawing together many of these different strands of affect and trauma, theorist Ann Cvetkovich develops a theory of trauma that attends to the everyday texture of people's lives and finds trauma located not just in catastrophic events but also in everyday acts of personal suffering. In fact, "catastrophic traumatic histories are embedded within everyday life experience. Trauma becomes the hinge between systematic structures of exploitation and oppression and the felt experience of them" (Cvetkovich 2003, 12). The felt experience of trauma is not just of "loss and mourning but also anger, shame, humor, sentimentality," love, and more (48). Trauma is not just debilitating and destructive; it can become the ground out of which new cultures and new cultural products emerge. These texts constitute an archive of feelings and the practices political counter-cultures. She defines an "archive of feeling" as "an exploration of cultural texts as repositories of feelings and emotions, which are encoded not only

---

1. For introductions to affect theory and biblical studies, see Koosed and Moore 2014; and Kotrosits 2016. For work that specifically examines the interactions between trauma, affect, and Scripture, see Kotrosits 2015.

in the content of the texts themselves but in the practices that surround their production and reception" (7). The Book of How (Lamentations) has been shattered and its pieces scattered. We gather them up and piece them together the best we can. This is a political act, and in brokenness there is power. Remember the genizah. A text is only in the genizah because somewhere on it is inscribed the name of God—a genizah is a garbage pile of sacredness. Even when we accidently destroy such holy trash in the process of recovering it, its fragments still can enter into us, making us sick but also making us transformed.

Prayer Book Primer

Judaism is a religion of the Book. The "Book" is not just the Bible (the Tanak) but the designation also includes a vast religious literature—Talmud, midrash, Tosefta, targum, mystical writings ... the list goes on. Whereas the Bible (especially the Torah) is at the center and the Talmud is crucial for normative Jewish practice, the prayer book (the siddur) is the most intimately known book for observant Jews. Traditionally, Jewish men are required to pray three times a day, in addition to saying a variety of blessings for common everyday activities—waking up, going to the bathroom, eating. Although they are not under the same ritual requirements, observant Jewish women also say prayers and blessings throughout the day from the siddur. As Jeremy Schonfield (2006, 4) notes: "The intensity of contact with the prayer-book, in terms of the number of separate encounters with it in the course of each day, thus makes this the text to which traditional Jews turn most frequently.... The hours of the day are enmeshed with the prayer-book and it is a matter of almost constant awareness."[2] The book is always close at hand; its words form the weft of the weave of life.

The prayer liturgies are the service of the heart, but Jewish prayer is not spontaneous and personal; rather, it is fixed and formal. Particular words are said in a particular order at a particular time. One should

---

2. In her introduction to affect theory as a research method in biblical studies, Maia Kotrosits (2016) chronicles the way in which encounter and relationship shape scholarship. In 1994–1995, I was a student at the Oxford Centre for Hebrew and Jewish Studies. While there, I took a course on Jewish liturgy with Jeremy Schonfield. The siddur was our only text. I have been thinking about Jewish liturgy through the lens of Schonfield's analysis ever since.

say these words with *kavanah*, feeling and intention, but the prayers are efficacious without this intention (or attention) (Schonfield 2006, 4). A powerful aspect of fixed prayer is that the words connect Jewish communities across the world and across time. Many of the prayers in the siddur have existed for millennia; for example, central prayers such as the Shema (said twice a day) and the Amidah (said three times a day) were already a part of Jewish liturgy in the time of the second temple. The siddur as a book, however, developed over centuries, beginning in about the sixth century CE (Elbogen 199, 7). The oldest complete prayer book dates from about 875 CE. During the Middle Ages, it was common for different sages in different communities to compile their own siddurim, including favorite liturgical poems called *piyut*. Since different communities liked different collections of *piyut*, this led to a lot of variety among siddurim, most of which has now been lost (8). Even so, the order of prayers that is used today among Orthodox and other observant Jews was "decisively influenced by [the rabbinical communities in] Babylon" (8–9), and the penetrating biblical erudition, theological complexity, and ambiguity that marks rabbinic literature as a whole also permeates the prayer book. If one were to open the book expecting quiet piety, one would be sorely disappointed. Instead, returning to the central motif of Cvetkovich, the prayer book is a vast "archive of feeling" and as a repository of all of the different affective responses to trauma, as it happened and as it is remembered, it is just as resonate as the Hebrew Bible itself.

Cvetkovich focuses on queer cultures, particularly the literature, music, and performance art that emerges out of twentieth-century lesbian communities. The traumas she investigates are primarily related to sexuality (homophobic violence, incest, AIDS), but she also looks at transnational trauma such as the dislocations caused by political exile. As Cvetkovich (2003, 28–29) herself asserts, a "queer sensibility" is not just the "property of lesbian or gay culture," and her basic framework and insights are applicable to trauma cultures other than LGBT ones.[3] In the history and ideology of Judaism, exile is not a single event. Rather, there are multiple exiles in Jewish history and story, from Abram's egress from Ur (Gen 12) to the episodes of forced migration happening across the Middle East today.[4] The idea of exile is embedded in biblical texts, from the expulsion from

---

3. She specifically references Art Spiegelman's graphic novel *Maus* as a text with a queer sensibility that can be analyzed through affect theory.

4. To give just one example: fifty years ago there were 15,000 Jews in Aleppo,

Eden to the Babylonian exile and beyond. In mystical texts, the creation of the entire world is predicated on an exile, the exile of God. God voluntarily exiles Godself, withdraws in an event called the *tzimtzum*, in order to make the space necessary for the world. In Judaism, exile becomes the ground of being.

The historical exiles have certainly been traumatic, soaked in blood and marked by profound suffering. Even so, Cvetkovich advocates a shift from a medical model that views trauma as a source of pathology, to an affective model that views trauma as productive of new forms of community and culture, especially new, experimental and ephemeral genres (Cvetkovich 2003, 7–9). Out of the Jewish exiles have come the Jewish books; out of the loss of political sovereignty and the land has come Judaism as a religious identity; out of the loss of the temple and sacrifice has come prayer, written in a book to be held close at hand.

Recovery from trauma includes reintegration into community, and one powerful path of communal connection is through religion, especially through participation in ritual. "Religious ritual can cultivate safety, nurture social bonds, and foster both discursive and nondiscursive modes of representing collective suffering" (Frechette and Boase 2016, 10). The ritual of Jewish prayer is an act of collective recovery in several ways. First, Jewish prayer creates intricate networks of community that transcend time, connecting the person praying to both past and future; and that transcend space, connecting the person praying to Jews all over the world who are saying the same words at the same times. Hence, Jews who pray integrate into multigenerational and multidimensional communities, not bound to any particular physical homeland. Second, prayer is accomplished with the aid of a book, a ritual object, picked up several times a day. According to Cvetkovich (2003, 118), "The fetishization of objects can be one way of negotiating the cultural dislocation produced by immigration" as the object travels as well and becomes a source of continuity and comfort. The ritual actions and objects become the mechanism, then, of creating an alternative way through the trauma of dislocation—the migrant neither returns to the point of origin nor completely assimilates into the new place but creates a culture connected to but not bound to either. The ritual of Jewish prayer especially brings together

---

Syria; today there are none, as Jews have either fled Syria as refugees or have been killed in the fighting (Prince 2015).

the physical, emotional, and intellectual as the body moves and speaks and feels the rhythm of the words. The siddur, with its opaque, complex, yet also deeply evocative meanings, provides both an embodied and an emotional experience, and, as such, may be the most under-explored site of the greatest affective archive in Judaism.[5]

Morning Blessing

From the moment an observant Jew wakes up, the prayer book is in his or her hands, the words on his or her lips. The first of the morning prayers—the *Modeh ani*—reads:

מודה אני לפניך מלך חי וקים שהחזרת בי נשמתי בחלמה רבה אמונתך

> I thank you, living and eternal king, for restoring my soul to me with compassion; great is your faithfulness.[6]

The day's opening statement contains within it "the seeds of the liturgy as a whole, both in its use of language—especially the citation or echoing of scriptural texts—and in the ideas it encapsulates" (Schonfield 2006, 67). There are a number of remarkable aspects of this seemingly simple statement. It does not begin with a typical formulaic opening; rather, it begins informally and seems to link directly to the last prayer spoken upon going to bed.[7] *Modeh ani* can be read as the end of this blessing rather than as a separate blessing, as if these words continue a prayer, temporarily interrupted, rather than begin a new one. The daily liturgy is a continuous cycle, again underscoring its pervasive presence in a traditional Jew's life. Moreover, instead of simple words of gratitude, the opening blessing

---

5. Schonfield (2006, 6) begins his study of the siddur noting the lack of commentary on Jewish prayer, especially when compared to the intense focus on the Tanak and the Talmud: "The prayer-book thus offers its users an experience so lively and unsettling that the lack of curiosity about its meaning is nothing less than astonishing." He then explores possible reasons for the collective reticence to exegete the siddur (22–46).

6. This prayer first appears in writing in 1599. For a fuller history of its inclusion in the siddur, see Schonfield 2006, 69–70. All translations of the siddur are my own.

7. The blessing before sleep reads, "Blessed are you, Lord, our God, king of the universe, who causes the bonds of sleep to fall upon my eyes and drowsiness upon my eyelids."

contains within it the memory of the Babylonian destruction of Jerusalem and subsequent exile through an echo of Lamentations.

In these first words of the day, a phrase from Lamentations is intoned. The quotation is from Lam 3:23. The full sentence reads: "But this I call to mind, and therefore I have hope: The steadfast love of the Lord never ceases, his mercies never come to an end; they are new every morning; great is your faithfulness [רבה אמונתך]" (Lam 3:21–23 NRSV). Alone, these verses seem like a ringing endorsement of the mercy, compassion, and faithfulness of God, and the connection to waking and renewal is clear. However, in the context of Lamentations, the positive message is not as clear. These verses are in the middle of a passage recounting, in anguished detail, the suffering the speaker has experienced from God's own hand: "I am one who has seen affliction under the rod of God's wrath" (Lam 3:1) begins the cry. The sorrowful speaker is standing in the middle of a city under siege, death lying all around, exile already begun. The images are both vivid and brutal. The speaker continues: "he has driven and brought me into darkness without any light; against me alone he turns his hand, again and again, all day long" (Lam 3:2–3). The light of morning never comes, the hope of a new day never dawns, as the man is continuously beaten by God. There are twenty verses describing physical pain (in v. 4, God has broken the speaker's bones; in verse 13, God has shot him through with arrows; in verse 16, God has ground his face ["teeth"] into gravel) and spiritual suffering (in v. 8, God has ignored the speaker's prayers; in v. 14, the speaker is the subject of cruel taunts). Suddenly, in typical lament fashion, the tone changes: "But this I call to mind, and therefore I have hope: The steadfast love of the Lord never ceases, his mercies never come to an end; they are new every morning; great is your faithfulness" (3:21–23). In context, these verses in Lamentations become less an endorsement of God's compassion, and more a plaintive appeal for the compassion of which the speaker is in desperate need.

The two contexts could not be more disparate—a man in the midst of war crying out to God and someone waking up from sleep, presumably having suffered nothing more traumatic than bright light through the window or a startling alarm bell. One event is singular, traumatic and historically specific; the other is universal, mundane, and commonplace. What is produced by connecting the everyday practice of waking up to the trauma of the Babylonian assault? Why reference Lamentations in the context of thanking God for restoring one's soul? And what does that mean, anyway? The siddur is a vast and chaotic web of scriptural citation and allusion, and it is in this way—through the fragmentation and juxtaposition of biblical texts—that prayers become deeply complex. Multiple contexts are present in almost every line, along with their concomitant ideas and emotions. Trauma has shattered the simply grateful, and the creative juxtaposition of biblical fragments highlights ambiguities and explores existential issues (Schonfield 2006, 68). Each word, each phrase, is taken from an original context and arranged anew to create a prayer, to archive a host of feelings.

In addition to this fragment from Lamentations, other biblical verses are assembled in this first morning prayer, adding other emotions and layers of meaning. Referring to God as מלך חי וקים ("living and eternal king")—is an unusual designation. The descriptors "living and eternal" occur together in only one passage in the Bible, albeit in Aramaic: Dan 6:27 (Eng. 6:26). Daniel, a Jewish exile living in a foreign court, has been cast into the lion's den for praying—the activity in which the speaker of the blessing is currently engaged. Prayer can bring punishment, and this hint of danger lies just under the surface of *Modeh ani*. God's protection prevails, however, and Daniel emerges unscathed. Brought before the Persian king Darius, he addresses him with words of praise. Darius, in turn, acknowledges Daniel's God as "living and eternal" (my translation). In this scriptural citation, the vulnerability of exile is referenced but also the salvation rendered by a responsive God. Although the involvement of God is different in the situations, both Daniel and the speaker in Lamentations are exilic survivors of foreign hostility. Both have escaped death.

Placing these allusions to Daniel and Lamentations in the first prayer spoken upon waking points to a question: what does waking up have to do with escaping death? In Jewish literature, there are a number of references underscoring the close relationship between death and sleep, which reflect a prescientific anxiety about the similarities between these two states of being. Sleep brings powerlessness, a surcease of communication and community, vulnerability. Sleep is obviously necessary, refreshing; but it is also scary, and the rabbis speculate about what happens to consciousness, to the self, and even to the soul when the body slumbers. These questions are explored but not answered, and the tensions that arise in the midrashic literature "about nocturnal existence and the separation of body and soul also serve as vehicles for speculation about the relationship between God and humans" (Schonfield 2006, 75). Does the soul leave the body during sleep, just as the soul leaves the body at death? If the soul does indeed leave the body during sleep, where does it go? If it goes to heaven, is this where the soul really belongs? If it belongs in heaven, does it belong to the individual, or does it really belong to God? Does the individual have a right to life (because the soul is his or her possession), or is life given by God (and therefore can be taken back at any time for any reason)? If sleep foreshadows death, does waking foreshadow resurrection? The questions are never resolved, and the prayer evokes these traumatic contexts and these unanswered questions every morning. The simple act of waking up takes on theological and even cosmic dimensions.

To return to where we started, with the echo of Lamentations in the final phrase of the blessing, we can see how the juxtaposition of scriptural citation along with the midrash develops a complex meditation on the nature of existence and the human condition. The one who awakes immediately enters into these conversations connecting sleep and waking to exile and return, creation and destruction, death and resurrection. Heady topics when one is still rubbing the sleep out of one's eyes. In addition, the connections are not stable but instead slip and slide, as exactly how the exile relates to everyday life is unclear, and the role of God in the suffering is ambivalent. As a whole, Lamentations presents the destruction of Jerusalem as God's punishment, Babylon as only an instrument of God's wrath. Yet, even in the midst of Lamentation's theodicy, other voices more critical of God emerge.

> Look, O Lord and consider!
>   To whom have you done this?
> Should women eat their offspring,
>   the children they have born?
> Should priest and prophet be killed
>   in the sanctuary of the Lord?
> The young and the old are lying
>   on the ground in the streets;
> My young women and my young men
>   have fallen by the sword;
> in the day of your anger you have killed them,
>   slaughtering without mercy. (Lam 2:20–21 NRSV)

Sleeping and waking become a perpetual cycle of exile and return—but exile from what and a return to where? God's restoration of the soul in the morning could be a rescue—God has rescued the individual from sleep/death/the lion's den/the Babylonian exile. Or, does God cast the soul out of heaven every morning; is waking the exile?

The suffering of exile has multiple dimensions. There is the actual everyday experience of living in exile. Although the speaker of the prayer has not him- or herself experienced the Babylonian trauma, the exile continues to have real effects as Jews continue to live in diaspora communities, vulnerable to any shift in the political and religious ideologies of the dominant culture. Their precarious political standing is felt in everyday slights and insults, in the foreclosing of economic opportunities, in a hundred different ways that the dominant culture marks them as different and therefore inferior. Even twenty-first-century Western democracies are not immune to anti-Judaism and antisemitism. But there is also spiritual exile and dislocation as the soul is removed from the presence of God, a suffering felt by all regardless of where they live or their material circumstances. What is the purpose of prayer? Prayer is often understood as communication with the divine—when we pray we talk to God. However, it is a one-sided conversation because, to state the obvious, God never talks back. We can certainly explore faith-based and theologically-oriented understandings of how God responds to prayer, but in every case, the person praying must interpret feelings and experiences as answers from God. At best, any communication from God is an ambiguous response rooted in silence. At worst, we are only fooling ourselves. The act of prayer does less to bridge the gap between human and divine, this world and the world to come, than to underscore that gap, bring it into sharper relief. This is particularly true if prayer isn't just an occasional exercise, or even a once a week activity, but if prayer is wrapped into your everyday life, then God's silence is particularly stark. "The associations of sleep with death and exile, and the paradoxical implication that these continue even in waking life" (Schonfield 2006, 79) in both physical and spiritual senses is embedded in the siddur from the first moment of waking, archiving the feelings of distrust, betrayal, fear, and despair, alongside the more positive feelings of gratitude and hope.

The Torah Service

A fragment of Lamentations appears in another common song—*Etz hayim hi*—which is a part of the public Torah service, sung at the end as the Torah scrolls are placed back into the ark.[8] What may have once

---

8. The song is part of a larger prayer. The whole passage is a collection of biblical verses that begin with Num 10:36 and includes a number of verses from Ps 132 before the lines from Proverbs and the final verse from Lamentations.

been a simpler reading of Torah is now, in the words of Ruth Langer (2005, 121), "a complex ritual drama in which Jews experience the living presence of God." The liturgy that has accrued around the Torah reading connects the revelation at Sinai, to the temple in Jerusalem, to the contemporary moment when the worshipers stand together in the synagogue around the scrolls. All three periods are collapsed in the sacred time of ritual, and in the last moments of this ritual drama, as the scrolls are placed in the ark and the curtain is left open, the congregation stands and sings:

עץ־חיים היא למחזיקים בה ותמכיה מאשר:
דרכיה דרכי־נעם וכל־נתיבותיה שלום:
השיבנו יהוה אליך ונשובה חדש ימינו כקדם:

It is a tree of life for those who hold fast to it and all of its supporters are happy.
Its paths are the paths of pleasantness and all of its ways are peace.
Turn us, Lord, to you and we shall be returned. Renew our days as of old.

The song is composed of three biblical verses assembled together in the common Jewish compositional strategy seen also in the morning blessings. The first two lines are from the book of Proverbs: 3:18 and 3:17.[9] In the context of Proverbs, "it" (literally "she") actually refers to חכמה or *wisdom*. Wisdom is a tree of life, a path of peace. Proverbs and the other wisdom books of Job and Ecclesiastes are noteworthy in their complete lack of reference to other biblical texts, stories, and figures (except for Solomon). Wisdom is a universal good, able to be sought by anyone (Job, for example, is not an Israelite). Later in the Jewish tradition, however, wisdom is transformed into Torah, a specifically Jewish work and therefore a specifically Jewish virtue. Ben Sira, for example, does much of this transformative work, building the equation between wisdom and Torah from a variety of directions (see especially Sir 24). As one stands before the open ark, the scrolls displayed in all of their ornamental glory, the transfer between wisdom and Torah is made manifest. The Torah is the tree of life; the Torah is, indeed, wisdom.

---

9. These verses are present in most Ashkanazi siddurim by the sixteenth century. See Langer 2005, 138–39, table 4.

The final line of the song is from Lamentations.[10] In the biblical book, this line is part of the last passage. The chapter begins with calling on God to look at the destruction wrought in Jerusalem—death, slavery, rape, torture. Then the final cry:

> Why have you forgotten us completely?
> > Why have you forsaken us these many days?
> Restore us to yourself, O Lord, that we may be restored;
> > renew our days as of old—
> unless you have utterly rejected us,
> > and are angry with us beyond measure. (Lam 5:20–22)

Not only do these lines end the passage, but they are also the concluding words of the entire book. They are an affective bounty, a cacophony of feelings and emotions. The words express anguish, longing, anger, dejection, hope, fear, and anxiety. They do not express confidence in the Torah or wisdom or anything else; and they most certainly are not about peace and happiness. In fact, within the context of Lamentations, they are a desperate plea to God, and they express a dark worry about God's wrath and the pain and suffering it causes. The verses also reiterate a theme found in the book as a whole—God's anger and fury has become unleashed and forgiveness, mercy, and compassion have been denied. An echo of Lamentations seems even more out of place here than in the morning blessing.

Just like in the morning prayer, the inclusion of Lamentations in the Torah service adds an undercurrent of protest, worry, anxiety, and lack of trust in God, all present in a moment of surface affirmation.[11] Langer argues that the Torah liturgy is to make God's presence manifest, as if one is standing again at Sinai or in the temple in Jerusalem. The Torah scroll becomes the "locus of revelation that had been located in the Temple" (Langer 2005, 131), and the service as a whole brings the worshiper before God as embodied in God's Torah, an intimate moment of connection. At the same time, as Lam 5:21 serves to remind us, Torah "goes out" from Zion into the diaspora precisely because of the destruction of Zion—the migrations were the result of the trauma of imperial violence. The verse

---

10. As documented by Langer (2005, 149), "this verse only becomes common (but not universal) in the mid-eighteenth century." Also, see table 5 (148–49).

11. Although he does not address the Torah service directly, Schonfeld (2006, 6) does argues that the entire prayer book is rife with these undercurrents of anxiety.

from Lamentations is a tremor of fear in a moment of intimacy. God's attention is not always safe or comfortable; after all, in Lamentations, God's attention brought disaster (cf. Job). Situating this verse from Lamentations next to the ones from Proverbs also opens up a space to doubt the Torah's ability to bring peace, happiness, and security.

Alternatively, the inclusion of Lamentations here can also work against the fear and worry expressed by the verses in their biblical context—like Rubin's illusion where subtle shifts in perception can reveal either a white vase or two faces in silhouette. By bringing Lamentations into this otherwise joyful and affirming context, the fearful emotions are domesticated and tamed by surrounding them with the peace of Torah and the body of the congregation. By including these penultimate lines of Lamentations, there is perhaps an implicit answer to the worries expressed in the last line—is God exceedingly angry, is forgiveness impossible? No. Around you is the evidence of love and forgiveness—in the survival of the Torah and in the survival of the people of the Torah.

The tension between the two different texts and contexts is never resolved. Langer only addresses the verse from Lamentations once in her analysis of the development of the Torah service. For her, it simply reiterates the expression of intimacy that she sees throughout; she writes that Lam 5:21 "speaks to this intimate sense of God's providential concern for Israel and the human desire to stand as a community in direct communication with God, as was possible at Sinai and Zion" (2005, 155). Yet, as Langer fails to mention, Sinai and Zion are also sites of violence where God's anger brought destruction. Intimate relationships are places of vulnerability, and being open to love always also entails being open to heartbreak. Singing Lamentations at the end of the Torah service, as the curtain on the ark is closing, as heaven is receding—all of the complexities of intimacy are assembled, expressed, and archived.

Cvetkovich (2003, 38) insists that we need "models that can explain the links between trauma and everyday experience, the intergenerational transmission from past to present, and the cultural memory of trauma as central to the formation of identities and publics." As the trauma of exile rolls through the centuries, with each new generation taking it up and transforming it, the liturgy evolves. Anxiety is present, but always anxiety embedded in other affects. Jewish liturgy and ritual stitches together multiple historical and geographical contexts, along with their multiple emotions and affective responses, like a mosaic or a crazy quilt. By doing so, not just the pain of trauma is present, but also the creative impulse to gather up that which has been broken, recover that which has been turned into trash, and reassemble it into a kaleidoscope of ever-changing meaning.

The Service of the (Broken) Heart

In the centenary edition of Simeon Singer's seminal English translation of the prayer book, there is an opening meditation on the Jewish idea of prayer. In this opening, Chief Rabbi Immanuel Jakobovits notes that in Judaism, prayer is not about communication with God and personal self-expression. The Hebrew word translated "prayer" is a *hitpael*, a reflexive verb, connoting an action performed on the self. The focus of prayer is not outward but inward, not God but the self. "In short," writes Singer (1990, xvi), "Jewish prayer is intended to *impress* more than to express oneself." According to this understanding, prayer is designed to cultivate a particular attitude and orientation in the reader—which is one of the reasons for a fixed prayer book. The person praying places him or herself under the routine of the words and is shaped by their force accordingly.

The word *impress* presents another entry into affect theory. Bringing together psychological and sociological models of emotion, understanding emotions as both interior states *and* cultural practices, Sara Ahmed (2004, 10) writes that emotions "produce the very surfaces and boundaries that allow the individual and the social to be delineated as if they are objects." Emotions produce both social and individual bodies because emotions have effects, emotions *impress*.

> To form an impression might involve acts of perception and cognition as well as an emotion. But forming an impression also depends on how objects impress upon us.... *We need to remember the "press" in impression.* It allows us to associate the experience of having an emotion with the very affect of one surface upon another, an affect that leaves its mark or trace. So not only do I have an impression of others, but they also leave me with an impression; they impress me, and impress upon me. I will use the idea of "impression" as it allows me to avoid making analytical distinctions between bodily sensation, emotion and thought as if they could be "experienced" as distinct realms of "human" experience. (6)

Praying the siddur entails both bodily and emotional sensations. Jewish prayer requires a book that is picked up, its pages turned. Jewish liturgy focuses on heavy scrolls, picked up and carried, kissed, and unfurled. There are certain postures and movements, along with a near constant awareness of orientation in space and time. The words of the prayers evoke emotional experiences. "Liturgies by their very nature hold the attention while simultaneously frustrating the understanding.... Opacity is essential to the genre" (Schonfield 2006, 9). The incomprehensibility does not matter "as long as the prayers are able to arouse deep emotions and a feeling of mystery" (10); prayers resonate in affective registers that, through ritual movements and sacred objects, embed emotions in the body and link bodies to bodies. The fragments of Lamentations especially intensify this bodily experience. Elizabeth Boase argues that somatic metaphors in Lamentations—particularly in chapters 1–3 but also present in chapter 5—are a mechanism for the community to remember: "Embodied language names experience in a form that is both individual and communal. We experience the world in our bodies. Evoking bodies connects us to other bodies. The language and metaphors help re-remember the body, to bring back together the communal body by the naming of shared experience" (2014, 206). Invoking Lam 3 every morning and Lam 5 every Shabbat is not only a way to express doubt and anxiety but can also be a way of healing the traumatized body by patching it back into the community, impressing it with the presence of others.

The Babylonian exile continues to have a long durational reach as the siddur transmits the trauma from one generation to the next in a type of intergenerational and transnational talk therapy. Yet, the transmission is also a transformation. The diaspora communities that form around and in response to the trauma of exile are testimonies not just to the suffering of dislocation, but also to the creative interplay that exists between minority and majority cultures and the way subcultures become vibrant producers of alternative realities and alternative cultural and religious practices. The public culture that is formed from these practices "create a collective audience for trauma," a way to negotiate it outside of the therapeutic context (Cvetkovich 2003, 4). Praying three times a day is a form of political protest as it creates communities that move to a rhythm utterly unlike the larger surrounding community; praying three times a day is a form of spiritual protest as it defiantly continues to communicate with a God who refuses to talk back.

Dalia Marx (2003, 61) notes how the loss of the temple operates in the rabbinic imaginary like the loss of a limb, and in the same way that people sometimes still feel their arm or leg or hand (the phenomenon of the phantom limb), the temple though no longer present is even more poignantly felt. The siddur is haunted by the temple, and all of the complex emotions and affective responses associated with its loss are inscribed not just in terms of its content, but also in the ways the words touch other texts and contexts, and in the way in which the activity of prayer forms individuals and communities. The siddur as both product and practice is an "archive of feelings." The ways in which trauma is present are not always obvious and sensational. Rather, the trauma manifests in sometimes subtle and elusive ways (Cvetkovich 2003, 43)—like the echo of a question, the echo of how—heard and held briefly, and then it's gone.

Bibliography

Ahmed, Sara. 2004. *The Cultural Politics of Emotion*. New York: Routledge.
Boase, Elizabeth. 2008. "Constructing Meaning in the Face of Suffering: Theodicy in Lamentations." *VT* 58:449–86.
———. 2014. "The Traumatised Body: Communal Trauma and Somatisation in Lamentations." Pages 193–209 in *Trauma and Traumatization in Individual and Collective Dimensions: Insights from Biblical Studies and Beyond*. Edited by Eve-Marie Becker, Jan Dochhorn, and Else Kragelund Holt. Gottingen: Vandenhoeck & Ruprecht.
———. 2016. "Fragmented Voices: Collective Identity and Traumatization in Lamentations." Pages 49–66 in *Bible through the Lens of Trauma*. Edited by Elizabeth Boase and Christopher G. Frechette. SemeiaSt 86. Atlanta: SBL Press.
Carr, David. 2014. *Holy Resistance: The Bible's Traumatic Origins*. New Haven: Yale University Press.
Cvetkovich, Ann. 2003. *An Archive of Feelings: Trauma, Sexuality, and Lesbian Public Cultures*. Durham, NC: Duke University Press.
Elbogen, Ismar. 1993. *Jewish Liturgy: A Comprehensive History*. Translated by Raymond P. Scheindlin. Philadelphia: Jewish Publication Society.
Frechette, Christopher G., and Elizabeth Boase. 2016. "Defining 'Trauma' as a Useful Lens for Biblical Interpretation." Pages 1–23 in *Bible through the Lens of Trauma*. Edited by Elizabeth Boase and Christopher G. Frechette. SemeiaSt 86. Atlanta: SBL Press.
Horn, Dara. 2013. *A Guide for the Perplexed*. New York: Norton.
Koosed, Jennifer L. and Stephen D. Moore, eds. 2014. *Affect Theory and the Bible*. BibInt 22.4–5.
Kotrosits, Maia. 2015. *Rethinking Early Christian Identity: Affect, Violence, and Belonging*. Minneapolis: Fortress.

———. 2016. *How Things Feel: Affect Theory, Biblical Studies, and the (Im)personal*. Leiden: Brill.

Langer, Ruth. 2005. "Sinai, Zion, and God in the Synagogue: Celebrating Torah in Ashkenaz." Pages 121–59 in *Liturgy in the Life of the Synagogue: Studies in the History of Jewish Prayer*. Edited by Ruth Langer and Steven Fine. Winona Lake, IN: Eisenbrauns.

Marx, Dalia. 2013. "The Missing Temple: The Status of the Temple in Jewish Culture Following Its Destruction." *European Judaism* 46:61–78.

Prince, Catheryn J. November 12, 2015. "The Stunning Tale of the Escape of Aleppo's Last Jews." *The Times of Israel*.

Schonfield, Jeremy. 2006. *Undercurrents of Jewish Prayer*. Oxford: Littman Library of Jewish Civilization.

Singer, Simeon. 1990. *The Authorized Daily Prayer Book of the United Hebrew Congregations of the Commonwealth*. Edited with Introductions by Immanuel Jakobovits. Centenary ed. London: Singer's Prayer Book Publication Committee.

The Affective Potential of the Lament Psalms of the Individual

Amy C. Cottrill

This essay explores the connection between affect and the experience of prayer, especially the lament psalms of the individual. The first-person subject position of the individual laments is a particularly intimate space, and the language of lament—through prayer—therefore shapes the experience of the supplicant. Affect theory provides an important avenue for exploring the embodied feelings generated by the performance of the language of the psalms in the act of prayer. How does the physically performed experience of the intensely complex, volatile, and multivalent language of the laments of the individual in the form of prayer create sensory registers of sensation in the one who prays the psalmist's words? Especially in the language of the laments specifically, how does the alternating language of violence and powerlessness and the mixture of evocative, embodied experience create an affective experience in the one who inhabits the subject position of the speaker? How might those bodily experiences and movements be or become politically relevant? This essay describes a methodology for investigating such questions.

I draw on previous work I have done on the laments of the individual but change the approach in order to address the embodiment of the psalmist. In the first section of this discussion, I briefly review my previous treatment of the laments of the individual in order to clarify how affect theory changes the range of possible questions and types of inquiry. Then, I discuss aspects of affect criticism that provide foundation for engaging the lament psalms of the individual in particular. Much of this essay sets out methodological guidance for approach to the laments that combines textual analysis with imaginative engagement with the psalmist as an embodied individual. My focus is on the affective potential of

Ps 109, which offers a particularly volatile and evocative subject position for the "I," alternating between submission and demand ("Oh God of my praise, do not be silent!" [v. 1b]), powerlessness ("Like a shadow when it spreads out, I am made to disappear. I am shaken off like a locust" [v. 23]) and aggression ("May there not be anyone to give him faithfulness, let there be no one to show compassion to his orphan" [v. 12]).[1] How does this shifting combination of images register in the body of the one who prays it, and how do those feelings and sensations become politically and socially relevant?

The Embodied Psalmist and the Laments of the Individual

Who is the "I" of the laments of the individual? Elsewhere, I investigated this question as a rhetorical one (Cottrill 2008b). I sought to isolate the ideological assumptions embedded in the language of the laments through analysis of cultural assumptions, narrative scripts, imagery, and privileged language in order to understand the figured world of the psalmist, not simply as a reflection of the psalmist's historical circumstances, but also as a figurative, linguistic world that offers a particular subject position to the psalmist and thereby shapes the psalmist's experience. Language, according to this reading, is a reflection of historical circumstances and simultaneously a place of generative world construction; the linguistic world of the psalmist both reflects and creates ideological and theological realities in an ongoing way. Though I attended to the psalmist's body language and description of distress, my attention to the body of the psalmist was as a linguistic artifact of a rhetorical world (Cottrill 2008a). I analyzed the language of the body as reflective and generative of theological and ideological assumptions and narratives.

Though I continue to value analysis of psalmic language for its theological and ideological assumptions, that analysis easily leads to a disembodied, abstract, and cerebral notion of the psalmist who becomes an ideological construct as opposed to an enfleshed pray-er.

This essay takes the question of the identity of the "I" in the laments of the individual in a different direction: what sensory experiences and feelings are generated in the psalmist as an embodied person in the performance of

---

1. All translations are my own. For discussion of translation issues, see my examination of Ps 109 in Cottrill 2008b, 138–56.

this language as prayer? Rather than thinking about the psalmist as rhetorically shaped and constructed in and through the language of the psalms, I extend the question to include how the psalmist as an embodied supplicant is shaped affectively by performing the language of the laments of the individual as prayer. What feeling is generated in the psalmist when he inhabits the subject position afforded by the "I" in the psalm? What happens to one's body when one performs these words as prayer? What happens between and amongst bodies standing together praying these words? How do those feelings and bodily sensations evoked by the images and narratives of the laments, not yet taken up by the conscious mind and categorized into emotions, become socially, ideologically, and politically persuasive in certain times and places? I forefront the embodiment of the psalmist in the act of prayer as a sensate, corporeal subject. In other words, what difference does the capacity of the human body to sense, register, and experience make in our understanding of how the language of the laments comes to signify and mean in particular ways? These are the questions of affect criticism (Koosed and Moore 2014, 386).

Affect Criticism and the Laments

In this essay, I provide initial orientation to the aspects of affect theory as they are "transmuted into affect criticism," a means by which to engage biblical texts.[2] Particularly relevant to this discussion of the laments of the individual in this chapter is affect theory's focus on embodiment, the social and political implications of embodiment, and understanding of language as replete with affective potentialities.

One of my touchstones for conceptualizing affect theory is the philosopher Baruch Spinoza (1959, 87), who said, "No one has yet determined what the body can do." Through this statement, Spinoza implies a question that has yet to be answered: what *can* the body do? Affect theory is concerned with what the body can do and takes as its starting point that first, all thought and emotion is embodied, not separable from bodily sensation and processes, and second, only a small portion of embodied experience reaches the level of conscious awareness, yet that preconscious,

---

    2. For an introduction of different ways affect is conceived and used, see Seigworth and Gregg 2010, 6–9. Affect in biblical interpretation is gaining scholarly attention. Examples include Kotrosits 2014; Moore 2014; Cottrill 2014; Waller 2014; Knust 2014; Koosed 2014; Runions 2008.

visceral response of the body is the context for conscious thought and later knowing.[3] Affect theorists Melissa Gregg and Gregory Seigworth (2010, 1) describe affect in this way:

> Affect is found in those intensities that pass body to body ... in those resonances that circulate about, between, and sometimes stick to bodies and world, *and* in the very passages or variations between these intensities and resonances themselves. Affect ... is the name we give to those forces—visceral forces beneath, alongside, or generally *other than* conscious knowing, vital forces insisting beyond emotion—that can serve to drive us toward movement, toward thought and extension, that can likewise suspend us..., or can leave us overwhelmed by the world's apparent intractability.

Affect theory is therefore interested in the totality of bodily experience, not only what rises to the level of conscious awareness. Affect theory asks about what is happening in our preconscious, prelinguistic responses. As it stretches what is important for consideration, affect theory often sounds more like poetry than argument-based scholarship, referring to the shimmers, intensities, forces, rhythms, sensations, resonances, movements, and vibrations that are part of the preconscious experience that affect theorists insist are vital parts of embodiment (Koosed and Moore 2014). Because affect theory makes a theoretical space for what is preconscious, much of the language used to describe the embodied experience challenges scholarship that assumes as its goal understanding and signification.

Affect theorists are concerned about bodily sensation and the sensory context of meaning-making, as well as how those sensations become connected to systems of power and political movements. In addition to this robust understanding of embodiment, affect theorists are also interested in the social and political implications of this preconscious sensory reality. Affective experience, or feeling, is not only a personal and therefore private matter within the study of affect, but has social and political implications that make feeling a matter of public interest as well. In short, sensory experience is a sociopolitical concern within affect theory (see especially Ahmed 2004; Kotrosits 2014, 477).

---

3. Affect theory challenges the mind/body dualism that has characterized much of Western thought, which has privileged the conscious and the rational as worthy of investigation and scholarship. For further discussion, see Lakoff and Johnson 1999; Ahmed 2004, 3.

Relationality is at the root of understanding of the body and affect, and that relationality means that affect is inherently political, according to affect theorist Brian Massumi (2017, ix). Bodies are not self-contained, isolated containers of individual experience; nor are sensory experiences, feelings, and emotions. Affect is transindividual, the result of microprocesses of interaction that register in individuals and pass in and through bodies. Before emotions become political in ways that pertain to systems and institutions of social order that reflect and structure ideological commitments, there is the affective interaction of bodies and feeling that is preconscious and undetermined. Massumi (2017, ix) describes affect as "proto-political," a term that captures the dynamism of affect, the potential in any interaction to create change, and the openness of processes and bodies to move, respond, react, resist, or transform.

The preideological nature of affect as process is central to the understanding of affect and the political. Before affect is taken up and channeled in ideological structures, affect is the responsiveness of the body to other bodies. That responsiveness is, for Massumi, an important way in which affect is inherently hopeful, not because the affective potential of interaction necessarily results in particular ideological commitments among individuals and societies, but precisely because it is *not* predetermined by interaction. Massumi connects the preconscious sensations and bodily movements with possibility that is different in every moment, tolerates opposing views, and allows for maneuverability in every situation. Affect, he says, is the "where we might be able to go and what we might be able to do" (Massumi 2017, 3). Affect, or hope—Massumi uses the terms interchangeably at times—is about the potential and possibility that our preconscious bodies register in any particular moment in response to other bodies, texts, linguistic experiences, images, and so on (2017, 3).

Poet and philosopher Denise Riley elucidates the means by which affective experience contributes to the ideological commitments of individuals and societies and the process through which some texts become particularly important in specific times and places. She discusses the process by which linguistic systems become both affectively and politically powerful. For Riley, much of what happens politically relies upon our willingness to understand ourselves in certain ways. The connection of language to politics happens through "the ventriloquy of inner speech," the ways we interiorize external definitions of ourselves, allowing dominant discourses to become our narrative of the self (Riley 2005, 6). For instance, Riley says the dominant story of the self today is one of a self that is radically individualized and static, independent of history, the body, and the bodies of others such that we experience "petrification" in the "politics of the personal," and we are "embalmed" in the "Museum of Me" (6). Affect confronts those assumptions of interiority, individuality, and stasis by positing a different notion of the self as profoundly embedded in history, highly responsive to the surrounding social world, including the bodies of others, constantly in motion in the experience of sensation, and constructed through language that is, as Riley says, "fat with history" (7). Riley's choice of the term *fat* to describe language is saturated with its own multivalence and sensory impact, evoking a robust and layered aspect of language, embedded with an accumulation of abundant sensory associations and memories that inhabit words. Affect criticism urges a fat understanding of language as saturated with possibilities, associations, and provocations.

Riley's concept of self-ventriloquy is especially relevant for my discussion of the lament psalms of the individual. As first person speech in texts detached from their original contexts, the "I" is not a historical referent to a specific speaker but a rhetorical placeholder for the speaker, a linguistic point of entry for anyone who prays these psalms as their own prayer.[4] In other words, when one assumes the subject position of the "I" in the laments, one steps into a specific linguistic and affective world. As is abundantly clear in the long history of praying, memorizing, and meditating on the psalms, these prayers have offered individuals and communities a linguistic experience in which they have come to see themselves through that language.[5] The laments have and continue to offer a particularly powerful place for affective experience, perhaps because they offer the speaker an emotional script, language that both reflects and creates feeling as one inhabits the identity of the "I." Affect criticism brings into focus the affective possibilities that are generated in the individual who sees herself through the language of the laments.

---

4. See my discussion of this distinctive rhetorical aspect of first-person language in Cottrill 2008b, 12. See also Carol Newsom's (2001, 9–10) discussion of the "I" as a discursive position for construction of the self.

5. For instance, see the following works for discussion of the influence of the Psalms in the devotional practices of Christian women: Trill 1996; Austern 2011; Beal 2007.

Affect Criticism and Methodology

There is no single theory of affect, and there is no single methodological approach to using affect theory as affect criticism. As Koosed and Moore (2014, 387) note, affect criticism resists a type of "snap-on, grid-like" application of theory and has privileged a more vital, interactive approach to reading texts affectively. Rather than an abstract introduction or manual-like instruction for use of affect theory in the context of exegesis, I offer these remarks in the spirit of loose guidance about the possibilities affect theory might offer the study of the laments of the individual specifically.

Medievalist Sarah McNamer's approach is instructive. McNamer offers a discussion of feeling generated by and within medieval texts, how individuals learn to feel in certain ways by the performance of scripted words. As opposed to conceiving of emotions as happening to people, McNamer, among others, argues that "intimate scripts" produce certain feelings that come to be named according to certain emotional categories that are culturally contingent. Intimate scripts embedded within texts produce feelings that can come to be "true" through repetition and performance (McNamer 2010, 13).

McNamer (2007, 247) recommends an approach that combines traditional textual and historical study with attention to the embodied, kinetic aspects of the performance of the text. The "affective stylistics" of texts include features such as emplotment, repetition, alliteration, rhythms of language, the development of images, creation of dissonance through contrasting imagery, pace, and progression of language that builds toward climactic resolution (248, 250; cf. Fish 1970). Many of these features are established features of literary and rhetorical analysis of biblical texts. The key difference in examining literary features within affect criticism is that affect focuses on how literary features of text generate feeling as opposed to how they communicate meaning. Situating attention to emotion as a development of the questions Stanley Fish posed in reader-response criticism, McNamer says: "As instituted by Stanley Fish and used by reader-response critics, this phrase has come to stand for the process through which literary texts make *meaning*. Let's make an honest term of it: how do texts make *feeling*?" (247–48, emphasis original). The somatic effect of linguistic events is the focus of affective literary criticism.

I turn now to how affect criticism attends to the reconstruction of the historical and cultural construct in which a text was first read or performed. In addition to traditional questions of historical reconstruction,

McNamer's (2007, 247, emphasis original) approach recommends attention to the bodily context in which the texts were performed or used, to what I call the sensory landscape: "what is likely to have been seen, heard, touched, even *tasted* at the moment of the text's performance." Additionally, the historical context includes the social and political landscape of the sensory experience (247). A central concern for affect theorists is the way embodied feeling, conscious and unconscious, serves particular social, political, and personal functions. Of course, the *Sitz im Leben* of the laments of the individual is much-discussed in Psalms research and notoriously difficult to determine (for a brief discussion of various theories, see Cottrill 2008b, 5–18). Depending on the context of the particular use of the laments of the individuals under consideration, the sensory landscape may not be documented with historically reliable evidence. Limited scholarly evidence of how the laments were used in ancient Israel is available. This slight evidence might create a methodological barrier in reconstructing the sensory and sociopolitical landscape for performance of the laments, but, as McNamer notes, performance is always studied as a combination of presence and absence because performance is temporary and fleeting. Therefore, performance theorists who have developed strategies of study that attempt to "actualize absence" may be particularly useful in affective study of the Psalms.[6] Moreover, the rich history of the Psalms' use in lives of individuals and communities offers significant opportunity for those interested not only in the use of the Psalms in ancient Israel, but in centuries of the Psalms' reception. In this way, attending to the affective experience of the embodied psalmist provides possible generative connections between affect, historical, reception, and performance criticisms.

In the next section I briefly discuss the affective stylistics of Ps 109 that I think would be a feature of the experience of the individual who inhabits the subject position of the "I" in the act of prayer. To be clear, there is nothing determinative about affect. I do not argue that an individual who allows himself or herself to be represented by the "I" of this lament will necessarily feel or respond to the language in a particular way. Affect is unpredictable. As Maia Kotrosits (2014, 501 n. 96) notes, "the 'stickiness' of affect may be shaping, but it is not determinative of one's experience of

---

6. I am indebted to McNamer's introduction of this concept in 2007, 247. McNamer takes the phrase from Franko and Richards 2000.

an object. Another dynamic of affect is its unpredictability. It is not compatible with straightforward models of cause and effect, and it is full of contradiction and conflict." Yet this sort of discussion sets the stage for enfleshed scholarship that engages vital questions about how bodies are shaped and shape others, examines how they become restrained or agentive in particular ways, and gives attention to the bodies of those who use these prayers, whomever and wherever they might be.

Psalm 109 and Affective Stylistics

In previous work on Ps 109, I isolated various strands of self-constructive language that I see in the laments related to the psalmist's relationship to God, the enemy, and the psalmist's representation of distress that appears primarily in descriptions of physical pain and distress (Cottrill 2008b). Each of those strands of identity discourse assumes a different audience for the psalmist's prayer. Though a lament as prayer is most obviously addressed to God, the linguistic structure of the prayer seems to be addressed to a community—possibly including the enemy who receives so much attention in the laments—and an idealized self, as well. The audience of the laments is diverse, as the psalmist explains the cause of his suffering, the expectations and hopes he has of God and his community, and his desires for his enemy who is often the cause of the suffering. More generally, laments are also a way that the psalmist organizes his suffering and explains it to himself, articulating for himself a narrative of his experience to bring some sense of order to the feeling of chaos.

In my earlier work, I analyzed each of these segments of the psalmist's audience independently (Cottrill 2008b). For instance, I attempted to isolate the theological assumptions of the psalmist's understanding of his relationship to God, examining the laments for the imagery and rhetorical strategies that reflect and create that relationship. In a similar way, I analyzed the psalmist's understanding of the enemy and his own suffering, all according to the embedded rhetorical assumptions of the prayers. In addressing God, the psalmist is likely to adopt a subject position of submission and dependence. In referring to the enemy, the psalmist is likely to adopt a position of rhetorical dominance and aggression. Describing his own suffering, the psalmist is likely to adopt a language of dissipation and powerlessness. The psalmist does not address one single entity in a psalm, however, and so while this strategy of isolating the various relational frameworks helps the reader to understand the complexity of the prayer as an utterance, it elides the fact that those rhetorical strands overlap and interact within any particular lament. Any single lament psalm, including Ps 109, contains abrupt shifts in tone and self-representation, reflecting the multiplicity of audiences and relational narratives addressed by the prayer, making for a complex and volatile theological and ideological experience for the "I" of the psalm. Though I alluded to that volatility in a brief discussion of Ps 109 in my earlier work, I did not pursue that observation at the level of affect. What is the effect of performing such a volatile prayer, of allowing the "I" of that particular lament to narrate and shape both one's ideological and somatic identity? Here, I am interested in how the different methods of self- and other representation mingle and accent one another, and stand in tension with one another in the same psalm, creating an interplay of affective potentialities.

To illustrate, because God is a prominent audience of the prayer, the psalmist employs rhetorical strategies that make use of dominant assumptions of the God/psalmist relationship; the psalmist assumes a subject position of submission and supplication, emphasizing God's responsibility and the psalmist's weakness and dependency on God for action:

> Oh God of my praise, do not be silent,
> For a mouth of wickedness, a mouth of deceit,
> They have opened against me.
> They speak to me with a lying tongue. (vv. 1b–2)

> You, YHWH, my Lord,
> Deal with me according to your name,
> For good is your loyalty. Save me! (v. 21)

At the beginning and end of the psalm (v. 1 and v. 21), the psalmist rhetorically emphasizes God's power and his own weakness, articulating his understanding of God's ultimate responsibility and the psalmist's dependence on God to alleviate the psalmist's suffering: "Help me, YHWH, my God, save me according to your loyalty" (v. 26).

Between these requests for assistance and expressions of submission and hope, which establish the psalmist's need and his dependence upon God, a much more rhetorically aggressive psalmist enters. In fact, one of the distinctive features of Ps 109 is its lengthy and imaginative curse section of fifteen verses, in which the psalmist lingers over his desires for the enemy's destruction:

> May his days be few,
> Let another take his position.
> Let his children become orphans,
> and his wife a widow. (v. 8)[7]
>
> May his descendants fall to destruction,
> In another generation may his name
> be annihilated. (v. 13)

This language offers the psalmist a different set of affective experiences from the language of supplication and powerlessness. In these curse verses, in which the psalmist describes his hopes for the enemy's social and personal destruction, the speaker adopts a position of rhetorical power over the enemy, impressing upon his audience his ability to dispatch his enemy through rhetorical violence if not through physical dominance.

In the final verses of the prayer, the psalmist moves from curse language to self-representation as one who is incapacitated and physically weak. Rhetorical empowerment that the psalmist may have experienced through the language of violent desire in verses 6–20 shifts abruptly to images of faintness and frailty in verses 21–31. The psalmist's description of his physical distress is particularly evocative:

> For I am poor and needy,
> My heart convulses within me. (v. 22)
>
> My knees tremble from fasting,
> My flesh is emaciated from fat. (v. 24)

On an ideological level, this transition from rhetorical rage in the curse verses to physical and social powerlessness in the final section of the psalm may help the psalmist and the audience validate, justify, and affirm the violence in verses 6–20; the extensive curse in the preceding verses might be considered by all (psalmist, audience, God) to be justified when articulated by one who suffers as the psalmist does in the last section of the prayer (see Cottrill 2008b, 151). Here, however, my interest is in volatile and unstable feelings generated within and between the psalmist and his audience by these abrupt shifts in tone and self-representation.

---

7. For further discussion of this verse in particular in a popular political context, see Cottrill 2012.

While literary and rhetorical analysis might focus the interpreter's attention on the linguistic features and their contrasting effects, affect criticism is also interested in the *movement* of images. The imagistic language of dissipation and need combined with aggression and violence offers a potentially combustive embodied experience to the one who performs this psalm in meditative reading, prayer, or other contexts of reception. These diverse subject positions of supplication, murderous hostility, and powerlessness exist side-by-side in the psalm and change abruptly as the psalmist moves through the language of this prayer, creating a volatile linguistic experience for the speaking "I." The "I" experiences sudden and intense shifts from a position of threat to a position of aggression. The kinetic effect of this psalm is as important as individual images in isolation. In Ps 109, the movement of the psalmist's language offers a volatile, unstable, and multivalent experience that generates conflicting affective potentialities for the "I" who uses this text as a means of knowing self and others. The particular rhythms of this psalm offer a powerful poetic experience, moving between and among images of submission and need to language of aggression and threat, especially perhaps for those who know and experience fear and threat on a personal and social level.

The psalm makes use of contrasting images of aggression and powerlessness that potentially evoke a multiplicity of overlapping and conflicting associations. So, on the level of the language itself, the multivalence of the psalm's imagery is palpable, evoking opposing reactions. Because the psalmist of Ps 109 directs his language to multiple audiences, he uses language that reflects different persuasive strategies and imagery. A diverse audience requires diverse rhetorical strategies. Affect criticism directs attention to the ways these subject positions of submission and frailty and then violent aggression oscillate and move, creating instability. How does that disharmony and tension between expression of powerlessness and violence combine in the sensory registers of the speaker? How does the volatility of this psalm both reflect and create a bodily experience for the speaker? As the "I" of the psalm, the one who prays this prayer encounters overlapping sensations in the urgent expression of both submission and aggression. That physical experience of volatility and movement undermines static interpretive attempts and forefronts the kinetic effect of the psalmist's language as central to its affective potential. A specific performance of the psalm that explores the use of the psalm and the affective response of the "I" in the context of a specific sociopolitical setting would contribute to a more complete analysis of the psalm; my hope is that this discussion of the affective potential of Ps 109 contributes to further investigation of specific ways that the psalms are used in concrete situations. Such investigation of the embodied use of the Psalms, whether in prayer, meditative reading, worship, or other kinds of performance, facilitates future affective analyses of the Psalms.

Conclusion

In this essay, I introduce affect criticism as a productive and generative means to address the identity of the psalmist as an embodied pray-er. This embodiment extends the concept of rhetorical identity to include explicit attention to the sensory experience of real bodies who take up the subject position of the "I" in the laments. I add a new layer to an old discussion: who is the "I" of the laments of the individual as a body who prays? In this essay I pursue largely methodological goals, setting up the question of identity as one of feeling and bodily experience as well as ideology and conscious awareness.

My observations about the affective stylistics of Ps 109 set the stage for further discussion about how this prayer (or others) becomes socially or politically persuasive for individuals and communities in certain times and places. Affect moves the interpretive conversation from the level of signification, the ways in which we find and discover meaning in texts, to another level: Why and how do we come to find certain texts meaningful in particular ways? And, how does the self as embodied factor create the context of interpretation for those meanings? The ability of affect theory to contribute to emerging understandings of the interactions among embodied selves, texts, and cultural contexts, how texts work on us physically and preconsciously as well as consciously is, I think, one of the greatest contributions of affect studies.

Bibliography

Ahmed, Sara. 2004. *The Cultural Politics of Emotion*. New York: Routledge.
Austern, Linda Phyllis. 2011. "'For Musicke Is the Handmaid of the Lord': Women, Psalms, and Domestic Music-Making in Early Modern England." Pages 77–114 in *Psalms in the Early Modern World*. Edited by David L. Orvis, Kari Boyd McBride, and Linda Phyllis Austern. New York: Routledge.

Beal, Lissa M. Wray. 2007. "Mary Anne Schimmel Pennick: A Nineteenth-Century Woman as Psalm-Reader." Pages 81–98 in *Recovering Nineteenth-Century Women Interpreters of the Bible*. Edited by Marion Ann Taylor and Christiana De Groot. Leiden: Brill.

Cottrill, Amy C. 2008a. "The Articulate Body: The Language of Suffering in the Laments of the Individual." Pages 103–12 in *Lamentations in Ancient and Contemporary Cultural Contexts*. Edited by Carleen Mandolfo and Nancy Lee. Atlanta: SymS 43. Society of Biblical Literature.

———. 2008b. *Language, Power, and Identity in the Lament Psalms of the Individual*. LHBOTS 493. London: T&T Clark.

———. 2012. "'Pray for Obama: Psalm 109:8': A Reception Critical Approach to the Violence of the Psalms." *Biblical Reception* 1:366–84.

———. 2014. "A Reading of Ehud and Jael through the Lens of Affect Theory." *BibInt* 22.4–5:430–49.

Fish, Stanley E. 1970. "Literature in the Reader: Affective Stylistics." *New Literary History* 2.1:123–62.

Franko, Mark, and Annette Richards, 2000. "Actualizing Absence: The Pastness of Performance." Pages 1–9 in *Acting on the Past: Historical Performance across the Disciplines*. Edited by Mark Franko and Annette Richards. Hanover, NH: Wesleyan University Press.

Knust, Jennifer Wright. 2014. "Who's Afraid of Canaan's Curse?: Genesis 9:18–29 and the Challenge of Reparative Reading." *BibInt* 22.4–5:388–413.

Koosed, Jennifer L. 2014. "Moses: The Face of Fear." *BibInt* 22.4–5:414–29.

Koosed, Jennifer L., and Stephen D. Moore. 2014. "Introduction: From Affect to Exegesis." *BibInt* 22.4–5:381–87.

Kotrosits, Maia. 2014. "Seeing Is Feeling: Revelation's Enthroned Lamb and Ancient Visual Affects." *BibInt* 22.4–5:473–502.

Lakoff, George, and Mark Johnson. 1999. *Philosophy in the Flesh: The Embodied Mind and Its Challenge to Western Thought*. New York: Basic Books.

Massumi, Brian. 2017. *Politics of Affect*. Cambridge: Polity Press.

McNamer, Sarah. 2007. "Feeling." Pages 241–57 in *Oxford Twenty-First Century Approaches to Literature: Middle English*. Edited by Paul Strohm. Oxford: Oxford University Press.

———. 2010. *Affective Meditation and the Invention of Medieval Compassion*. Philadelphia: University of Pennsylvania Press.

Moore, Stephen D. 2014. "Retching on Rome: Vomitous Loathing and Visceral Disgust in Affect Theory and the Apocalypse of John." *BibInt* 22.4–5:503–28.

Newsom, Carol. 2001. "Apocalyptic Subjects: Social Construction of the Self in the Qumran Hodayot." *JSP* 12:3–35.

Riley, Denise. 2005. *Impersonal Passion, Language as Affect*. Durham, NC: Duke University Press.

Runions, Erin. 2008. "From Disgust to Humor: Rahab's Queer Affect." *Postscripts* 4.1:41–69.

Seigworth, Gregory J., and Melissa Gregg. 2010. "An Inventory of Shimmers." Pages 1–25 in *The Affect Theory Reader*. Edited by Melissa Gregg and Gregory J. Seigworth. Durham, NC: Duke University Press, 2010.

Spinoza, Benedict. 1959. *Ethics: On the Correction of Understanding*. Translated by Andrew Boyle. London: Everyman's Library.

Trill, Suzanne. 1996. "'Speaking to God in his Phrase and Word': Women's Use of the Psalms in Early Modern England." Pages 269–83 in *The Nature of Religious Language: A Colloquium*. Edited by Stanley E. Porter. Sheffield: Sheffield Academic.

Waller, Alexis G. 2014. "Violent Spectacles and Public Feelings, Trauma and Affect in the Gospel of Mark and The Thunder: Perfect Mind." *BibInt* 22.4–5:450–72.

Public Suffering? Affect and the Lament Psalms as Forms of Private-Political Depression

Fiona C. Black

Might the lament psalms be incorporated into a history of depression?[1] How might their unique representation of pain and suffering figure in our understanding of depression's cultural legacy? Following Ann Cvetkovich, this essay takes up the idea of depression not only as an interior, individual affliction—as we might typically think of it—but as a complex, affective picture, which reveals a publicly produced register of feelings in response to various social and economic forces. Usually not understood as the representations of actual sufferers in response to specific traumas, it is often noted that the psalms are homogeneous in terms of the scenarios they explore, and that the wealth of imagery used to describe the suffering has a compendial quality (Culley 1988; 1991; 1993; Broyles 1989; Miller 1986). What, politically, might this manufacture of feeling represent? At the same time, and as Cvetkovich's work anticipates, there is still the matter of the memorializing of the traces of individual feelings, located in time and place. How are these represented, and how might one distinguish between the personal in these works—the subjective recording of despair, even if as

---

1. I use this imprecise language of *lament psalms* because, though I often deal with the language of the complaints (laments of the individual, which follows Gunkel's [1967] influential formulation), I am not here working uniquely with one specific form; actually, I am going rogue on formal categorizations of the psalms. The use of these designations remains the norm in psalm scholarship, but it seems that the psalms often resist their formal categories, and lament language can be found in other form types. One psalm considered below, Ps 91, would be an odd fit in a study of the formal complaints, for example, but it is useful for beginning and ending my discussion. I therefore use *lament psalm* or *lament* to signal psalms that use typical lament language of grief, isolation, bodily degradation, and threat from outsiders.

literary device—and the public, sociopolitical response they might indicate as an archive of feeling?

One might object that it is misleading to attempt to separate individual (*true*?) emotion from that which appears to be a cultural product, aimed at reflecting, and ultimately shaping, a society's response to certain events, and not necessarily intended as an accurate representation of how people *actually felt*. Indeed, might not affect theory's insights generally indicate that emotion is always complexly intertwined with culture? Where such objections are appropriate, I phrase things this way because I am interested in the passages between what is *felt* and what is *produced*, and between what is *produced* and what is *received*. Put another way, and with reference to the psalms, I wonder what might change in psalm criticism if we were able to gauge feeling in the psalms in a way that allowed (at least the idea of) subjective, individual experience to exist on a continuum with emotion's rhetorical purposing in the hands of the genre. To me, the laments are unique in both their encapsulation of feeling (evidenced by their long intertextual history and their use as private, devotional texts) and their politicization of the individual body and its subjectivity. More specifically, in my opinion the memorialization of the/an individual speaker's feeling and its context is essential to the production of feeling as a corporate response to trauma and its potential therapeutic cure. We might call this the rhetoric of the personal. Interestingly, I also find such a trajectory to be present in depression's representation in our contemporary age.

I choose to see depression or lament in the psalms as a complex state that encapsulates many affects, most compellingly *happiness* (in particular, its lack), *fear*, and *pain*.[2] Where it would be enough to explore just

---

2. There is an extensive body of literature on lamentation in the Hebrew Bible; its scholars might be troubled at seeing it used interchangeably with depression (though the connection has been explored for pastoral work, e.g., Christenson 2007). From the simplest perspective, lament is considered action generated by emotion, which has produced certain types of literary texts. Such phrasing might indicate a temporal relation between feeling (grief), action, and literary product, but I am not sure this is necessarily the case. One of the interests of this paper is whether literary products could actually transmit or grow emotion. My insistence at inserting depression into this picture is to try to gauge some of the emotion behind texts we have habitually designated as forms of lamentation (the act and its generic product). Where the former is often perceived as a response to bereavement or trauma, could we not say that depression is a constellation of responses to these and other events? Via Cvetkovich and others, we have cause to consider it as such a cultural product.

one of these in what follows, I have a persistent curiosity about how such affects might coexist, bounce off each other, and perhaps be interrupted or manipulated by others: this seems to me to reflect how emotions work. In this study, then, I explore several instances of lament language in the psalms in terms of these three emotions, particularly with respect to the body's implication in that affective picture; I also consider their political and social implications. These investigations are laid alongside contemporary theoretical and popular-cultural work on depression. To begin, though, I seek clarification on whether, or how, psalms might belong in a history of depression at all.

Depression in the Psalms/The Psalms in the History of Depression

The laments are known for their brief but intense reckonings with despair: an unnamed speaker bemoans his isolation, his extreme physical and emotional pain, and his fear of death.[3] But is such lamentation predicated on or connected to *depression*? I resist the urge to pull out the *DSM* (*Diagnostic and Statistical Manual of Mental Disorders*) to check, because it is precisely the relationship to the medical history of depression that scholars such as Cvetkovich (2012) and Elizabeth Wilson (2015) wish to query, and for good reason. Such thinking about depression, though important, tends to diminish the social and cultural causes and manifestations of it, rendering it as something that skirts any relationship to culture altogether (Cvetkovich 2012, 90–91). The laments incorporate several qualities and experiences into their semantic and figural field: despair, fear (of harm or loss of life), physical pain and suffering, ostracism (or the perception thereof), alienation, sadness, and so on. Bearing in mind that depression figures differently across time and geography (cf. Greenberg 2010; Watters 2010) and is widely defined, it seems that these are directly in depression's purview, and that it is reasonable to explore the psalms as products of depression, memoirs of suffering that is sometimes alleviated by a divine reprieve and at other times left unresolved.[4]

---

3. I assume the speaker in the psalms is male; this is a reasonable conclusion given the realities of ancient/biblical social roles and literary conventions. In addition, I make no comments on his particular identity. For some comprehensive discussion on the identity of the speaker of the complaint psalms, see Croft 1987.

4. Cvetkovich (2012, 78–80) discusses the idea of memoir and its relation to the writing of depression as both a way to show "ordinary feelings embedded in ordinary

The context of the laments, however, could render their presence in a history of depression suspect, in a way similar to that encountered by Teresa Brennan (2004) and Cvetkovich (2012) in their respective discussions of *acedia*.[5] As Cvetkovich (2012, 87) explains, scholars of depression have tended to dismiss *acedia* as unsuitable for their work, on the grounds that it is "the sign of a distant, alien, or false conception of depression; although sometimes exotic, it mostly carries negative connotations." Cvetkovich (2012, 88) writes, "For many popular writers on depression, the medieval framework of sin stands as the opposite (in a psychically charged way) of the lifting of the burden of agency and responsibility that comes with medical diagnosis." *Acedia*'s putative spiritual origins, therefore, invite the dangerous attribution of depression to such unscientific elements as sinfulness or demons, and thereby threaten to negate the reality of the disease—or more significantly, blame the sufferer for it.

Something closer to home might further act to impede the inclusion of the laments in our history, too. Psalm scholarship has seen faithful adherence to the generic categories established by Gunkel (1967) and Mowinckel (1962), with plenty of debate over the parameters or suitability of individual psalms for those categories (e.g., Culley 1993; Nasuti 2004), but little querying of the entire system of classification. The expectation of the laments of the individual, for example, is that they follow a specific pattern of complaint, petition, and surety of rescue/vow: in short, suffering and its delineation follow a natural course. With this course comes the habit of psalm scholars to "read for the ending," subordinating suffering to rescue (cf. Villanueva 2008; Williamson 2003; compare Black 2012a).[6] On

---

circumstances.... I wanted to capture how depression feels—the everyday sensations that don't immediately connect to any larger diagnosis or explanatory framework" and as a way to politicize the genre and to "[exemplify] the activist principle of presenting criticism in the form of a productive or alternative suggestion."

5. *Acedia* is the medieval affliction of the soul described by Cassian (one of the eight faults articulated by him). Literally meaning "carelessness" (Cvetkovich 2012), though the meaning is hard to pin down (Brennan 2004, 98–101), *acedia* came to encompass weariness or distress of the heart. (In Cassian's hands, it later became laziness or sloth; cf. Brennan 2004, 101, 188 n. 3.) Manual labor can correct *acedia* (Cvetkovich 2012, 113), so Cassian urges that the world-weary monk who succumbs to such temptations needs to find a way to refocus his mind away from his sin and back on God.

6. See, for example, in their commentaries: A. A. Anderson ("Psalm 22: God is able to deliver"; 1972, 184); George A. F. Knight ("Does God really forsake us?"; 1983,

the surface, therefore, to query or resist the generic confines of the psalms or to focus on the unpleasant or depressive moments means swimming against the tide of an interpretive tradition that urges us to look away from the grim moments and towards prosperity and relief.

Several factors, though, indicate that the inclusion of the psalms in depression's long cultural-historical catalogue is not only sensible, but essential. As Cvetkovich (2012, 87) urges us, history and religion should not be seen as liabilities, but instead negative stereotypes about them should be exposed, so that they are thereby free to offer a way to critique "constructions of modern culture as enlightened or civilized." In addition, Cvetkovich (2012, 91) cautions that medical models, in addition to being "significantly bolstered by powerful economic and institutional interests, … [relieve] people of individual blame or responsibility and [make] for a tangible set of solutions that contrast with the overwhelming, diffuse and messy tendencies of social or cultural analysis." The messiness of social and cultural contexts is key. It is not that these contexts are to be *preferred* in the exploration of depression's contours, but that they must *also* be considered alongside medical models.[7] Further, we might make such considerations not only for biblical times and spaces, but also for our contemporary biblically-inflected cultures and politics as well.

There is good cause for the psalms' inclusion in depression's history in the literary contours of the poems themselves, too. Generic (in)stability, the precarious, shifting nature of the psalmic body, and the artifice with which it appears to be constructed indicate the complexity with which the psalms simultaneously reflect and manufacture lament, putting these texts squarely in the social and cultural sphere to which Cvetkovich points. To me these shifts and instabilities are not only accurate reflections of the challenges and vulnerabilities of depression, but might in fact be essen-

---

106). These readings are not unique to the commentarial tradition, but also seem to be demonstrated in literary readings as well. For example, see Robert Culley's (1991) study of the rescue patterns of the laments and Patrick Miller's (1986) discussion of the laments in chapter 4. An extreme example comes in the form of H. G. M. Williamson (2003), who, noting the difference between the retrospective perspective of the psalm and the speaker's present condition, suggests reading the Psalms backwards, so that the suffering of the speaker is understood as retrospective.

7. Cvetkovich's intention (which is one that is shared here) is not to argue for one model over the other, nor to diminish gains made by the medical profession in diagnosing and treating depression (see especially 2012, 95–104).

tial poetic vocabularies for it.[8] The laments' ability both to explore and subvert society's normal expectations around suffering and death appears integral to their nature, both necessary and alienating, at once legitimating the speaker's suffering and threatening to undermine his subjectivity. This ability also makes them an intriguing subject for considering depression's past.

As part, then, of a cultural history of depression, the task here is to look at how the psalms work to reflect some of how depression *feels*. The texts are taken as representatives in a body of literary exploration of feelings. The psalms are explored as part of a public register, or as Cvetkovich has elaborated elsewhere, an "archive of feelings" (2003), wherein cultural texts function as "repositories of feelings and emotions, which are encoded not only in the content of the texts themselves but in the practices that surround their production and reception" (2003, 7). Cvetkovich's study is specifically directed at queer trauma, noticing that it is differently configured, challenging the typical contents of an archive and putting pressure on conventional forms of representation, because trauma "can be unspeakable and unrepresentable" (2003, 7). In *An Archive of Feelings* Cvetkovich (2003, 9, 10) is specifically concerned with what results from representations of trauma, namely, the emergence of new publics and practices, which both reflect and reorganize existing cultural norms.

Such publics and practices naturally have political implications. As we authorize the placing of the psalms in depression's history, we thereby prompt questions about the shaping and governance of (depression's) culture. This would offer that even biblical poets can be depression's public intellectuals (Cvetkovich 2012, 91), and as such, and like *acedia*, they offer an important counterpoint to depression's contemporary cultural representations, which tend to be removed from personal and cultural histories. While care is needed to avoid co-opting Cvetkovich's activist, queer culture-work for the biblical context, we might take the opportunity to explore her observations that depression prompts us to rethink (what counts as) the political (2012, 110). The intriguing possibility is that, following Cvetkovich, the pain, fear, and failure of happiness in depression points to alternate histories of dispossession and isolation. Might depression therefore—in

---

8. Previously, I pondered the laments' similarity to the transgressive cultural-historical spaces of madness and possession (Black 2012a), likening them to the religious, economic and social worlds that Michel de Certeau (1990) painted in his study of the possession at Loudun in 1634.

the biblical context at least—prompt a counterreading of, for example, the Bible's colonial narrative? As Cvetkovich argues, despair does not have to be converted into contentment to elicit action; its presence can generate political action all the same.

A Demon, Old Shucksy, and a Bird on the Roof: Fear as Affect

Importantly, Cvetkovich and Brennan draw our attention to *acedia* as a component of depression's origins, for *acedia*'s formulation relies in part on a psalm. That is to say, Cassian's "noonday demon" in his influential description of *acedia*/sloth, is not Cassian's at all but the psalmist's.[9] Psalm 91, which appears to be a paean to trust in YHWH, mentions the noonday demon as part of a catalogue of things that the speaker need no longer fear (Ps 91:5-6). (The text literally reads "the destruction that threatens at noon," מקטב ישוד צהרים; the idea of the demon comes to us via the LXX.) The destruction's actual nature is disputed (Tate 2015, 448, 454–55; Weiser 1962, 608); indeed in the psalm the catalogue in vv. 5–6 may be intentionally elusive (Tate 2015, 155). This is significant. Whatever their exact meaning, the elements listed seem to trade on indistinct—but nonetheless familiar—sources of fear, such as the darkness, the midday hour, and so on. For both Brennan (2004) and Cvetkovich (2012), the evocative figure is notable here for its strangeness and for its identity as an agent that is not integral, but external, to the subject's psyche, only visiting or bothering him from time to time. The idea of the external agent also usefully gestures to the idea of the mutability of depression, to the idea that such a state might be subject to external stimuli—not so much in terms of its cause and effect, as might be assumed—but its cultural representation and reception. Seemingly, this is depression's bailiwick, from psalm to Prozac, and beyond.

I find a related figure in the lonely bird of Ps 102:8 ("I lie awake; I am like a lonely bird on a rooftop"). Where commentators are tempted to pin down its species and purpose as it idles there, it would seem that its efficacy is due in large part to its strangeness. Out of place, and behaving out of character, it aptly sums up the speaker's alienation and isolation as he sinks deeper into his depressive state. Indeed, it would seem that the

---

9. David's? Or is it Moses's? Tate discusses whether Pss 90–100 reflect an exilic or postexilic sensibility (Tate 2015, 452–53).

bird on the roof is an emblem of the speaker's own disassociation from his humanity; bird-other and human-other reflect each other well. The figure may not be menacing, as the noonday demon is, but it eerily lingers in the mind (the speaker's and the reader's) as a sign of the fears of one who falls away from his community and all that he had come to expect (see Black 2015 for fuller discussion of this figure).

All is not always strange, however: the laments normally list some tangible sources of fear (animals and enemies), perhaps drawn on for their familiar cultural resonances. Lions roar, dogs menace with open maws, enemies wait to ensnare (Pss 22, 31, 88, 102); in the latter image, in an effective collation, the subject also becomes the enemy's prey. But such feared objects are often repeated throughout the laments and remain fairly general, except where by accident or intent, they are modified, as in Ps 22:17b, literally, "like a lion my hands and feet." As scholars such as Robert Culley (1988; 1991; 1993), Craig Broyles (1989), and Patrick Miller (1986) have pointed out, this language appears to display a vernacular for suffering. The idea of the noonday demon, or the lonely bird, hints at something more complex behind the psalmic sources of fear, gesturing towards the imprecision or futility of trying to pin down what—as fear persists—is the source of the speaker's anxiety. This has an important connection with Sara Ahmed's thinking about fear, as we shall see. In more recent historical contexts, a similar, culturally weighty and strange presence might be visible in the figure of Winston Churchill's black dog, an oft-used symbol of his own depressive states. Churchill was likely not the originator of the phrase (McKay 2006), but popularized a formulation stretching at least as far back as Samuel Johnson, and possibly linked to the British folk/dog figure Old Shucksy, known not so much as a source for bad feeling, but as a menacing and potentially harmful presence. Old Shucksy and indeed Churchill's black dog run the gamut of depression's ability to shift about and evade definite representation, along with the fear that those who suffer navigate concerning *real* physical harm. These shadows and unknowns aptly embody the fearful *why-me*'s (Riley 2005) and *what-if*s of the depressive.

How, then, might we think about fear in the psalms more complexly? In Ahmed's formulation, the feared body is given a shape or surface by the one who fears, as she shows in her discussion of Franz Fanon's representation of a white child fearing a black man. As Ahmed (2015, 62–63) explains, fear brings these bodies into relationship, establishing proximity, but also maintaining a distance that is fueled by stereotype and misunderstanding. And bodies in fear are "surfaced" by their anticipation of the feared other. Sometimes, depending on the body and the circumstance, some bodies suffer a kind of shrinking, as they retract from the world and the potential harm they perceive there. Yet, what precisely is being feared? Ahmed indicates that fear has no proper object, but relies on the threat of the/an object approaching or making contact, though not necessarily being successful. "The more we don't know what or who it is we fear *the more the world becomes fearsome.* In other words, it is the structural possibility that the object may pass us by which makes everything possibly fearsome" (2015, 69, emphasis original). This renders the world "a space of potential danger, a space that is anticipated as pain or injury on the body" (2015, 69). The nonspecific threats in the laments, and especially the unspecified menace (the dark, the demonic, the pestilent) in Ps 91:5–6, make the gap over which this uncertainty presides more effective. Fear looms in the mind of the speaker; it keeps him always tense and alert.

The fearful one's integrity as a subject is what is at stake in the psalms. Ahmed refers to Fanon's example of the white child fearing that the black man will eat her up to explain that fear encompasses the threat that the feared other "will *threaten to take the self in*" (2015, 64, emphasis original). She observes: "Such fantasies construct the other as a danger not only to one's self as self, but to one's very life, to one's very existence as a separate being with a life of its own" (2015, 64). Most interestingly, the political implications of this fear are that they might serve to justify violence against the feared other (2015, 64), or alternately that they prompt bodies to withdraw or be diminished. In both cases, the economics of fear seems in many ways to be spatial; one party must lose ground or physically deplete the other, in the quest for presence in an uncertain world.

Ahmed's dynamics of fear are easily visible in the more overt lament palms, such as Pss 22, 88, or 102. The majority of the threatening forces in lament language are elements, as we have seen, that can consume or overcome the speaker. If it is an animal, the animal threatens to attack or devour. If it is an enemy, the enemy threatens entrapment or death. If it is an illness, the illness overcomes the beleaguered body, abjectly rendering it in the throes of wasting away, as the bones melt, the mouth dries up, the skin shrivels. In all of this, the language shares much in common (even if not as direct quotation) with other psalms, keeping things general, as we saw. What the psalms do not do is to build a picture of the enemy, the animal, or even illness in any great detail that might contribute to their diminishment as subjects, as Ahmed has envisioned. Instead, they seem wholly concerned with the speaker's (the fearful one's) subjectivity. The speaker recoils from these threats. His body shrinks (melts, breaks, dries up), turning inward the negotiation with the other about which Ahmed writes. The ground he loses is perceptible.

Psalm 91, which offers lament as retrospective (we might even call it lament's alter ego) elaborates this internal process in a sophisticated way: it constructs a drama around fear that includes an interlocutor, the one-who-may-still-be-afraid ("you"), but who might learn from the speaker's contemplation on how he came to move on. This is a counterpoint, we are led to infer, to the interlocutor's persistent failure in this regard. Whether an actual or a rhetorical other, fear persists in the figure of the one needing advice, having been transferred from the rescued speaker to become stuck to his inner self/auditor (see Ahmed 2015, 89–92 on the stickiness of affect). One could even go further to speculate that the complainant's presence depends on this other for his existence, as if *fearful* and *no-longer-fearful* are mutually constructed by the other; for one to gain ground, the other fails, and vice versa. Each party's presence only makes gains when the other serves as counterpresence, as when he functions as auditor for the speaker's claims, or supplies an explanation for the other's fear persisting, despite insistence that the object of fear will pass by (Ahmed 2015, 69).

The consideration of this first affect, fear, shows us already that there is a curated, public component to affect in the psalms, and that, by virtue of fear's literary presence in a lament text, what is ostensibly an interior negotiation also banks on interlocutors or audiences. As we saw above, in Cvetkovich's (2012, 102) appraisal, the *acedia* connection in depression's history is fundamentally important because it "plac[es] the medical model of depression within the longer history of notions of not only health but embodiment and *what it means to be human*" (emphasis added). So, too, with the laments, we might say that fear is about the public exploration of what it means to be human, which here involves an interrogation of subjectivity's manipulability, action-orientation, and rhetorical purposing. This fear is not a personal matter for the lamenting subject alone, it is a culturally inflected quest. Fear here requires a cultural sounding board; it invites a response. The longstanding question of the depressive, *Why me?*, which is so beautifully elaborated by Denise Riley, seems straightforward, and it appears deeply interior: "Why is this [illness] [attack] [isolation] happening to me?" Yet as Riley points out, there is always an assumed response (*why not you?*) and an embarrassment to it, since the questioner knows the answer cannot be forthcoming in any tangible sense. In real terms, it is a rebuke, a confrontation, but the target (society? God?) is not fully engageable.[10] In the most direct sense, it is

> a shorthand for this event has happened and I fear (or hope) that I am present in it while I simultaneously fear (or hope) I am absent. So *why me* boils down to, What is the status of "me" here? or, Where is me? The answer is: Nowhere. The questioner, however, valiantly persists. (Riley 2005, 63)

The questioner persists. This is the (ash-covered) bread and butter of the lament psalm. The urgent questioning refers, as we know, to the status of the questioner (Will he live? Will he die?), but also to the need for such texts to exist, to validate the speaker (in addition to showing his feelings), and to create a reason for him to speak in the first place. And the more such texts exist, the more they are needed; they proliferate and a culture develops. What the psalms might also add to Ahmed's exploration of fear as affect, then, is the rhetorical nature or *constructedness* of it all. This is the possibility that fear here has a purpose that both exhibits feeling—with real political consequences in the form of the fearful one's impending dissolution—but is culturally useful in that it creates or licenses a space from which the depressive might speak. The *why me?* therefore is the central component of the fear of un-becoming that plagues the speaker, but it is not a nihilistic question. As Riley observes, there is hope for absence *and* presence in it. Her remark that *me* is "nowhere" refers here, I think, to *not-one-place*—to everywhere—since the speaker is dynamic, subject to the onslaughts of his condition, but also performing it with a well-timed sigh here and a well-chosen word there, as he replies to those who might respond *why not you?* (Riley 2005, 64). His fear keeps him on the move; it also keeps him on display.

---

10. Brueggemann (1986, 59) even goes so far to suggest that lament language "shifts the calculus and *redresses the redistribution of power* between the two parties, so that the petitionary party is taken seriously and the God who is addressed is newly engaged in the crisis in a way that puts God at risk." This is an interesting proposition, but I am not convinced that the texts are able to effect such an equalizing shift.

Dreams of Home: Domesticity and the Ordinary, or, Where Happiness Resides

In the contemporary, medicalized understanding of depression, the risk is that the body will be estranged, as afflicted minds are separated from their bodies.[11] Our psalmist, though, keeps the alienated, afraid, and dissolving body at the forefront and thereby refuses this arrangement. But what else is he *feeling*? Fear's ubiquity suggests the presence of other affects in the psalmist's depressive world, too, such as happiness, our second affect. Disappointed, he sorely misses happiness; his fear gets in the way of it, he feels longing for what he cannot have and he realizes that loss keenly. We are speaking pointedly here, then, of happiness's absence, and of the objects over which he obsesses, which have come to stand in for it.

What, then, does the estrangement of the body actually show up? Cvetkovich ventures that depression might be intimately linked to isolation and dispossession. She asks: "What if depression, in the Americas at least, could be traced to histories of colonialism, genocide, slavery, legal exclusion, and everyday segregation and isolation *that haunt all of our lives*, rather than biochemical imbalances?" (Cvetkovich 2012, 115, emphasis added). Her work here takes us to important conversations about race and colonization, whose fuller exploration is beyond the scope of the present project. However, what I am wondering is if the psalmic figurative vocabulary helps to fill out contemporary depression's connection with dislocation, since it lays down the emotional and literary patterns of despair by creating powerful connections between the lamenting subject and the question of where (or if!) he belongs. If he cannot belong, he cannot be happy.

We might explore perhaps the most obvious example available to us, Ps 137, which is an exilic lament for Zion (see especially Ahn 2008, 270–74). This psalmist's complaint is that the speaker is unable to function; he is overcome with grief at his dislocation. Using the psalm's ubiquitous language of tears and weeping (Bosworth 2013), the speaker tells those who

---

11. The pharmaceutical industry seems to have appreciated this gap in recent years. One thinks of the widespread add campaign for Cymbalta™, *Depression Hurts*, which served to enter physical pain and feeling into the list of depression's symptoms (https://www.youtube.com/watch?v=Nf6Mm__M5RU; or www.depressionhurts.ca). An important exploration of the relations of the mind, the pill, and the body is to be found in Elizabeth Wilson's work *Gut Feminism* (2017).

are listening that he weeps in his memory of Zion. He remains taunted by his captors, who ask him to sing of his homeland, while he and his compatriots remain in exile. The psalm here has a few of the typical bodily images and ideas of depression that I have already discussed, as in the wasting or desiccating body, suggested in his vow that his right hand may shrivel or his tongue stick to the roof of his mouth, if he forgets (137:5, 6). (Both the hand and the tongue obviously have relevance to his identity as singer and musician as well.) This psalm also has one more feature, to which I return below: it ends with an imprecation on the enemy, and a particularly heart-wrenching and violent one at that.

In Ps 137, the loss of land is the dominant cause for weeping, but one wonders if it is not the specter looming behind all the laments. Cvetkovich suggests that, in her context and for whites at least, sadness is about the failure of the American dream. Analogously, one might come to the fairly straightforward conclusion that there is a perceptible dream (the Israelite dream?) behind the psalmic corpus in its final, redacted form and penned by the tradition's privileged elites. This state is one where stability, domesticity, and security reign supreme and would indicate that, for the tradition generally, signs of geopolitical security, prosperity, and health are signs of the dream being successfully realized. Their reverse, which is now sadly experienced by speakers of the laments as they navigate enemies and illness, marks a failure of that dream. These events of the laments thereby situate the speakers as always at risk for dislocation, for separation from the markers of YHWH's favor.

This proposal of a failed Israelite dream is supported not only by the laments' display of threats against stability and integrity (political and somatic), but also by its constant use of the everyday or routine to remind us of what is normal. We often see the speaker at risk of having the everyday activities of life in which he participates disrupted: he cannot eat, he cannot sleep, and so on. In order to familiarize emotion, to trace its impact on politics and social constellations, Cvetkovich has promoted the importance of the everyday in appreciating and evaluating emotion as it plays out in the public sphere (cf., the Public Feelings Project; also Cvetkovich 2012). This work has the effect of bringing the "things that happen" or the "stuff that seemingly intimate lives are made of" (Stewart 2007, 2, 3) to our attention. Kathleen Stewart notes that the ordinary (or, ordinary affects) "is a circuit that's always tuned into some little something somewhere. A mode of attending to the possible and the threatening, it amasses the resonance in things." In this circuit, the body seems to be at the whims of daily life: "It goes with the flow, meets resistance gets attacked, or finds itself caught up in something it can't get out of" (Stewart 2007, 75).

We can think of the psalmic body—the depressed body—with its peculiar corporeal inflections, as being built out of layers of the everyday (Stewart 2007), itself remaining as a register of ordinary feelings in ordinary time (Cvetkovich 2012). These layers may be the intensities or forces that pass between individuals (Seigworth and Gregg 2010, 1)—maybe the animals, the enemies, or God—but they may also be the everyday objects of life. For the speakers of the laments, the everyday things that happen occur so frequently and so mundanely, it is easy to miss them. These are events such as eating bread (Ps 102:3), the use of trees for shelter from the sun (Ps 137:1–2), a fire burning, grass withering from the heat (Ps 102:4), the pouring of water (Ps 22:10), or giving birth (Ps 22:14). The everyday, moreover, is wrapped into the body's suffering or its dissolution, as with the body that burns with fire, or the mouth that tastes ash instead of bread. More than simply referents for images of decay and despair, these features of everyday life link the body to its everyday exercise of simply existing. What is visible here is the utopic dream of everyday life (compare Cvetkovich 2012, 189–93, where this is explored via art). When the expectation of the everyday itself is threatened, so too is the broader picture of the dream that is at the heart of the psalter.

Importantly, however, one should not see the body as passive in this exchange. Stewart notes that:

> The body surges. Out of necessity, or for the love of movement. Lifestyles and industries pulse around it, groping for what to make of the way it throws itself at objects of round perfection. *The way it builds its substance out of layers of sensory impact.* The way the body is submerged in a flow and both buoyed and carried away.... Agency lodged in the body is literal, immanent, and experimental.... *The body knows itself as states of vitality, immersion, isolation, exhaustion, and renewal....* The body is both the persistent site of self-recognition and the thing that always betrays us. It dreams of redemption, but it knows better than that too. (2007, 113–14, emphasis added)

Stewart's vision of the body could be read as a rather exuberant one—or, at least, agentive. Where sometimes the speakers would have us believe that they are the passive, innocent recipients of violence, or of YHWH's displeasure, the conflict in the laments between the experience of suffering and the contrived, manufactured presentation of distress as rhetorical device to effect change remains paramount. For, at the same time as it is suffering, we also know that the body is caught up in the rhetorical fray of the exile and thereby evidences the demands placed upon it by the conservators of the faith to be of specific use in this context. If, indeed, it is in the everyday that affect seems most appreciable, then it is in the everyday that the trauma and expectation prompted by the exile is located. To put it another way: the mundane offers a commentary on the crisis of the present, which itself is an actual or perceived loss of the ideal. I like Stewart's presentation of the affective body as being caught somewhere between agency and passivity, between self-recognition and betrayal, as if the body both directs its role in life's theater, and is at the same time caught off guard by it. This dichotomy aptly sums up the dual intention of the laments, and it also captures the divergences of suffering as the speaker exhibits them. But the ultimate repercussions of his bodily descent into dissolution are beyond his control: as the body fails (or threatens) simply to exist, so the Israelite dream in which it is implicated loses its sharp features around the edges, until it too fades and is gone.

Suppose, then, that the land—especially in its idealized forms (the Zion of the psalm) might be viewed as an object of happiness, and that happiness (or its lack thereof) is as much a part of depression's affective picture in the laments as fear was. To be sure, the speaker of the psalms does not always comment directly on the land, but surely the everyday objects to which he does frequently refer might be ciphers for it. In her essay "Happy Objects" (2010), Ahmed explains that happiness is related to certain objects, which might be physical things or things that happen; these are affixed with certain qualities, and so in effect the recipient subscribes to their value. Moreover, the experience and/or the value ascribed to the objects is catching—happiness, like other affects, spreads or is contagious. Happiness's absence—in the sense that an object may become known as an unhappy object—might also be transmissible. In the laments, it appears that everyday objects are layered on/over each other (water, bread, the bones), some standing in for this happiness object, others pitifully showing its absence. Noteworthy for my purposes here is Ahmed's turn to the melancholic migrant for consideration; he fixates on his injury, focusing on some small sign of it, and thereby (it is perceived) blocks happiness. In her analysis, he holds on to the unhappy objects of difference, insisting that the difference they represent is the key to his identity (2010, 48).

In Ps 137, the harp fulfills this role of unhappy object of difference. An everyday object, it is imbued with multiple meanings, such that it reveals signs of bodily suffering (the tears), grief (a feeling), and then points beyond these to something more abstract. The harp is the sign over which the speaker and his captors wrestle (137:2). Yet in that psalm, this item indicates something deeper: he must relegate his harp to the branch, just as his claim on his land can no longer be satisfied; it has been removed to the hand of another. In the affective system here, there could be no possibility of playing whatsoever. Not simply a matter of the speaker *feeling too sad to play*, but that, without the physical object of the land, the harp has no correlate. Play is literally and figuratively impossible. And for the not so obviously exilic lament texts? The land still looms as the desired object, or, one might say, the object whose status (Will I lose it? Will I remain in it?) causes anxiety *or fear*. Will it be the source of happiness, or will happiness evade the speaker? An outsider perceives that the speaker becomes stubbornly attached to the everyday, to what is not there: the injury of the failed sleep, the dried mouth, the bread that tastes like ashes, are at the forefront of his complaint. Happiness remains unattainable.

The Body in Pain, and, What about the Happy Endings?

Cvetkovich's query that depression might be linked to histories of displacement, isolation, and colonialism includes the possibility that such dislocation might cause emotional wounds. In the lament psalms, the speaker is in pain—our third affect. This much is clear to anyone. But what is the wound? As ever, the language remains generalized—aching bones and melting bodies—and though some have tried to identify the mysterious afflictions of the speaker, this work risks forcing the collapse of the public-private tension that the psalms so beautifully explore. For, problematically, to diagnose the speaker with a unique somatic affliction is to cement the affliction firmly in the realm of the particular and the personal (e.g., Lindström 1994). For Ahmed (2015, 26), pain's intensity brings one back to an awareness of the body, which does not mean that one is unaware of it in the first place, but that in interactions with others, the body has become absent. Because pain involves the violation or transgression of the border between inside and outside, one becomes aware of such borders (2015, 27)—a factor that troubles the understanding of pain as somehow wholly personal or private (2015, 29).

This transgression of borders—inside and outside—would be the case, also, for emotional wounds. In the psalms, the emotional wound may not have the same physical signs of distress, but there are others: isolation, alienation, fear for one's life, desperation—all these are attested. Again, like physical injury, these have a sociability to them, in that others witness this pain and confirm its existence (Ahmed 2015, 31–32). Furthermore, it is not only individual bodies that are affected, but there may also be injury to the "skin of the community," a collective pain, especially of those who have suffered the injustices of colonization and dislocation (Ahmed 2015, 34). In this way, it is easy to see how here, as in the presence of fear and the absence of happiness, the individual's emotional experience (the rhetoric of the personal) is a model for collective feeling. This passage between what is felt and what is produced for the collective is barely traceable *as a passage*; instead, the two conflate, thanks to the body's wounds.

The injuries apparent in a text like Ps 22 are an excellent case in point. In this psalm, the language of pain and injury pervades, either in the form of showing the physical body at the point of destruction (the heart is like wax; the bones melt; the body is skeletal; the tongue is dried up; the body is desiccated: Ps 22:15, 16, 18), or the threat to it from external forces (wild animals surround him; enemies wait to attack; 22:13–14; 17–18; 21–22). On the face of it, this seems a deeply interior poem of suffering. Seemingly, the poetry was so effective that its initial declaration of isolation was put into the mouth of Jesus by Mark and Matthew (Mark 15:34; Matt 27:46). But, the vision here moves from the interior to the total; the suffering spans everything from the speaker's birth to his death. His pain must be witnessed, and his witnesses are nothing less than all Israel and the ancestors of the people; they are generations unborn, and the entire universe over which YHWH presides. As witnesses, they not only see, but they share in this suffering; they have a stake in its relief.

Oftentimes, therefore, wounds are co-opted by institutions and empires. Put another way, what is felt is transformed into cultural products, which are received and used by various entities. Consequentially, we need, Ahmed notes, to make ourselves aware of how wounds enter politics (2015, 32–33). This can be through a form of fetishization, for example, directed in the legal profession at compensation, or it can be about the co-option of pain to serve an ideological purpose, as with the translation of Ps 22:17's textual issues to reflect a christological event (cf. KJV, NIV, NAS, RSV [all 16b]; compare NRSV [16b], JPS). Ahmed, however, encourages different forms of remembrance that allow us to memorialize the past but not to create fetishes from our wounds. In the psalms, the speaker perhaps unsurprisingly holds on to, or even fetishizes, signs of his injury, displaying them for all to see—and to put to political use in the future. So, such signs of pain become the markers that readers latch on to, and which might be used as a point of connection. These points of connection can be positively inflected, or, as I discuss below, directed towards destruction.

When readers connect personally with these texts—which of course they do—it becomes apparent that they make demands on them, and on the suffering speaker. The melancholic migrant's injury, discussed earlier, is not the subject of critique for Ahmed, but an observation about what is expected from those who appear to be unable to be happy—those who are suffering the pain of dislocation, which can never be salved. As she explores, the expression of such pain might be tolerated for a time, even being the object of sympathy, but eventually there will be impatience on the part of the witnesses. ("When will he get over it?" or "When will he assimilate?") The speaker of Ps 137 is staging a montage for the reader. Picture it! It is hot; the cicadas are humming. He sits weeping on the banks; his idle captors, lazy in the heat, demand a song; but he will not be a laughingstock. The harp hangs above him, instead, taunting them both. But even the genre itself demands that the complainant get over it; move on, get out (Ahmed 2010, 50). Where is the rescue? What will happen in the end? Will YHWH intervene? This scene cannot stay static forever; the speaker cannot leave us hanging. We expect that all will be resolved, and indeed most laments make some indication in the form of a vow that resolution may come. (But: will it?)

Most scholars of the laments would aver that the endings typically signify resolution, either in the form of hope, an assertion of trust, or a statement of rescue. So perhaps, given what I have just discussed, the norm to read for the ending that I indicate at the beginning of this essay is well-placed after all. I am not convinced, however, that whatever upswing is visible in the psalms provides closure that *counteracts* depression's affects as they are articulated throughout. They do not seem to match the dynamics of the affects as Ahmed and Cvetkovich have described them. Can one who is feeling fear talk oneself out of it? Does pain dissipate on the assertion of hope alone? What seems more useful, given what has been explicated so far in this essay, is that these putative happy endings indicate two trajectories. The first is the expectation from outside that the speaker get over it. The second is that, at the least, these moments signify movement, action. For me, they signal where Ahmed hopes we might move upon recognizing politicized pain, and the place to which Cvetkovich traces depression as she pursues its implications. For both of these thinkers, pain is not an ending, but a beginning.

Endings, Beginnings, and Lament's Alter Ego

At least three of depression's affects are traceable in the laments; these are somatically inflected and effect deep connections between the speaker, his community, and the physical world around him. The relationships between things and people would indicate that depression here could never be thought of uniquely as an interior, personal affliction. As we saw, the speaker would not appear to want it this way; a private-public elaboration of how he is feeling points to a poetic performance of feeling, a cry for help, or a rhetorical representation of emotion, intent on making change—or perhaps all three. Moreover, it seems that depression's manifestations are brought out in relation to something or someone. Depression's affects work via the outside, not on the inside. In addition, depression's body in the psalms is a malleable, manufactured entity. Things that happen or threaten it, or objects that collide with it, help to shape it. And the malleable body is also able to be shaped by the speaker for certain ends. Or to be used effectively by others. To what end? I cannot conclude with the impression that depression's profile in the psalms is all about manufacture and artifice. What I make apparent is that feeling for the speaker is multivalent and *useful*, as much as it reflects the speaker's state of mind (and body!). In terms of its place in the cultural history of depression, the subject's corporeality indicates a rejoinder to a contemporary focus on the interiority and *minded* nature of depression. The unstable subject signals the struggles but also the possibilities of the depressive position; put another way, its usefulness marks it as a place for action (more on this below). One might also venture that the malleable depressive body here is mirrored by contemporary ideas of depression, which themselves seem subject to the shaping of various cultural contexts and discourses.

One example of many stands out. In his exposé of the mental health industry, Ethan Watters (2010) traces the marketing and introduction of the SSRI (selective serotonin reuptake inhibitor) Paxil by its makers, Glaxo Smith Kline (GSK), into Japan. A few points of this story, as told by Watters, are of interest here. The first is the malleability of cultural beliefs about the self and depression (the subject of his entire book), which in the case of Japan, was reportedly exploited by the pharmaceutical company following a high-profile suicide case and the subsequent use of the drug by Princess Masako. Those key players are the second point of interest. Both the public witness of trauma and class/status are essential factors (so argues Watters) for Paxil's success. The third issue is that several marketing trials took place until the right language was found for the symptomology that GSK sought to identify and market, as well as its cure. Depression being like a "cold of the soul" was ultimately the successful model, and Paxil's promise of increased productivity was the successful cure (Watters 2010, 225). Watters ultimately argues that, because of Paxil's presence in Japan, there appeared to be a significant increase in the case of people being diagnosed, or using the language of depression to describe their feelings. The question is thus: could the targeting of the culture by GSK have simply provided those with depression with a language for their experience, or did GSK actually grow depression?

Possibly, the more lament language proliferated, in response to the traumatic events of exilic Israel, the more it was needed? Could it be that psalmic depression spread, becoming a *lingua franca* for exilic times? One could never prove such a conjecture, but the sheer volume of psalmic texts (canonical and extracanonical) is suggestive of their ubiquity and efficacy, as is their pervasive use in the history of reception. Also thought-provoking is the idea that the present forms that we have imply there was a *right* or appropriate language for the Israelite context and for response to trauma. As with the GSK/Japan connection, one suspects that lament language became itself a tool for exploring what it means to feel fear, pain, and the loss of happiness, as much as it reflected those feelings. Certainly, the appropriation of this language by the tradition for political ends suggests as much. Additionally, it indicates why biblical psalmic language is still available to be co-opted in certain political settings today (see, e.g., Runions 2009; 2015).

The malleable body and the feelings of depression thereby signals readers'—and my own—interventions with it. As Brennan Breed (2014) points out throughout his study of Ps 91, the flexibility of the psalms creates space for readers to interpolate themselves. We are led to the brink with the speaker, but it would seem that we never actually fall over; neither does he. But readers do get drawn into the speaker's suffering. In its piecemeal, stylized representations, the body shifts about and resists determinate form, or diagnosis, but it seems that this is exactly the point (cf. Black 2012a). It is neither useful to pin down the exact nature of the malaise nor to see it entirely cured. Rhetorically full of potential, it is something discussed along the way in the journey to salvation; the body helps to make the case to the deity. The body also helps to make the case to the public that there is something to be lamented. This kind of interpolation ultimately interests Cvetkovich. Depression for her is not finally an ending, but a beginning.

She notes that it need not be something from which the subject is urged to recover, but that action, especially political action, can come from fear, sadness, or any of the other affects seen here.

We saw one such action included in Ps 137, which takes the form of a sudden shift to an imprecation directed at the enemy. The speaker asks for the opportunity to crush his enemy, to dash his enemy's children against the rocks (137:9). Never a usual ending for laments, this one is shocking in its desire for retribution against a specific demographic. Psalm 91 makes a series of more abstract assertions, that YHWH's angels will protect the hearer, that God will rescue the one who takes refuge in God, that with God the speaker might crush the lion and cobra under his feet. As Breed (2014) traces, these in turn have been applied, however, to specific contexts: for example, by Charlemagne, by Catholic gothic cathedral builders, by Crusaders, by Henry VIII, and, most surprisingly and recently, in recent American political discourse. One of the more memorable examples that Breed (2014, 306) brings to light is actor Chuck Norris's book, urging Americans to remember the God of 9/11 (that is, Ps 91:1) in the fight against Islamo-fascism.

More needs to be said on the matter of psalmic reception—but not now. What I wonder instead is if Cvetkovich's call to action, to activism, is a better place to stop. Can pain and grief (even as retrospective) be brought to bear—to bear witness—to other voices, as in her development of a trauma archive for queer communities? One might find the seeds of such witness in the psalmist's refusal to play for the captor (Ps 137), or the persistence of the speaker's voice in the midst of suffering, evident in all of the psalms. Such a move would see the language of lament not as a stopping place, but as a place to start. To open up pain and grief could mean an opportunity to pry apart the biblical colonial narrative and insert or explore the voices of dissent—because if this language meets the needs of the people as captives, might it not also be utilized by those whom they have captured at earlier points in their story and indeed by other captives who were schooled by these texts centuries later? The point here would not be to see if a match could be made—as if to imply that all the displaced really need is a nice psalm to sing, or a literary text in which they might find themselves reflected. What Cvetkovich, Ahmed, and Riley are all indicating in their own ways is that affective language is generative—of cultures of transformation and therapeutic or healing spaces, and of course, of the diminishment of others or of their further harm. The risk, then, is that depression's language might be co-opted for violent and oppressive ends, as much as it might be for the inclusion of marginal voices and experiences that figure differently. In Cvetkovich's vision, there is no option for the former.

Bibliography

Ahmed, Sara 2010. "Happy Objects," Pages 29–51 in *The Affect Theory Reader*. Edited by Melissa Gregg and Gregory J. Seigworth. Durham, NC: Duke University Press.

———. 2015. *The Cultural Politics of Emotion*. New York: Routledge.

Ahn, John 2008. "Psalm 137: Complex Communal Laments." *JBL* 127:267–89.

Anderson, A. A. 1972. *Psalms (1–72)*. New Century Bible. London: Oliphants.

Black, Fiona C. 2012a. "Formless but Not Void: Some Reflections on the Psalmist-Subject from Clay-Level." Pages 21–40 in *Far from Minimal: Celebrating the Work and Influence of Philip R. Davies*. Edited by Duncan Burns and John W. Rogerson. London: T&T Clark.

———. 2012b. "Lamenting or Demented: The Psalmist-Subject of the Complaints and the Possession at Loudun." *BCT* 8.1:28–37.

———. 2015. "A Bird on the Roof: Trauma and Affect in Psalm 102." Pages 89–106 in *Poets, Prophets, and Texts in Play: Studies in Biblical Poetry and Prophecy in Honour of Francis Landy*. Edited by Ehud Ben Zvi, Claudia Camp, David Gunn, and Aaron Hughes. LHBOTS 272. New York: Bloomsbury.

Bosworth, David. 2013. "Weeping in the Psalms." *VT* 62:36–46.

Breed, Brennan. 2014. "Reception of the Psalms: The Example of Psalm 91." Pages 297–312 in *The Oxford Handbook of the Psalms*. Edited by William P. Brown. Oxford: Oxford University Press.

Brennan, Teresa. 2004. *The Transmission of Affect*. Ithaca, NY: Cornell University Press.

Broyles, Craig. 1989. *The Conflict of Faith and Experience in the Psalms: A Form-Critical and Theological Study*. Sheffield: JSOT Press.

Brueggemann, Walter. 1986. "The Costly Loss of Lament." *JSOT* 36:57–71.

Certeau, M. de. 1990. *The Possession at Loudun*. Chicago: University of Chicago Press.

Christenson, Randall. 2007. "Parallels between Depression and Lament." *Journal of Pastoral Care and Counseling* 61:299–308.

Croft, Stephen L. 1987. *The Identity of the Individual in the Psalms*. Sheffield. Sheffield Academic.

Culley, Robert C. 1988. "Psalm 88 among the Complaints." Pages 289–302 in *Ascribe to the Lord: Biblical and Other Studies in Memory of Peter C. Craigie*. Edited by Lyle Eslinger and Glen Taylor. JSOTSup 67. Sheffield: Sheffield Academic.

———. 1991. "Psalm 3: Content, Context and Coherence." Pages 29–39 in *Text, Methode und Grammatik: Wolfgang Richter zum 65. Geburtstag*. Edited by W. Gross et al. Saint Ottilien: EOS Verlag.

———. 1993. "Psalm 102: A Complaint with a Difference." *Semeia* 62:19–35.

Cvetkovich, Ann. 2003. *An Archive of Feelings: Trauma, Sexuality and Lesbian Public Cultures*. Durham, NC: Duke University Press.

———. 2012. *Depression: A Public Feeling*. Durham, NC: Duke University Press.

Diagnostic and Statistical Manual of Mental Disorders: DSM-IV. 2000. Washington, DC: American Psychiatric Association.

Greenberg, Gary. 2010. *Manufacturing Depression: The Secret History of a Modern Disease*. New York: Simon & Schuster.

Gunkel, Hermann. 1967. *The Psalms: A Form-Critical Introduction*. Philadelphia: Fortress. [Orig. 1930]

Knight, George A. F. 1983. *Psalms*. Vol. 2. Daily Study Bible. Philadelphia: Westminster.

Lindström, Fredrik. 1994. *Suffering and Sin: Interpretations of Illness in the Individual Complain Psalms*. Stockholm: Almqvist & Wiksell.

McKay, Megan. 2006. "Churchill's Black Dog? The History of the Black Dog as a Metaphor for Depression." Pages 175–92 in *Tracking the Black Dog: Hairy Tales and Historical Legwork from the Black Dog Institute's Writing Competition*. Edited by Kerrie Eyers. Sydney: University of New South Wales.

Miller, Patrick D. 1986. *Interpreting the Psalms*. Philadelphia: Fortress.

Mowinckel, Sigmund. 1962. *The Psalms in Israel's Worship*. Nashville: Abingdon.

Nasuti, Harry P. 2004. "Plumbing the Depths: Genre Ambiguity and Theological Creativity in the Interpretation of Psalm 130." Pages 95–124 in *The Idea of Biblical Interpretation: Essays in Honor of James L. Kugel*. Edited by Hindy Najman and Judith H. Newman. Leiden: Brill.

Riley, Denise 2005. *Impersonal Passion: Language as Affect*. Durham, NC: Duke University Press.

Runions, Erin. 2009. "Disco-Reggae at Abu Ghraib: Music, the Bible and Torture." *Religion Dispatches* June 22. https://tinyurl.com/SBL0696b.

———. 2015. "Political Theologies of the Surveilled Womb." *Political Theology* 16:301–4.
Seigworth, Gregory J., and Melissa Gregg. 2010. "An Inventory of Shimmers." Pages 1–25 in *The Affect Theory Reader*. Edited by Melissa Gregg and Gregory J. Seigworth. Durham, NC: Duke University Press.
Stewart, Kathleen. 2007. *Ordinary Affects*. Durham, NC: Duke University Press.
Tate, Marvin E. *Psalms 51–100*. WBC. Dallas: Word.
Villanueva, F. 2008. *The Uncertainty of a Hearing: The Sudden Change in Mood in the Psalms of Lament*. Leiden: Brill.
Watters, Ethan. 2010. *Crazy Like Us: The Globalization of the American Psyche*. New York: Free Press.
Weiser, A. 1962. *The Psalms*. Old Testament Library. London: SCM.
Williamson, H. G. M. 2003. "Reading the Lament Psalms Backwards." Pages 3–15 in *A God So Near: Essays on Old Testament Theology in Honor of Patrick D. Miller*. Edited by Brent A. Strawn and Nancy R. Bowen. Winona Lake, IN: Eisenbrauns.
Wilson, Elizabeth. 2015. *Gut Feminism*. Durham, NC: Duke University Press.

Prophecy and the Problem of Happiness: The Case of Jonah

Rhiannon Graybill

The story of the prophet Jonah is a story about unhappiness. The book opens with the prophet fleeing from God; it ends with him sitting outside of Nineveh in the blistering heat, "angry enough to die" (Jonah 4:9).[1] That the precise cause of Jonah's anger is unclear only underscores the intensity of his response. The lack of detail is also notable given that Jonah, unlike nearly all the other prophets in the Hebrew Bible, is a *success*: he successfully persuades a city to repent and as a result, its inhabitants are spared. In spite of these prophetic accomplishments, he is neither pleased nor satisfied. Instead, the book of Jonah, and its final chapter in particular, is dominated by what Sianne Ngai calls "ugly feelings" (Ngai 2007, 2–3, 6–7). Jonah is disappointed; Jonah is truculent; Jonah argues with YHWH before retreating into a sulky silence. Jonah is angry enough to die. Whatever else he is, *Jonah is certainly not happy.*

Many readers and scholars have found themselves compelled to argue against Jonah's unhappiness, painting the prophet as petty, provincial, or even comedic in his small-mindedness (e.g., Craigie 1984, 218; Gottwald 1985, 1999; see further discussion of this tendency in Frolov 1999, 86–87). Others have suggested that there is something pitiable or even tragic in the limitations of Jonah's empathy or his failure to comprehend theological universalism (see discussion in Sherwood 2000, 21–32). Unlike these readers, I

I am thankful to Steven L. McKenzie and John Kaltner, my partners in thinking about Jonah. Portions of this argument were previously presented at the 2016 Annual Meeting of the European Association of Biblical Studies in Leuven, Belgium, and the 2016 Annual Meeting of the Society of Biblical Literature in San Antonio, Texas (the latter presentation together with McKenzie and Kaltner).

1. Unless otherwise noted, all biblical translations are mine.

am not interested in passing judgment on Jonah's response. Instead, in this paper I explore *how unhappiness works* in the final chapters of Jonah, circulating between the prophet, the objects he encounters, and the text itself. I am equally interested in *what work unhappiness does* in the text. In order to draw out the text's critical relationship to happiness and unhappiness, I advance two linked arguments: the book of Jonah is organized around happy and unhappy objects, and the prophet Jonah is an affect alien. Unhappiness is not a temporary crisis to be resolved; neither is it a personal shortcoming of the prophet. Instead, it is essential to the chapter, the prophet, and even prophecy more broadly. Prophecy is a practice of unhappiness. Following the winding trajectory of unhappiness leads to new forms of meaning.

Both (un)happy objects and the affect alien are terms that I adapt from Sara Ahmed and her work in *The Promise of Happiness*. In that text, Ahmed explores the way happiness comes to be associated with certain objects. She emphasizes that it is not that good things make us happy but rather that "happiness *participates* in making things good" (Ahmed 2010, 13). Furthermore, happiness, like other affects, is "sticky" (Ahmed 2010, 44, 230 n. 1). It clings to and is transmitted between objects, which then become "happy" or "unhappy" (a concept I explore in greater detail below). The final chapter of Jonah contains a number of unhappy objects; taking these objects and their unhappiness seriously offers new ways of understanding the text and brings unity and meaning to the often-confusing final chapter.

The "affect alien" is Ahmed's name for the subject who rejects, resists, or is otherwise excluded from the dominant orientation toward happiness. The affect alien refuses to be oriented toward proper and previously established objects of happiness, instead finding happiness in unhappy objects; she may likewise refuse happiness entirely. As a consequence, "the affect alien is the one who converts good feelings into bad" and kills joy in the process (Ahmed 2010, 49). As I show, this is precisely the activity of Jonah, particularly in chapter 4, which is my focus here.

In addition to providing descriptive insights into the Hebrew Bible, reading Jonah with Ahmed's theoretical concepts reveals the political significance of the question of happiness as it figures in the biblical book, and the biblical text more broadly. Jonah, I suggest, dramatizes the political and ethical stakes of the demand to be unhappy. Both of these concepts—the happy object and the affect alien—prove useful in thinking about the Hebrew Bible. My reading unfolds as follows: After a brief overview of *The Promise of Happiness*, I turn to a closer examination of happy and unhappy objects in the text. Objects lead to subjects, and the essay then shifts to the prophet Jonah and his status as affect alien. The final section of the essay explores what Ahmed (2010, 192) names "the freedom to be unhappy" and prophecy as a practice of unhappiness.

As I allude to above, my focus here is on the events of Jonah 4, which occur after Jonah has prophesied to Nineveh and YHWH has decided to spare the city. The earlier chapters of the book (Jonah 1–2), which include Jonah's encounter with the sailors and sojourn within the fish, contain their own complex interplay of alienated prophet and happy and unhappy objects. First among them is the fish itself, an object into which Jonah is literally, if also temporarily, incorporated throughout chapter 2. There is also the question of whether Jonah desires either to enter the fish, or to exit it. He demands that the sailors throw him overboard (Jonah 1:12); otherwise, his desires vis-à-vis the piscine remain opaque. For the sailors, Jonah himself is an unhappy object and one they hope to dispose of. In chapter 3, Jonah prophesies to the people of Nineveh and they repent. Objects figure here as well, as the people and their animals dress in sackcloth and fast (3:7–8). Their actions are effective, and YHWH changes his mind—a happy event for the people, though not for the prophet. While I cannot address these objects and dynamics in detail here, I hope to demonstrate the efficacy of an affect-oriented approach in reading and understanding Jonah, thereby opening the possibility of further affect-oriented readings of the prophet and the text.

The Promise of Happiness, the Problem of Happiness

In *The Promise of Happiness*, Ahmed follows the sticky traces of happiness as they move between subjects and objects. Unlike most documentarians of the happy, she does not begin by asserting (or assuming) that happiness is *good* as either a personal or social end; she likewise suspends the assumptions of meaning and value that circulate around it. Instead, *The Promise of Happiness* opens with a critique of the "happiness industry" and other cheerfully coercive discourses of happiness, which engender what she terms the "happiness duty" (Ahmed 2010, 61, 91). One problem lies in the use of happiness to justify structures of oppression, as well as to silence dissent.[2] In the same vein, the appeal to happiness—the happiness

---

2. As Ahmed notes, building on substantial traditions of feminist, queer, and critical race critiques, figures such as "the happy housewife" or "the happy slave" are

duty—is used to justify or shore up the status quo while foreclosing the possibility of imagining or effecting a different sort of world. This *refusal to be happy* presents a significant challenge to the dominant system. Much of Ahmed's text is an exploration of figures who resist or otherwise stand outside the discourse of happiness, including the figures she terms affect aliens.

I return to these figures at a later point in this essay. For now, I consider the issue of the promise as it relates to happiness. Happiness is a *promise* insofar as it is directed beyond the present object or moment; it is not present to itself or intrinsic to objects. Not that good objects make us happy, but rather that "happiness *participates* in making things good." As such, happiness is a sort of orientation:

> Orientations register the proximity of objects, as well as shape what is proximate to the body. Happiness can be described as *intentional* in the phenomenological sense (directed toward objects), as well as being *affective* (having contact with objects). To bring these objects together, we might say that happiness is an orientation toward the objects we come into contact with. (Ahmed 2010, 24)

This orientation has a promissory structure, even when the object associated with happiness is located in the past. Ahmed borrows from John Locke the example of a man who loves grapes (Ahmed 2010, 22–25). This pleasure is not limited to the moment of eating: if I also love grapes, I may become happy when I think about how much I like eating grapes; I may look forward to buying grapes when they are in season (Locke's example, at least, assumes an agricultural calendar still tied to the seasons); I may remember past meals involving grapes I ate and enjoyed. Of course, happiness is bound up in disappointment: if I anticipate the taste of grapes, go to buy them, bite into a grape and find it flavorless (or perhaps simply *different* than I expected), I will experience unhappiness. Of course, I may also get what I want and then still feel what Locke terms "uneasiness"—a feeling that is nevertheless directly linked to satisfying my desire. Was this *really* all that I wanted? Really? *Grapes*?

---

harmful fantasies that use the language of happiness to silence accusations of sexism, racism, or other structures of oppression.

Happy and Unhappy Objects in Jonah 4

Grapes? Or, we might ask with Jonah, a *qiqayon* (קיקיון) plant (Jonah 4:6)?[3] Or, for that matter, a hut (4:5), a larva that comes in the night (4:7), a blistering wind (4:8), a penitent city of more than 120,000 people "and many animals" (4:11)? As even this brief list suggests, chapter 4 of the book of Jonah is largely organized around objects. The chapter opens after Jonah has prophesied to Nineveh (3:4), the people have repented (as well as undertaking a fast and clothing themselves and their animals in sackcloth, 3:5–9), and YHWH has decided to spare the city (3:10). Chapter 4 shifts from Nineveh to Jonah and his anger. In spite of this preordained outcome, Jonah sits on a hillside to the east of the city, waiting to see what will happen to it (4:5). He makes himself a hut of some sort; YHWH causes a plant to grow up and provide shade, until,

> at dawn the next day God appointed a larva; it attacked the plant and it withered. Then as the sun rose, God appointed a scorching east wind. The sun beat down on Jonah's head until he felt faint and asked to die, saying, "It's better for me to die than live!" God said to Jonah, "Is it right for you to be angry over the plant?" He replied, "Angry enough to die." YHWH said, "You have pity on the plant—which you did not cultivate or grow—which came in a night and perished in a night. So shouldn't I have pity on Nineveh, that great city with 120,000 people who don't know their right from their left, as well as many animals? (Jonah 4:7–11)

Jonah never answers. Instead, here the text concludes, with YHWH's words and Jonah's silence.

Though the chapter is only eleven verses, it deals significantly with objects (on objects, see chapter 1 of Ahmed 2010, especially 21, 25). Most important is the plant that so pleases Jonah. In addition, there is the worm that destroys the plant, as well as the hut Jonah builds. Insofar as in chapter 4 the city of Nineveh is only observed from afar and functions more as

---

3. The precise sort of plant represented by the Hebrew קיקיון is unclear; it is sometimes taken to refer to *ricinus communis*, the castor bean plant. Interestingly, given the unhappiness circulating in and around Jonah, *ricinus communis* is the source of the deadly poison ricin. In the text of Jonah, its most salient feature is its ability to create shade. The term *qiqayon* appears nowhere else in the Hebrew Bible. I have translated as simply "plant" to preserve the ambiguity of the referent.

object of desire and frustration than as space/place in which action occurs, it too is an object. I analyze these objects using Ahmed's work.

Bodily Orientation and the Phenomenology of Happiness

Happiness is bound up with the question of orientation. In *Queer Phenomenology*, the precursor to *The Promise of Happiness*, Ahmed explores in detail the question of orientation. Ahmed suggests that orientations are not given, but rather they are forms of attention shaped by histories; furthermore, "orientations involve different ways of registering the proximity of objects and others" (2006, 3). This interest continues in *The Promise of Happiness*, where she writes,

> to be affected by something is to evaluate that thing. Evaluations are expressed in how bodies turn toward things. A phenomenology of happiness might explore how we attend to those things we find delightful. (Ahmed 2006, 23)

In the case of Jonah, this link between orientation, evaluation, and the body is made explicit. Jonah goes out of the city precisely so that he can sit opposite and observe it. In turning toward the city, Jonah's body says what otherwise remains unspoken. Without needing words, his posture telegraphs his desire: to see Nineveh destroyed. The future ruined city becomes a happy object toward which Jonah orients himself; its pull is so strong that it threatens to overcome the object that is present: the still-vibrant, now-penitent, but manifestly *not destroyed*, city of Nineveh. Jonah, however, refuses to orient himself toward this present city. Instead, in going out of the city and then turning back to look upon it, he makes clear that the object that orients his happiness is not the present city but its future destruction.

Ahmed's general comments about orientation gain specific support vis-à-vis the book of Jonah when we consider Gert Prinsloo's work on spatiality and spatial axes in the text. As Prinsloo notes,

> Spatial orientation can be plotted along two axes. Horizontally, primary orientation is to the east, hence 'in front' is east, 'behind' is west, 'right' is south, 'left' is north.… East–west orientation represents the temporal dimension. 'In front' is the past, 'behind' is the future. One moves backwards toward the future, with the past receding in front of him/her. As the past becomes remote, it becomes the realm of myth. (Prinsloo 2013, 9)

Jonah goes out of the city to the east; thus in looking upon it, he must face west. For Prinsloo, this is proof of Jonah once again doing the wrong thing: the prophet "ends his journey outside the city (4:5), sitting down 'east of the city' (4:5), thus again facing west (as in Jonah 1). *Jonah constantly and deliberately defies facing in the right direction*" (Prinsloo 2013, 23, emphasis added). The language of defiance, which Prinsloo uses here, is frequently deployed against those who refuse to conform to normative scripts of happiness (Ahmed 2010, 61, 116; Lorde 1997). Thus Jonah's orientation becomes *more* meaningful with the contextual background Prinsloo provides. Jonah goes to the *east*, associated with *in front* and *the past*; he looks *west*, which carries the meanings of both *behind* and *the future*. Jonah thus moves his body to a location from which he can look out onto the future he wishes to see. His bodily position enacts the anticipatory structure of happiness—though the city has not been destroyed, Jonah wishes it to be so. At the same time, his posture uses the text's own spatialization of temporality for a practice of meaning making.

An additional level of meaning emerges when we consider the gap between the narrative world of the story and the historical moment in which the text is written and, subsequently, encountered by readers. In the world of the story, Nineveh, "that great city," is not destroyed; it remains assertively present. The book of Jonah, however, is the product of a later historical moment, in which Nineveh has lost its great status. Thus the object that Jonah *wants* to see, and that he positions his body *in order to see*—the ruined or diminished city—is the real and present object in later historical moments. As Ahmed (2010, 25) writes: "Pleasure creates an object, even when the object of pleasure appears before us. The creativity of feeling does not require the absence of an object"—or, we might add, of a city.

Anticipatory Causality and Clusters of Promises

In describing the ways in which pleasure creates objects, Ahmed borrows from Friedrich Nietzsche and his arguments about retrospective causality. In *The Will to Power* (1968), Nietzsche argues that it is only retrospectively that we assign causality to feelings and affects. For instance, first I experience a burning sensation, then I notice that I have set my hand on the hot stove; only then do I associate the pain I feel with the action. Thus, as Ahmed (2010, 27) writes, "the object of feeling lags behind the feeling." Ahmed adds to retrospective causality a notion of anticipatory causality; an object causes feelings even before it is present. "Objects can become 'happiness-causes' before we even encounter them" (Ahmed 2010, 28). Similarly, the destruction of Nineveh can cause happiness before it ever really happens. For Jonah, this anticipatory causality is reinforced by the message he is made to prophesy in chapter 3: "forty days more and Nineveh will be destroyed!" (3:4). This repetition trains Jonah to associate the destruction of Nineveh—a destruction he avidly anticipates—with his own happiness. Lauren Berlant (2006; cf. Ahmed 2010, 30) describes objects as "cluster[s] of promises"; Nineveh is such a cluster of promises to Jonah.

Anticipatory causality and clusters of promises are also useful in reading the peculiar scene with the hut, the plant, and the larva that follows on Jonah's exit from the city. Jonah builds himself a hut; God causes a plant to grow over Jonah and shade him; Jonah "was extremely happy about the plant" (4:6). Why Jonah needs the plant when he already has the hut is never addressed by the text and has proved a thorny problem for interpreters (e.g., Winckler 1900, 260–65; Duhm 1911, 115; Lohfink 1961, 185–203; for a review of the history of the problem, see McKenzie, Graybill, and Kaltner 2016). Affect theory suggests one possible solution to this problem: the plant is a cause of happiness not because of the specific comfort or even pleasure it provides, but because it functions as a cluster of promises from YHWH to Jonah. If YHWH's decision to spare the city is taken by Jonah as an affront and a cause of humiliation, then the plant represents a change in trajectory. It represents YHWH's return to Jonah's side. The object of the plant is thus what Ahmed terms a "happiness cause" (Ahmed 2010, 28).

The plant as promise and anticipatory causality also explains Jonah's fury at its destruction. Ahmed (2010, 29) writes, "The very expectation of happiness gives us a specific image of the future. This is why happiness provides the emotional setting for disappointment, even if happiness is not given." Jonah has been disappointed once, as Nineveh is *not* destroyed; the destruction of the plant and the cluster of promises it represents is too much.

Happiness and Freedom; Encouragement as Coercion

YHWH's response to Jonah's unhappiness over the plant is basically an admonishment to be happy. God's first comment (which I have translated "Is it right for you to be angry?") is another way of expressing "Why can't you be happy?" This question can carry a certain aggressive or coercive force, as when it is reformulated into the deceptively kind statement of "I just want you to be happy" (a phrase Ahmed [2010, 19, 92–94] analyzes in detail with reference to parents and their children). Here, happiness functions as a practice of orientation, taste, and coercion.

In considering the social context and constraints of happiness, Ahmed draws on Pierre Bourdieu's work on taste. As Bourdieu (1984, 466) argues, "taste is an acquired disposition to 'differentiate' and 'appreciate'" as well as "a practical mastery of dispositions which makes it possible to sense or intuit what is likely (or unlikely) to befall—and therefore to befit—an individual occupying a given position in social space." Learning which tastes are acceptable, and which should be shunned, is a practice of social class. This is a practice of, in Ahmed's (2010, 32) words, "learning to discern what tastes good and what is disgusting: delight and disgust are social as well as bodily orientations." In the case of prophecy, this means learning which objects of worship are appropriate objects of delight (YHWH) or disgust (other gods). Jonah, for his part, must learn how to orient himself as a prophet; in his case, he must overcome his disgust toward Nineveh and the deliverance of its inhabitants. Furthermore, taste is a practice of orientation; as Bourdieu (1984, 466) describes, "it functions as a sort of social orientation, a 'sense of one's place,' guiding the occupants of a given place in social space towards the social positions adjusted to their properties." As with food, so too with other objects of happiness. Ahmed (2010, 34) writes, "to become oriented means to be directed toward specific objects that are already attributed as being tasteful, *as enjoyable to those with good taste*." YHWH's object lesson to Jonah is a lesson in how the prophet is improperly oriented: he does not enjoy the deliverance of the city of Nineveh because his taste is improperly aligned. He does not find the right objects happy; his happy objects, such as the hut, are not right.[4]

The process of educating taste involves the erasure of all signs of the educative process. Taste and happiness should not only be directed toward

---

4. The theological use of Jonah, especially in Christian religious contexts, introduces another layer of complication here. The book of Jonah frequently becomes a teaching tool to show readers or listeners why their happy objects are not right and to reorient them to new happiness trajectories. The popular cartoon Veggie Tales, which includes a feature-film length Jonah narrative, is one especially popular example. I thank Meredith Minister for suggesting this to me.

the proper objects; they should also appear effortlessly to do so. This is an argument made strenuously by Aristotle in his *Nicomachean Ethics*, where he insists not simply on moderation but on effortless moderation. Thus, "a happy life, a good life … involves the regulation of desire" (Ahmed 2010, 37). Jonah, however, refuses either to regulate his desire (that is, to respond with moderation) or to align it with proper objects (the repentance of the Ninevites, the merciful sparing of the city). And in the course of Jonah's refusal, the coercive logic of YHWH's message becomes clear. YHWH is attempting to orient his prophet, to force him to find pleasure in certain appropriate objects and not in others. The violence that this lesson engenders—the nocturnal destruction of the plant by a worm—is supposed to go unmentioned. Jonah's preoccupation with the plant is a way of naming and calling out the otherwise unspoken process.

It is possible to read YHWH's words not as chastisement but as encouragement, meant not just to instruct but to revive his weary prophet. But encouragement, too, can be coercive. Ahmed (2010, 47–48) writes,

> To be encouraging is often thought of as generous, a way of energizing somebody, of enabling them to be capable. To encourage can be to give courage. But to encourage can also be forceful. Being encouraged can be a way of being directed toward somebody else's wants. The generosity of encouragement can hide the force of being directed somewhere.

In Jonah's refusal to go along, this structure is made clear. YHWH's encouragement that his prophet adopt an attitude of mercy and compassion is experienced, by said prophet, as coercion. I, now, shift to consider Jonah's refusal more thoroughly, and in particular to set forth an argument for reading Jonah as an affect alien.

Jonah as Melancholic Migrant and Affect Alien

In mapping who is outside—willingly or otherwise—the structures of happiness, Ahmed offers the figure of the *affect alien*. The affect alien is the subject whose affect does not line up with what is expected; instead, the result is alienation. As Ahmed (2010, 240) explains, "affect aliens are those who do not desire in the right way"; their desires are misaligned with the demands of the happiness duty. The affect alien represents a disjoint between general happiness and messy particulars. Ahmed gives a number of examples of such affect aliens:

1. the *bride*, who doesn't, or can't, feel happy on her wedding day, "the happiest day of your life" (Ahmed 2010, 41);
2. the *feminist killjoy*, who refuses to be a "happy housewife" or to laugh at a rape joke (a related figure is the *angry black woman*; Ahmed 2010, 50–87, 67–68);
3. the *unhappy queer*, who either refuses to be heterosexual or refuses to be unhappy about not being heterosexual (Ahmed 2010, 88–120);
4. the *melancholic migrant*, who refuses to forget his old country and cheer for his new one in the rugby match (Ahmed 2010, 121–59).

The bride who refuses to act happy at her wedding kills the joy of her family. The feminist who refuses to laugh at a rape joke kills the joy of happy hour. And to their ranks, we might add Jonah, the prophet who refuses to be happy over the deliverance of a doomed city. The prophet who refuses to act happy after his prophecy succeeds kills the joy of both YHWH and the text's readers. Perhaps he even kills the joy of the Ninevites, who have oriented themselves toward his message so thoroughly.

Ahmed (2010, 49) describes the affect alien as "the one who converts good feelings into bad, who as it were 'kills' the joy of the family." The character of Jonah frustrates us because he does not respond appropriately throughout the book but more particularly to the Ninevites' repentance. His response—anger, then silence—goes against both what YHWH wishes (as is evident from their conversation in chapter 4) and what the intended Hebrew reader would expect. Jonah becomes an affect alien.

The Fixation with Injury

One of recurrent characteristics of the affect alien that Ahmed describes is the "fixation with injury." Insofar as happiness assumes a common orientation, the affect alien is alienated by his refusal to fall into line. In particular, he is fixated on his own past injury. Here, Ahmed's clearest example is the "melancholic migrant." Her focus is on nonwhite immigrants to Britain, especially those from former British colonies, and the impossible demands placed upon such migrants: to let go of the hurt of racism, to forget the harms of colonialism, to invent happy memories of empire. As Ahmed (2010, 130) writes of her own particular context, "I would argue that contemporary race politics in the UK involves … a social obligation to remember the history of empire *as* a history of happiness." In the face of such demands, migrants are melancholic insofar as they cannot let go of past trauma (whether the effects of colonialism, the hurt of racism, or some other cause of pain). The melancholic migrant is unwilling to "just get over it," remaining, instead, fixated on injury. Often, this fixation becomes a refusal to convert unhappy objects into happy ones. This may refer to large concepts (renarrating the history of colonialism as a story of happy diversity) or specific objects (the turban or headscarf appropriated into larger discourses of nationalism and patriotism; on this process, see as well Puar 2007).

Jonah, we here remember, is also a migrant. He journeys from his home under compulsion and ends up in an unfamiliar city; at least within the space of the narrative, he never returns home. Jonah, too, is melancholic; he refuses to let go of his past experiences or past hurt. Jonah is angry; Jonah is fixated on the harm he perceives. Ahmed (2010, 144) writes,

> The melancholic migrant's fixation with injury is read as an obstacle not only to his own happiness but also to the happiness of the generation to come, and even to national happiness.

If we replace *national happiness* with *Yahwistic happiness* or even *universal happiness under vaguely Yahwistic or biblical auspices*, this is a key description of Jonah and his refusal of letting go of hurt.

What is Jonah's hurt? The humiliation of being sent to prophesy, or perhaps even the humiliation of succeeding? The three days in the fish cannot have been pleasant, though Jonah never protests that portion of his prophetic journey. Then there is the hurt Jonah expresses directly in the text: the anger over the loss of his plant and the heat of the sun beating down on his head. In the face of all these affronts, Jonah cannot let go.

The Refusal to Remember a History of Happiness

The melancholic migrant's fixation with injury is linked to a refusal to perform certain types of memory work: specifically, to fabricate a history of happiness. As Ahmed explores in detail in her reading of the contemporary melancholic migrants to the United Kingdom, empire demands that it be remembered happily. This demand plays out in a number of ways: the so-called civilizing project is reremembered as a project of happiness, the "gift of happiness is imagined here in terms of civility," "empire is justified as *liberation from abjection*," "the colonial project is thus imagined as a form of moral training or habituation," "diversity ... becomes a way of remembering empire" (Ahmed 2010, 124, 127, 129, 131). Furthermore, migrants are disproportionately required to participate in this work of happy remembering. Thus,

> migrants are increasingly subject to what I am calling the happiness duty, in a way that is continuous with the happiness duty of the natives in the colonial mission. If in the nineteenth century the natives must become (more) British in order to be recognized as subjects of empire, in a contemporary context, it is migrants who must become (more) British in order to be recognized as citizens of the nation. Citizenship now requires a test: we might speculate that this test is a happiness test. (Ahmed 2010, 130)

I quote Ahmed at length because this passage is useful in thinking through how, precisely, the happiness duty is activated in Jonah 3 and 4. The duty of the residents of Nineveh is, clearly, not one of happiness but of penitence. However, as I sketch in detail above, the Ninevites are successful in orienting themselves toward appropriate objects (YHWH) and in embodying specific affects (through the practices of repentance.) The scene in chapter 3 is, in its barest form, a test; the people of Nineveh pass.

Jonah's test is different. As with other melancholic migrants, Jonah's test is a happiness test. Jonah is *supposed to be happy*. There are, moreover, multiple temporalities of happiness at play here. Jonah should be happy in the narrative present that the city has been spared; this is the thrust of YHWH's comments in 4:9–11. Jonah should also *remember* his prophecy happily; he should not dwell on past hurt. And, more broadly, the God of the Hebrew Bible should be remembered happily, as a universal God who shows mercy to all. Frequently, interpretations of Jonah 3–4 argue that this is the central theme of the book of Jonah, what Kevin Youngblood (2013) terms "God's scandalous mercy," directed not simply to Israel but to all.

In spite of his claim, Youngblood's reading almost entirely emphasizes mercy, not scandal; the latter term is used mostly to disparage Jonah's small-minded response. I suggest, however, that the term *scandalous mercy* is more fitting than Youngblood lets on. From Jonah's perspective, the mercy YHWH shows is, indeed, a scandal. He refuses to respond with happiness. And his refusal threatens the larger narrative of a universal and merciful God that so many commentators seek to find in the book (and that may even be the *intent* of the book, if such a thing exists).

Melancholia

Ahmed's description of migrant affect aliens as melancholic draws on Sigmund Freud, and in particular on "Mourning and Melancholia." For Freud, melancholia represents the failure to mourn properly. The melancholic subject is unable to give up a lost love object, instead incorporating the lost object into the ego (Freud 2005, 204–5). Ahmed suggests that the migrant is also a melancholic subject, unable to *let go* of certain objects and experiences that the new homeland would prefer to be lost. Jonah's refusal to accept YHWH's mercy and his insistence on clinging to his own pain are clear examples of such melancholia. As Ahmed (2010, 140–41) describes, the melancholia experienced by melancholic migrants and other subjects may well be the loss of an abstract ideal; Freud also raises the possibility. That nothing *real* is lost in Nineveh—no people, no animals—does not preclude Jonah's melancholic response. Of course, what Jonah has lost in being called to Nineveh is not addressed by the text—which does not negate the possibility of melancholia around those objects (a home? a family? a life before prophecy?) as well.

Melancholia also helps explain the peculiar succession of objects in Jonah 4. Jonah builds a hut; Jonah gains a plant; Jonah loses his plant to a larva that comes in the night; Jonah hates the hot sun. The reaction of the prophet to this rather muddled sequence of events—why does Jonah need the plant for shade if he has already built himself a hut?—becomes clearer when we consider melancholia. The plant represents, and to some degree substitutes for, the abstraction that is at the center of Jonah's loss. The plant gives material form to an otherwise abstract process. Thus, Jonah's claim that he is "angry enough to die" and YHWH's rebuke both are and are not responses to the proximate event of the destruction of the plant. Jonah is angry that his plant has been destroyed; Jonah is unable to mourn what cannot be admitted as lost. Anger and melancholia are intimately bound up together; the result is still more unhappiness.

The Freedom to be Unhappy

What if unhappiness were not a failure or an oppression, but a freedom? Ahmed (2010, 195) considers what it would mean to "radicalize freedom *as* the freedom to be unhappy." She elaborates,

> The freedom to be unhappy is not about being wretched or sad, although it might involve freedom to express such feelings. The freedom to be unhappy would be the freedom to be affected by what is unhappy, and to live a life that might affect others unhappily. The freedom to be unhappy would be the freedom to live a life that deviates from the paths of happiness, wherever that deviation takes us. It would thus mean the freedom to cause unhappiness by acts of deviation. (Ahmed 2010, 195)

Though Ahmed couches her comments in the conditional mood, the stakes are clear. The freedom to be unhappy is one key to dismantling the oppressively enforced happiness duty, and to clear space for other forms of subjectivity and belonging. What Jonah demands, first with words, then with silence, is the *freedom to be unhappy*. His refusal to go along, to reorient his desires and to align his happiness with YHWH's program, is also a demand for freedom. Even if the ending of the book of Jonah is a universalizing appeal to theological or even ecological justice, then Jonah's unhappiness summons us to recognize that this path of mercy is also one of compulsion.

Furthermore, I suggest, the centering of Jonah's unhappiness in chapter 4 directs attention to the problematizing of happiness earlier in the narrative. Jonah's flight to Tarshish, as well as his somnolent descent into the hold of the ship, may be read, as well, as acts of unhappiness. His demand to be thrown overboard, often read as an act of piety or even faith, is also, equally likely, driven by a desire for self-destruction. Or Jonah may simply be demanding to pursue his own (un)happy trajectory, one that fails to align with the dominant desire of the sailors, who resist throwing him overboard (1:12–16). At the narrative's beginning as at its end, *Jonah demands the freedom to be unhappy*.

Prophecy as a Practice of Unhappiness

Jonah's unhappiness opens onto the larger possibility of conceptualizing prophecy as a practice of unhappiness. Jonah is hardly the only prophet to voice unhappiness or even the wish to die. Among the company of prophets, perhaps best known for his unhappy affect is Jeremiah. The book of Jeremiah contains a number of complaints (often called "confessions" and found interspersed in Jer 12–20); these complaints include not just bodily suffering and social alienation, but profound unhappiness. Even Moses suffers from prophecy, as when he voices his frustration at being called to lead the ungrateful Israelites (Num 11:12).

Naming prophecy as a practice of unhappiness means taking seriously the affective and emotional edges of prophecy as much as the message the prophet transmits, or the social contexts in which the prophecy is executed. Reading prophecy as a practice of unhappiness means, first, listening for hints of unhappy prophets, or prophets unhappy with prophecy. Reading this way also means resisting the desire to subsume specific moments of prophetic unhappiness into a larger explanatory narrative, whether substitutionary suffering (the prophet suffers for the people), moral education for the reader (the prophet suffers so we can learn from the text), or even the prophet as tragic figure. Instead, we can pause with unhappiness, and listen to it.

Often, the unhappiness of the prophet is bound up with a practice of memory. As Ahmed draws out in her analysis of migration and empire, one significant form that the happiness desire assumes is the imperative to remember the past happily. In the case of the contemporary United Kingdom, Ahmed (2010, 130) describes "the social obligation to remember the history of empire as a history of happiness." The prophet, too, faces an obligation to remember the past (and to experience the present) as happy. Often, the tension in prophecy arises over a refusal to forget past harms, whether political or theological. Insofar as happiness (with the present, with the past) functions as "a technology of citizenship" (2010, 133), the prophet who rejects the happy story of the past becomes unhappy. This is one reason the prophets are often told that their messages will fail to be heard (e.g., Isa 6:9–10; Isa 29:11–12; Ezek 2:7): because the prophet refuses to remember happily.

Describing prophecy as a practice of unhappiness also directs attention to larger structures of organization and meaning. Unhappy prophets frequently have unhappy alignments. Because "we align ourselves with others by investing in the same objects as the cause of happiness" (Ahmed 2010, 38), the prophet who refuses to share in the accepted alignment becomes both unhappy and an unhappy object. In Jonah, this alignment is enacted via Jonah's anger at Nineveh (and, subsequently, at YHWH's didactic efforts). In other prophetic stories, the unhappy alignment of the prophet plays out in other ways. Jeremiah is mocked for his alignment to YHWH (Jer 20:7). Elijah's alignment toward YHWH is the cause of his conflict with the prophets of Baal (1 Kgs 17) as well as Jezebel. And the many stories of conflict between prophets and monarchies are stories of varying—and conflicting—object alignments.

Finally, describing prophecy as a practice of unhappiness opens a space to accommodate the transformative impulse in prophecy without slipping into simple fantasy. On hope, including the hope for a better world, Ahmed (2010, 183) writes,

> I want to suggest an intimacy between anxiety and hope. In having hope we become anxious, because hope involves wanting something that might or might not happen. Hope is about desiring the "might," which is only "might" if it keeps open the possibility of the "might not."

In its unhappiness, prophecy holds open this space. The promises of transformation and rebirth that appear scattered in the prophetic literature are promises that depend upon more than—*other than*—happiness. It is only when prophecy becomes a practice of unhappiness that such hope becomes possible.

To return to Jonah, the story of the prophet Jonah is a story about unhappiness, yet unhappiness is not the same as sadness, tragedy, or grief. Unhappiness is not always avoidable; equally, it is not always something to be avoided. Unhappiness may do the work of critique; it may also open the possibility of imagining other ways of being. Riffing on Judith Butler and *Gender Trouble*, Ahmed (2010, 115) writes: "We can think of trouble as an affective politics; acts of deviation mean getting in trouble but also troubling conventional ideas of what it means to have a good life that puts things into certain places." Jonah, I suggest, undertakes such an affective politics of trouble. Throughout the book, he repeatedly gets into trouble (on the ship, in the fish, under the plant); more importantly, he *troubles conventional ideas of what it means to have a good life, or to be a good prophet*. The book of Jonah represents a summons to take trouble seriously, to name and to resist the coercive thrust of the happiness duty. The unhappy prophet gazing back at Nineveh wants nothing more.

Bibliography

Ahmed, Sara. 2006. *Queer Phenomenology: Orientations, Objects, Others*. Durham, NC: Duke University Press.
———. 2010. *The Promise of Happiness*. Durham, NC: Duke University Press.
Berlant, Lauren. 2006. "Cruel Optimism." *Differences* 17.3:20–36.
Bourdieu, Pierre. 1984. *Distinction*. New York: Routledge & Kegan Paul.
Craigie, Peter C. 1984. *Hosea, Joel, Amos, Obadiah, Jonah*. Vol. 1 of *Twelve Prophets*. Daily Study Bible. Philadelphia: Westminster.

Duhm, Bernhard. 1911. *Anmerkungen zu den Zwölf Propheten*. Berlin: Töpelmann.

Frolov, Serge. 1999. "Returning the Ticket: God and His Prophet in the Book of Jonah." *JSOT* 24:85–105.

Freud, Sigmund. 2005. "Mourning and Melancholia." Pages 201–8 in *On Murder, Mourning and Melancholia*. Translated by Shaun Whiteside. Modern Classics. New Penguin Freud. New York: Penguin.

Gottwald, Norman K. 1985. *The Hebrew Bible: A Socio-literary Introduction*. Philadelphia: Fortress.

Lohfink, Norbert. 1961. "Jona ging zur Stadt hinaus [Jon 4, 5]." *BZ* 5:185–203.

Lorde, Audre. 1997. "The Uses of Anger." *Women's Studies Quarterly* 25.1–2:278–85.

McKenzie, Steven L., Rhiannon Graybill, and John Kaltner. 2016. "Slippery as a Fish: The Instability of the Jonah Story." Paper presented at the Annual Meeting of the Society of Biblical Literature, San Antonio, TX. 19 November.

Ngai, Sianne. 2005. *Ugly Feelings*. Cambridge: Harvard University Press.

Nietzsche, Friedrich. 1968. *The Will to Power*. Edited by Walter Kaufmann. Translated by R. J. Hollingdale. New York: Vintage.

Prinsloo, Gert T. M. 2013. "Place, Space and Identity in the Ancient Mediterranean World: Theory and Practice with Reference to the Book of Jonah." Pages 3–25 in *Constructions of Space V: Place, Space and Identity in the Ancient Mediterranean World*. Edited by Gert T. M. Prinsloo and Christl M. Maier. New York: Bloomsbury.

Puar, Jasbir K. 2007. *Terrorist Assemblages: Homonationalism in Queer Times*. Durham, NC: Duke University Press.

Sherwood, Yvonne. 2000. *A Biblical Text and Its Afterlives: The Survival of Jonah in Western Culture*. Cambridge: Cambridge University Press, 2000.

Winckler, H. 1900. "Zum Buche Jona." *Altorientalische Forschungen* 2.2:260–65.

Youngblood, Kevin J. 2013. *Jonah: God's Scandalous Mercy*. Hearing the Message of Scripture: A Commentary on the Old Testament. Grand Rapids: Zondervan.

The Disgusting Apostle and a Queer Affect between Epistles and Audiences

Joseph A. Marchal

Nose twitches, eyebrows shoot up (or sometimes just cinch), lips curl, as a mouth spits out: "Ugh. How could you study that?" Sometimes I am the object of disgust: how could *you* study that? What makes a pervert like you qualified to say anything of value about such sacred texts? Yet oftentimes, such texts—and especially Paul's letters—are what instigate such reactions: how could you study *that*?

A lot of people don't like Paul. Fairly or not, people are disgusted by Paul. In many cases this is because of the many, even the persistent, ways that Paul's letters have been used to target all kinds of people—women, and queers, and Jews, and slaves, and the poor, and the conquered (just to start)—to cast them as disgusting and thus deserving of discipline or destruction. Fairly or not, it appears that Paul—or at least the version he projects in and through these letters we still study all these centuries later—*this* Paul is disgusted by people. At the least, his letters depend upon a number of figures and practices of disgust. The appeal of his claims often relies upon the notion that his audiences will (also) find certain vilified figures disgusting (with shaved heads, castrated and enslaved bodies, intemperate gentiles, among others).

But what should one do with this apostle, these letters, these claims, or just these figures? For some, rejection is an option, but that just doesn't seem to stick. Paul's letters and these disgusting figures—they persist, they return, they stick out and stick around. For others, conciliation and apologies for Paul provide an imagined amelioration. The object of their affective attachment remains with Paul (or at least the version that they project in defending their identification with the saint and the religion to which most of them adhere); in their view Paul deserves our sympathy—our fellow feeling.[1] They are disgusted by those so disgusted by Paul. Some of them are even disgusted by me, by my limited forays in the study of Paul's letters (but never quite as a scholar of Paul), by my body, or by what some small limbs of my body of scholarship have suggested. Am I disgusted by Paul or his letters? By myself? By others?

Many of these options and this last batch of questions seem to me to evade more pressing issues when it comes to the affect circulating in and between and after the epistles and their audiences—in the first and the twenty-first centuries. What else can we do with these letters and the figures deployed, even targeted, within them? I suggest that the insights of affect theory can help us trace—or is it feel?—how these operate, even still. Indeed, disgust is perceptively and often playfully reconsidered within this affective turn, especially in work by Sara Ahmed, Eugenie Brinkema, and Sianne Ngai (among others). In what follows, then, I do not survey the massive, still-growing bodies of scholarship around disgust, most especially those developing in cognitive science or moral psychology (see Kelly 2011 for a survey of some of these). To be sure, this work has been of some use to those thinking about ancient texts, whether classical (Lateiner and Spatharas 2017) or biblical (Shantz 2009). In the case of the former, affect itself appears as a charged (even disgusting?) figure, as the editors object from the outset: "this volume is not a case of highfalutin, dilettantish degustation in the thriving field of 'affect studies'" (Lateiner and Spatharas 2017, 1). Affect, then, can function as a point of contrast for those concerned with (ostensibly) weightier matters of cognition in relation to emotion. Of course, the dissociation between reason and emotion, thinking and feeling, is a persistent one. The subject was hardly foreign to the contexts of Paul's letters and audiences. If one was aware of ancient rhetorical practices, one could recognize that appeals were generated on the basis of *pathos* (emotion) as well as *logos* (reason) and *ēthos* (character), even as emotional appeals were often cast as especially suspect (see Olbricht and Sumney 2001).

But, as I often do, I start with another kind of suspicion, particularly as one who comes to affect belatedly and obliquely, as an embodied creature already invested in particular ways, a scholar and a human (animal)

---

1. On the politics of identification with Paul, see Schüssler Fiorenza 2000.

with feminist, queer, race-critical, and postcolonial accountabilities, sympathies, and hopes. In some contexts (some or all of) this makes me an object of disgust; in others it makes these texts disgusting. I cannot pretend that one kind of approach to these materials can either lend me an air of authority or objectivity (even if I wanted either) or defuse in advance any particular position in these encounters. But one potential use for affect theory is its attention to such encounters, to what passes between bodies and, or as, objects. When imagined as those "visceral forces beneath, alongside, or generally *other than* conscious knowing, vital forces insisting beyond emotion" (Seigworth and Gregg 2010, 1), affect problematizes the (imagined) comforts of a divide between reason and emotion. Affect may just gesture critically to both cultural and corporeal vectors, and these tend to coalesce in disgust. Disgust is not just an embodied reaction, as it also proceeds from and performs powerful cultural functions.

There is something particularly biblical about this combination, as other queerly affected and inclined scholars have already demonstrated in reconsidering disgust at two different sex worker figures (Rahab and Rome/Babylon) within the bulky biblical corpus (Runions 2011; Moore 2014).[2] In what follows, and in following after Runions and Moore, I treat *porneia* in only glancing fashion, but I interact with some of the same interlocutors (Ahmed, Brinkema, and Ngai) from two of the more common domains of what we in biblical scholarship tend to call theory (critical or otherwise): cultural studies and contemporary (often continental) philosophy. To be sure, Paul is also exorcised about contact with sexually improper (likely sex-working) females (in places like 1 Cor 6:15–20), given the potential taint of contamination sticking to the bodies that belong to him and his audiences. While such moments highlight the stickiness of disgust, they do not even begin to scratch the surface of this affect between the apostle and the assemblies that received his letters. This dynamic draws my attention, particularly as one drawn to people beside Paul (Marchal 2015b). Along these lines, then, Ahmed's explicitly intersectional approach to and as this theory should give the following an edge and an angle, an orientation and a feel, even a commitment and an accountability to people prone to be targeted by dynamics of disgust first, over a commitment to Paul, or a church, or a discipline, or even to my own self (however these might be assembled or felt).

---

2. For distinctive reflections upon how sex worker texts might affect sex workers, and vice versa, see Ipsen 2009.

Getting Sticky

To many, disgust feels like an instinct—one that perhaps goes back to primal concerns about risk and danger and difference, when it comes to issues of food or sex or strangers (or strange food, strange sex, or strangers and their food/sex).[3] Disgust seems automatic and involuntary, especially since it provokes an immediate, physical reaction—revulsion, a gag, a retch, or a sneer. Disgust is not just a feeling, it's a gut feeling. For the feminist, queer, and antiracist cultural studies scholar Ahmed (2004, 83), however, it is more than that, since "our relation to our guts is not direct, but is mediated by ideas that are already implicated in the very impressions we make of others and the way those impressions surface as bodies." Disgust is an affect and an idea, or an affect mediated by ideas (and perhaps also vice versa). Indeed, even those inclined to think of disgust as a rigid set of (potentially unconscious) responses, recognize that disgust is also open-ended in how it is acquired, since the *disgusting* is defined by its cultural variety (Kelly 2011, 6). Disgust is not seated within the individualized body, occasionally bursting out in sensations of revulsion; it travels between bodies and reflects broader cultural politics. In her own provocative examination of disgust, film and media scholar Eugenie Brinkema (2014, 117) insists that "it is neither immediate nor visceral; ultimately, I will claim that one must read for disgust." Above all, Brinkema is interested in the forms of affects and how they are reflected in textual (and visual) forms. For an audience like ours, invested, even obsessed with texts, and what we can historically, rhetorically, ethically, and even politically do by engaging them, this attention might come as some relief, particularly as many of the rhizomatic branches of affect theory seem intent on avoiding, even rejecting, an emphasis on textuality (see discussion in Moore 2014; and, more critically, Kotrosits 2016).

Affect theory does tend to emphasize dynamics of embodiment, as does Ahmed, since she stresses the way disgust works in the relations between and on the surfaces of bodies, particularly through the dynamics of proximity and touch. Disgust is not, then, strictly a sentiment of distancing; rather,

---

3. For a psychological differentiation between *primary* disgust (in relation to primal survival instincts) and secondary *disgust* (in relation to morality and socialization), see Lateiner and Spatharas 2017, 7–8; applying Kelly 2011 and Korsmeyer 2011.

disgust is clearly dependent upon contact: it involves a relationship of touch and proximity between the surfaces of bodies and objects. That contact is felt as an unpleasant intensity: it is not that the object, apart from the body, has the quality of "being offensive", but the proximity of the object to the body is felt as offensive. The object must have got close enough to make us feel disgusted. (2004, 85)

Of course, disgust repels, but only in relation to this proximity:

Disgust brings the body perilously close to an object only then to pull away from the object in the registering of the proximity as an offence.... That distancing requires proximity is crucial to the intercorporeality of the disgust encounter. The double movement (towards, away) is forgotten. (2004, 85)

Disgust, then, reflects a push and a pull, rearing back and drawing toward, *or* a leaning in that leads to a recoil. Indeed, in sticking my nose into disgust, my own words have already started to recede. I have leaned, pushed, and possibly even fallen into disgust, so that others' words are sticking to the page. Or is it that disgust has already acted upon me, oozing, spewing, expelling all over, on, and around me? For a while, at least, I won't resist (some of) its ambivalent pleasures.

Disgust is profoundly, even intimately spatial. To Brinkema (2014, 131), disgust is "the forsaken outside that is nevertheless immediate and too close, a threatening proximity from which one recoils, but never with sufficient spacing, an exteriority without distance." Indeed, disgust might actually move according to two contradictory models of space, since disgust is characterized not only by proximity and contact, but also by excess and exclusion: "they cannot be mapped on the same set of axes, for the one involves a coming-too-close, while the other involves a going-too-far: figured onto a singular site, the pull-me-push-you tension might rip a body apart" (2014, 131).

In charting the history of philosophy's consideration of disgust, Brinkema foregrounds how it is treated as a figure of the excluded, the other, even in an absolute fashion. Yet, it is more than a revulsion or rejection, sensed "as something more than a powerfully felt refusal, but as 'an inability *not* to say no,' a grammatical pile-up of undoings appropriate for the affect of abyssal negation" (Brinkema 2014, 124; quoting Menninghaus 2003, 2). Disgust forces a response, in relation to both pleasure and desire. To be sure, its required exclusion is figured often as the retch or vomiting.

Yet if one follows Derrida's (1981, 22) claim that "vomit is represented in advance as forcing pleasure, and that is why it disgusts," then, as Brinkema (2014, 127) argues, "the disgusting or revolting is too much of the object that it purports to represent." This excess is related to both its proximity and its exclusion:

> Disgust just comes too close—it forces itself down your throat and yet cannot be digested, only expelled forever, utterly—hence, "the disgusting can only be vomited."... This is the particular perversion of disgust: in giving far too much enjoyment, it eats the conditions for the possibility of pleasure—in other words ... disgust "makes one desire to vomit." (Brinkema 2014, 128; quoting Derrida 1981, 23)

This association between disgust and desire is almost canonical among studies of affect. Feminist literary scholar Sianne Ngai's (2007, 335) own reflections upon disgust, for instance, stress: "what makes the object abhorrent is precisely its outrageous claim for desirability. The disgusting seems to say, 'You want me,' imposing itself on the subject as something to be mingled with and perhaps even enjoyed." William Ian Miller (1997, x) also stresses the paradoxical attraction-aversion dynamic at the heart of disgust: "Even as the disgusting repels, it rarely does so without also capturing our attention. It imposes itself upon us. We find it hard not to sneak a second look or, less voluntarily, we find our eyes doing 'double-takes' at the very things that disgust us." Again, this element of attraction is not simply sub- or unconscious, since "curiosity about or fascination with the disgusting is something we are often quite conscious of even as we turn away in disgust" (Miller 1997, 110).

For Ahmed, disgust involves attachment as well as attraction; it sticks or is sticky. This aspect of disgust, again, stresses contact and proximity, in considering the transmission of the affect as a kind of contamination: "It sticks to that which is near it; it clings" (2004, 87). Thus, disgust calls up images of certain objects, even certain kinds of people (even if these objects or people vary across space and time): "feelings of disgust stick more to some bodies than others, such that they become disgusting, as if their presence is what makes 'us sick'" (2004, 92). These bodies are, of course, those that belong to the marginalized, the oppressed, and the excluded; disgust reflects the power relations of a culture. Thus, Ahmed insists that affects are mediated by and grounded within histories, particularly histories of oppression and marginalization. These histories are, once more, reflected in the spatial dynamics of disgust. Disgust reflects competing geographies, not only of proximity and contact and of excess and exclusion, but also of hierarchy and vertical positionality. Disgust indexes a doubled hierarchy of bodies: on a body and between bodies.

> Lower regions of the body—that which is below—are clearly associated both with sexuality and with the "waste" that is literally expelled by the body. It is not that the low is necessarily disgusting, nor is sexuality necessarily disgusting. Lowness becomes associated with lower regions of the body as it becomes associated with other bodies and other spaces. The spatial distinction of "above" from "below" functions metaphorically to separate one body from another, as well as to differentiate between higher and lower bodies, or more and less advanced bodies. As a result, disgust at "that which is below" functions to maintain the power relations between above and below, *through which "aboveness" and "belowness" become properties of particular bodies, objects and spaces.* (2004, 89, emphasis original)

These spatially affective properties are affixed on certain bodies, perhaps because women, sexual minorities, and racially minoritized groups (and those bodies that are more than one of these) are frequently figured as especially sexualized or primarily somatic entities. When Brinkema turns to disgust, she also sees a different, if potentially related hierarchy: the hierarchy of the senses in Western philosophy. Certain critical faculties are disembodied or at least distanced from the materiality of bodies, whose lower senses experience affects like disgust (2014, 119–20). Brinkema, at least in part, appears to agree with Ahmed that such philosophical work "breaks the body apart at its seams to segment it into zones of propriety" (2014, 120). Yet, Brinkema's counterintuitive, even iconoclastic project is to insist that what matters most about affects are their forms—*not* their contents or their materiality. The form of disgust holds her critical attention: "The form of this affect is thus a structure organized around a process of exclusion and not a content that fills it in or gives it definition, shape, coherence, substance. Disgust names the opening up that is *worse than the worst*" (2014, 129, emphasis original). This structure of disgust compels definition-giving, but Brinkema (2014, 129) wants the critic to resist this compulsion:

> It is the lure of disgust to give it content, either substantives to its law or rules for determining that membership … the rabid critical gesture

of taxonomizing, category-making, boundary-drawing and -violating, and determining what is inside and what is outside propriety involves neutralizing the risk of disgust by privileging the object over the affect.

From this vantage point disgust must be seen as more than "a set of itemized disgusting things" (2014, 130).

Yet in conversation with Ahmed, I cannot help but come back to certain kinds of bodies, treated as objects of disgust, and thus to certain histories that have filled in the content of the affective form that is disgust. The stickiness of disgust is useful here as well. In a faint echo of Brinkema, Ahmed notes that the stickiness does not naturally belong to certain objects; rather,

> we can think of stickiness as an effect of surfacing, *as an effect of the histories of contact between bodies, objects, and signs.* To relate stickiness with historicity is not to say that some things and objects are not "sticky" in the present. Rather, it is to say that stickiness is an effect. That is, stickiness depends on histories of contact that have already impressed upon the surface of the object. (Ahmed 2004, 90, emphasis original)

Through the repetition of this form, disgust becomes affective and effective. Both Ahmed and Brinkema argue, along different lines, that disgust moves, it transfers and transmits, slides and sticks. To Ahmed and to myself, it matters a great deal to whom disgust has been stuck. Histories matter, you know, because movements like #BlackLivesMatter, matter! Yet, Brinkema's attention to form might also be useful if and as we consider whether there is any potential utility for disgust in counter-kyriarchal praxis.[4]

To pursue such a line, though, I must consider not only the spatial, but also the temporal dynamics of disgust. For Ahmed, disgust functions along an awkward temporality, particularly in its generation of border objects:

> As a result, disgust involves a "time lag" as well as being generative or futural ... so the subject feels an object to be disgusting (a perception that relies on a history that comes before the encounter) and then expels the object and, through expelling the object, finds it to be disgusting. *The*

---

4. Schüssler Fiorenza created the term *kyriarchy* to describe the intersecting and mutually influencing pyramidal structures of domination. See, for example, the discussion in Schüssler Fiorenza 2001, 1, 118–24, 211.

expulsion itself becomes the "truth" of the reading of the object. (Ahmed 2004, 87, emphasis original)

Disgust precedes the affective response, but the affective response does more than reinforce disgust, it performs it.[5] As Ahmed (2004, 91) considers in light of the ethnoracial, national-colonial slur *Paki*, the stickiness of disgust is achieved in history through repetition. Here, she elaborates upon Judith Butler's conceptualization of performativity:

> On the one hand, the performative is futural; it generates effects in the constitution or materialisation of that which is "not yet". But, on the other hand, performativity depends upon the sedimentation of the past; it reiterates what has already been said, and its power and authority depend upon how it recalls that which has already been brought into existence. This model of performativity relates to my argument about the temporality of disgust: it both "lags behind" the object from which it recoils, and generates the objects in the very event of recoiling. (2004, 92–93; on performativity, see Butler 1990.)

A performative conceptualization of disgust foregrounds the importance of repetition, temporality, and ultimately audience. Interpreters like Ngai (2007, 335) and Miller (1997, 194) agree that disgust, in particular, seeks and expects agreement or concurrence from others. Disgust, then, in some ways also depends upon acts of communication, like "that's gross" or "you disgust me":

> The speech act is always spoken to others, whose shared witnessing of the disgusting thing is required for the affect to have an effect. In other words, the subject asks others to repeat the condemnation implicit in the speech act itself. Such a shared witnessing is required for speech acts to be generative, that is, for the attribution of disgust to an object or other to stick to others. (Ahmed 2004, 94)

Disgust at once requires and creates a community, a collective that can assemble and commune in common through their condemnation of who or what disgusts.

---

5. Thus, it is possible that Brinkema might be arguing, by other means, that disgust is performative, its form drives categories and boundaries and definitions; its form is endlessly performative.

In some ways, these performative qualities of disgust present utopian or at least counter-hegemonic potentials. As an attentive reader of Butler, Ahmed (2004, 93) recognizes this possibility: "If the performative opens up the future, it does so precisely in the process of repeating past conventions, as to repeat something is always to open up the (structural) possibility that one will repeat something with a difference." But what can this difference be? It is true that movements arrayed along the political right have effectively and affectively used disgust (see Ngai 2007, 339; Miller 1997, 235–54; and Kelly 2011, 101–36), but interpreters like Ngai assert that it could be used on the left, "particularly if the harmful and contaminating qualities it identifies as intolerable are those of racism, misogyny, or the militarism of a political administration" (2007, 339). As an ostensibly minor affect, or ugly feeling, though, Ngai is convinced that other emotions would be more politically efficacious (2007, 354), perhaps because "disgust does not so much solve the dilemma of social powerlessness as diagnose it powerfully" (2007, 353). Ahmed (2004, 99) considers this possibility as well, but she recognizes "that critique requires more time for digestion. Disgust might not allow one to get close enough to an object before one is compelled to pull away." Because disgust is organized around expulsion, it obstructs or short-circuits other trajectories. "Such an expulsion will never be over given the possibility that other others 'could be' the cause of our disgust; the unfinished nature of expulsion allows its perpetual rejustification: we must be sick, to exclude the sick, again and again" (2004, 98). Disgust, in other words, is never done.

So, Brinkema might be onto something about the form of disgust. By ignoring some of the politics of how disgust has materialized, about the objects to which disgust has been stuck, and just considering its form, we have arrived at something like disgust's exponential apocalypticism. Vomit, then, is not just the reaction and possibly even a cause for disgust. As Brinkema (2014, 132) sees it:

> Indeed, disgust's emesis compels a reversal of metaphorical energies: less the black hole vacuum of meaning that its zero-point function as the excluded of philosophy might suggest, disgust is far more like the hypothetical white hole, an emissive, productive horizon ejecting matter in place of absorbing it.

Disgust is more than contagious, sticky, and thus aggregative. Again, recall that Brinkema describes disgust as "worse than the worst." Perhaps, then, disgust is not even primarily aggregative or assembling, since:

in place of a structure that can only suck things in, disgust continuously spits things out. One might say that disgust continually vomits that which it never took in ... Because there is always a horizon beyond which the worse than the worst may be put into play, opening up yet another affective deferral, it is not the case that disgust is distinct, immediate, and viscerally overpresent but that disgust as such is impossible. The worst can be exceeded by the ever worse; it is therefore never fully arrived. Certainly, and ineluctably, disgust advises us that the worst is always yet to come. (Brinkema 2014, 132)

The performativity of disgust is persistently futural, and particularly apocalyptic, promising, threatening with things worse still to come, paradoxically worse than the worst. Whenever disgust takes a particular form, it is not yet done, always signaling the "possibility of something more disgusting than the disgusting" (Brinkema 2014, 130).

What, if anything, comes after disgust, besides more disgust and possibly despair for those seeking to get unstuck without sticking it elsewhere? Can rethinking our temporal and spatial relations, here and now and in relation to an ancient assemblage of there and then, do anything else?

The Disgusted Apostle

Having pulled away from Paul's letters, one set of potentially disgusting objects, I am stuck if I do not push back into them, but perhaps you are curious to see if these ideas and affects about disgust can also stick to these epistles and their audiences. Disgust is in more than the guts, it is mediated and thus must be read—conveniently enough, since you are reading these words and we still mostly just read these letters. Disgust moves according to three different, even contradictory geographies: of proximity and contact—too close!—excess and exclusion—too far!—and hierarchy and debasement—too low! Disgust is intimately tied to desire and materially ground to history; it is both sticky and hierarchical. Its temporality is at least doubled—attaching to some, due to the past, but it keeps repeating, indicating an open future. Thus, disgust is also performative, in an unfinished, even apocalyptic register.

To this *reader*, at least, this feels like much of the movement in the figurative practices of Paul's letters and could account (among other things) for the ambivalence they reflect about the embodied practices of and between Paul and his gentile audiences. These reflections about affect offer more for our encounters with these epistles and audiences than traditional rhetorical analysis provides. I am not particularly interested, for instance, in simply tracing how Paul *uses* disgust toward particular goals, with the goals being the actual matter of interest. Instead, I dwell on disgust for some space and time, since disgust alternately affixes on me, the subjects of my affection, as well as the ancient auditors and authors in view in biblical materials, and then occasionally in the connections between these in contemporary circulations of disgust. As Thomas H. Olbricht (2001, 7) highlights, however, ancient rhetoricians like Plato and Aristotle, Cicero and Quintilian "did not set out to produce an exhaustive treatment of *pathos* but to provide ample insight in order that speakers could utilize emotional appeals to obtain their ends." I hope that my investment in disgust is not as instrumental as the practitioners of ancient rhetoric, even as they certainly depended upon the social dynamics of disgust, its existence prior to their rhetorical acts, and its sensational impact within them.[6] Approaching disgust affectively blurs and complicates not only the imagined division between reason and emotion—categorized as *logos* and *pathos*—but also between author/speaker and audience—each presumably addressed by *ēthos* and *pathos*. In affect and action, then, the role of the interpreter can be more than just taxonomizing and cataloguing the rhetorical forms (see, for instance, the critiques of Amador 1999), in line with Brinkema's (2014, 130) insistence that we do more than itemize a list of disgusting things.

Of course, there are plenty of disgusting people and practices in these letters. Paul, anxious about other bodies and ultimately his own vulnerability, repeats ancient stereotypes about gentile bodies. The one that most stands out is their association with sexual impropriety or immorality—*porneia*—in several letters, but especially 1 Corinthians and Romans.[7] He calls up a range of vilified figures—castrated bodies in response to perverting the gospel through a focus on the flesh (in Galatians);[8] viceful bodies excluded from the kingdom yet to come and androgynous bodies with shaved heads disgracing themselves and the community (in 1 Corinthians).[9] After only a few of these initial encounters with affect

---

6. On the use of disgust in Demosthenes and Aeschines, see Fisher 2017 and Spatharas 2017.

7. On sexual slander in the contexts of ancient Christianities, see Knust 2005.

8. Hans Dieter Betz (1979, 270), for instance, stresses how "Paul uses the public disgust" at castration to target and isolate those preaching a different message than his. See also Rauhala 2017.

9. On sexualized vices and gentile stereotypes in 1 Corinthians, see Ivarsson 2007.

theory, I now realize that the subjects of my own attention have recurrently been such objects of disgust for Paul (see especially Marchal 2019). I may have been preoccupied with disgust for over a decade now, without even knowing it! (Am I doing things that I do not want ... or just did not know I was doing?)

Strangely, in calling up a range of disgusting figures, Paul wants his gentile audience to feel a similar repulsion. In Galatians he stresses: "We ourselves are Jews by birth and not gentile sinners" (2:15).[10] In 1 Corinthians he expresses shock that the assembly community allows "a sexual immorality among you, and of a kind that is not found even among gentiles" (1 Cor 5:1). His rhetoric even depends upon this disgusting association: he is seeking to transfer disgust, to make it stick via contact with already disgusting objects. Generically, this often just means repeating the stereotyped association of gentiles with idolatry and sexuality (see Ivarsson 2007; Shantz 2013). This association also works when Paul connects sexual and food practices in letters like 1 Corinthians—see the associations of *porneia* with leaven and dough (5:6–8), or food and stomachs (6:12–18), or simple exclamations "Do not even eat with such a one" (1 Cor 5:11) (see also Hartman 2019).

These expressions center around the notion that disgust attaches to certain kinds of bodies, particularly gentiles. Paul even alludes to the history of these bodies and their contact with or proximity to the disgusting (in places like 1 Cor 6:11; Gal 3:23; 4:3, 8–11; or Rom 6:17–22), as he tries mightily to insist that these were things that represented their past ... and yet Paul keeps bringing these disgusting things up in the *present* of the epistles. And, again, Paul wants his gentile audiences to feel a similar repulsion ... at gentiles ... hmmm.... To me, at least, this is affectively puzzling. Though disgust oozes and drips and sticks to and from these corpora—epistolary and ethnic—in what remains I focus more on the Letter to the Romans, at first just the edges, but eventually getting stuck in the middle, and trying to get out, hoping perhaps to be the thing vomited out of it (again).

Romans aptly reflects the stickiness and circulation of disgust, since its opening arguments depend upon the image of an idolatrous *them* in a heap of gender and sexual trouble (1:18–32). The argument maps

---

For three different takes on the *androgynous* Corinthians, see Townsley 2006; Marchal 2014; and Matthews 2015.

10. Unless otherwise noted, all biblical translations are mine.

a sensory difference onto this ethnoracial, gender, and sexual differentiation: "they became futile in their thinking and their senseless minds were darkened" (1:21). This *them* is disgusting because of the desire to which God hands them over: they are overtaken by passions of dishonor (1:24–27). Both the females and males among this *them* slide upon divine impulse to passions away from the "natural use" (*psychikēn chrēsin*, vv. 26, 27) and (at least the females) toward a use that is *para physin* (v. 26), something that is contrary to, even *beyond* nature.[11] "Their females" (v. 26) are excessive and uncontrolled by their males, males who are consumed, or enflamed by passion with other males (v. 27), making the kind of contact that would have been too intimate, too close especially for elite males, who imagined themselves as impenetrable penetrators (see Walters 1997). *Our* implied disgust at *them* should correspond to a geography of excess and exclusion—they have gone too far![12] Their gendered and sexual perversity sticks out, but also attaches to an impossible range of vices (1:29–31; see also 1 Cor 5 and 6), and ultimately, to their death (Rom 1:32). Paul deploys this scare figure that is not only religiously and sexually different, but also perversely racialized. As has long been acknowledged, Paul is making use of certain stereotypes of gentiles, those who are nationally and ethnoracially different from ancient Jews, in Rom 1. Stanley K. Stowers (1994, 109), for instance, notes that this letter's fentile figure is "what moderns would call an ethnic cultural stereotype." The passage and the disgusting figure it recirculates reflect interwoven factors of gender, sexuality, race, ethnicity, and even empire (see Marchal 2015a). Certain bodies have not only gone too far, but they are also debased in an affective hierarchy, as they are politically and culturally. Paul expects that the audience will get the reference, because disgust reflects histories of contact, sticking to certain kinds of bodies.

But the affective argumentation is not only conditioned by revulsion and rejection at stereotypically excessive and thus hierarchically debased and inferior figures. For, looking backwards, in the letter and in time, once even these gender-troubled fentiles were rather close to what Paul wants from his audience, since they too knew what was apparently plain about

---

11. For a comprehensive study of the females targeted by this kind of argumentation, in this letter and the wider setting, see Brooten 1996. On the problem of excess in this text, see Martin 1995.

12. For more focused reflections on spatial dynamics in Paul's letters, see Johnson-Debaufre 2010; and Nasrallah 2012.

God, at least before they turned away (1:19–23; for further reflection on these temporal dynamics, see Marchal 2011). Apparently the divine contact was not quite sticky enough: how else could gentiles themselves have engaged in this primordial proximity and withdrawal, pull in-push away pattern? Is there something disgusting-desirable about (at least this concept of) God? Yet, moving forward, again in the letter and in time, to the *present* of the epistle, the argument shifts to address a second-person "you" who "are doing the very same things" (2:1).[13] The implicit "us" in the opening us-versus-them argument slides over and tries to swallow up the "you" (2:1–6) who is ostensibly a part of this us all along. The disgusting was close at hand, too close, right off to the side, but now crashing into the foreground. As a border object, this disgusting figure is not doing a good job of maintaining the differences between us and them. Apparently, there is still something rather desirable about doing these things. The awkward temporality of disgust indicates that this disgust is not only a figure of the past, but is a persistent past that is not yet past. Paul repeats the disgusting figuration, and the disgust keeps repeating, beyond the opening figure of vilification. They are not done with disgust, disgust is not done with them. Though judging other people, the you of Rom 2:1 displays something like an "inability not to say no" (Menninghaus 2003, 2). For Paul's purposes, this appears to help him demonstrate that everyone needs his version of Jesus, and he can then just leave disgust behind....

Or can he? Certainly, further figures of disgust crop up in the chapters to follow, especially reflecting debasing affects around flesh and enslavement (as he argues here and in so many of his other letters). Paul may have thought he was done with disgust, but disgust is not done with him. The "I" of Rom 7 seems downright tortured by a similar "inability not to say no," to doing things he does not want.[14] Disgust is tied firmly to desire and is almost performative. For example, "if the law/torah had not said: 'You

---

13. For the possibility that this is specifically aimed at Stoics, or Stoicized figures, see Swancutt 2003.

14. Leander Keck's (2001, 88–90) rhetorical analysis of *pathos* in Romans links the condemnation in 1:18–31 to the appeals in 7:7–25. Teresa Hornsby (2001) emphasizes idolatry in relation to sacrifice and violence (via the work of George Bataille) as the link between Rom 1 and Rom 7. The (potentially idiosyncratic) use of Bataille for a consideration of disgust (as in Brinkema 2014, 123) indicates the possible value of bringing biblical studies in closer contact with Bataille (still sadly missing in valuable collections such as Biles and Brintnall 2015).

shall not desire,' I would not have recognized desire" (7:7). This problem of desire is an embodied issue, and one with a history of past struggle: "I was once living without law/torah" (7:9), a time characterized slightly earlier as: "While we were living in the flesh, our sinful passions, aroused by the law/torah, were at work in our members to bear fruit for death" (Rom 7:5). This famously leads to a seemingly involuntary, precognitive problem for this "I": "For I do not do what I want, but I do the very things I hate.... nothing good dwells within me, that is, in my flesh, I can will what is right, but I cannot do it. For I do not do the good I want, but the evil I do not want is what I do" (7:15, 18–19). This affective state ultimately leads to a rhetorical dissociation: "Now if I do what I do not want, it is no longer I that do it, but sin that dwells within me" (7:20); "But I see in my members another law at war with the law of my mind, making me captive to the law of sin that dwells in my members" (7:23).[15]

Some scholars have resolved the historical, rhetorical, and potential affective problem of Rom 7 by identifying it as an example of *prosopopoeia*, or "speech in character" (see, for example, Stowers 1994, 258–84; Stowers 1995). Here, scholars have done some valuable labor, pulling the apostle away from the disgust-desire that would seem to cast him as an introspective sinner struggling with an anti-Jewish image of the law or torah (see especially Eisenbaum 2009). Paul, then, is not speaking for himself but is speaking in the style of another character, to present the subject from a different angle. Though interpreters cannot settle on exactly what kind of character Paul is "putting on," one of the more intriguing suggestions, by scholars like Stowers (1994; 1995) and Pamela Eisenbaum (2009), is that Paul is speaking as a gentile ... or at least how he imagines a gentile.[16] This suggestion not only pushes Paul away from the image of an anti-Semite, but it also distances the Pauline interpreters identified with the apostle from both ancient and more recent modes of disgust. In following inter-

---

15. For an initial consideration of this text from a cognitive-science perspective, see Shantz 2015. On sin (or "Sin") as the central figure or character in certain apocalyptic readings of Rom 7, see Gaventa 2013. On the double participation (that looks like affectively conflicted participation to this reader) of this "I, yet not I, but sin" figuration, see Eastman 2013.

16. Only some interpreters see *prosopopoeia* at work in this passage; many debate whether it refers to Paul, before or after the Damascus experience, to Adam, or to all of Israel. Even among those who perceive an example of speech-in-character, many still want it to refer to some aspect of Paul's identity or autobiography. For a brief survey of the options for the referent of the "I" in this passage, see Jewett 2007, 441–45.

preters like Krister Stendahl (1963), they seem right to stress that this is not the product of an introspective conscience. Yet, perhaps a brief turn with affect theory gets us further away from such individualized modes of understanding the epistle and its audiences, to grapple with the cultural politics of shared affect. The meaning of this passage and the disgust it is ostensibly trying to evoke are socially, culturally, even politically mediated.

After all, the apostle puts the disgust on in the epistle—or is it that the epistle puts the disgust on the apostle, even as it might try to put it on the audience? Try as we might to pull disgust away from the author and even the epistle, it tends to be sticky. Disgust is stuck on the apostle, even if temporarily ... but perhaps for even longer. Since, in rearing back from it, in epistle and in interpretation, the disgust evokes a disgusting and disgusted response, it achieves its affect. The "I" constructed by or for Paul does more than make contact with the disgusting, this "I" is disgusted and disgusting, even if just for a few sentences. If *prosopopoeia* is meant to provide a new or different angle on a topic by inhabiting a character in speech, what do we do when we recognize that this figure is repeating the figurative work that preceded it several chapters earlier? This figure fits with the previously vilified figure, particularly in the ways that the gentile is associated with desire and the trappings of flesh. There is a history to this figure, a history of affects sticking to certain kinds of bodies.

In this light, this argument does not look so different from the opening "us" who become "you." In repeating these rhetorics of disgust, the letter brings the apostle closer and closer to disgust ... and is it starting to stick by the time this character comes to speech? As before, those who were confidently judging those who do such things were shortly accused of doing these things. Disgust slides and sticks. If that dissociation between "us" and "you" is short-circuited so quickly, how can an interpreter be so confident that this "I" is dissociated from an authentic Pauline "I" and that the "you" Paul addresses can be dissociated from what "you" were (or even still are, since Paul keeps bringing this figure up). Exactly how, if at all, could or should these "you's" and "I's" be assembled or disassembled?

Keeping in mind that this was *Paul's* view of gentiles is helpful,[17] a view that might better be cast as a projection (not to suggest an anachronism via

---

17. Eisenbaum (2009, 236), for instance, parenthetically, but frankly notes: "I want to stress that I am in no way endorsing Paul's damning view of Gentiles. It is important to realize that this is just a bias of Paul's."

psychoanalysis, just a different anachronism, through affect).[18] Of course, when it comes to disgust, such projections are also projectiles: thrown at bodies so as to throw them out. Paul wants to expel certain kinds of bodies out of these assemblies, push them out so as to pull others close. This may just be a matter of expelling certain qualities from his concept of the community, but affective work on disgust teaches us that such qualities stick to certain kinds of bodies. Indeed, the form of disgust suggests it will keep projecting, ejecting, and spitting things out.... It cannot help but get some on the flesh of Paul's own members. After a while, for those who stick around later to read and think and feel about these letters (like us), the targets of such figures may be beside the point, as the effects can slide and the affect can be redeployed, to chilling, worse than worst ends. Indeed, disgust at the apostle might also be misdirected, since the cultural dynamics that keep affect circulating are not about individual agency, but can still be about our collective accountability. Still, these more recent accounts of disgust can account for one potential contradiction in our constructions of Paul: how he can repeat so many stereotypes of gentiles, feeling disgust for them (and apparently anticipating that they too will feel this disgust), and yet feels called or sent to them specifically?[19] The relation of apostle to his gentiles, and possibly, they to him, and each other, can be rethought through this attraction-revulsion, these contradictory geographies of too close (proximity), too far (excess), and too low (hierarchy), its sticky, yet unfinished historicity and temporality.

Indeed, this disgusting character comes into being through speech, but speech about disgust requires an audience with whom it must be shared. Paul puts disgust on several figures, including one version of himself, in an attempt to put it on the audience.[20] This practice raises one lingering puzzle for me: how exactly is this supposed to appeal to an audience that includes gentiles (primarily, and quite possibly exclusively)? What kind of gentiles would be disgusted by gentiles, or at least this disgustile/dis-

---

18. For some uses of the psychoanalytic and, more importantly, reflections on the racialized projection and sexualized stigmatization in Paul's treatment of gentiles, see Liew 2008, 75–97, 175–88. On Rom 7 with and after Lacan, see Blanton 2014, 169–81.

19. This dynamic presents difficulties, for instance, with more optimistic takes about Paul's radical sympathy and solidarity with the non-Jewish nations in Lopez 2008 and Kahl 2010.

20. On the turbulent affective terrain crossed, shaped, and shared by Paul and another assembly community (in Corinth), see Kotrosits 2011.

gentile figure? This speech in character is, after all, how Paul puts on his image of gentiles. Does Paul, then, imagine, risking another racialized anachronism, self-loathing gentiles?! Or, in following the insights about the form of disgust, is it just that once disgust slides into Paul's letters they stick to those bodies, not just the figures targeted within the letter, but the bodies of the letters themselves? Would they, by necessity, stick to whomever came close to or made contact with them, even if they were, in turn, repelled by them?

Queering Affect between Epistle and Audience

Now that we're stuck in the middle of this disgusting letter, what do we do with this epistle, or at least these figures circulating between it and its audiences? If one agrees that disgust is performative, there always remains the possibility that disgusting arguments, letters, or figures can be repeated differently. Erin Runions (2011) has highlighted that humor could both echo and disrupt dynamics of disgust. Both can be experienced through involuntary bodily reactions; they can be triggered, but not entirely captured, by words. They often cover some of the same cultural ground: habits around food, sex, and strangers. Yet, laughter has a way of breaking in and disrupting expectations, a bodily response that runs ahead of individualized cognition, agency, or will (2011, 54–55).[21] To Runions (2011, 55–56), humor is "a kind of queerness that makes odd connections, that moves toward usually reviled objects rather than pushing them away."

Indeed, there might be *something funny* (which might also be queer) about the arguments in the Letter to the Romans. Paul may just be trying to elicit laughter at the object of his disgust, if he is punning on the receptivity of those males who "received in their own persons the due penalty for their error" (1:27). This "they" are the butt of the joke, then; but the letter also hoists the audience on their own petard by claiming that "you" do the same things as those receptive males and their out-of-control females. Even just a cursory familiarity with the poet Martial reminds us that such figures are the objects of both disgust and humor in the ancient Roman imperial setting. Yet, if this is not only ironic, but humorous, the same punchlines persist in the prosopopoeic Paul in Rom 7. This "I" struggles

---

21. Here Runions draws upon ideas about the emotional capture of affect in Massumi 2002.

mightily with involuntarily passionate body parts (7:5, 23), a body part with a mind of its own, doing what the "I" does not want it to do (7:15–20). The letter has progressed to dick jokes, but affect signals the ways that Paul's attempts to project the disgust onto others only ends up sticking to him as well. In trying to hoist the gentile assembly members once more on this particular petard, it is Paul who ends up stuck. This might look especially funny, not just to contemporary connoisseurs of bawdy routines, but also to ancient auditors in this assembly: one which already assembles the ostensibly disgusting gentiles with Jews in their homes and synagogues (as the greetings of Rom 16:1–16 make clear).

But, laughing *at* Paul and his embarrassingly erect member (stuck in front of class at an imagined adolescent chalkboard?) almost seems too easy. What is more, it reminds me that humor easily slides into derision, not exactly defusing disgust, but reusing it, without much difference: this form persists with only slightly altered targets. Can disgust be affecting for more radical departures from kyriarchal orders? If the sexual is a persistent locus for disgust, it can help to take a few more turns with queer theory and its affects. While scholars of affect recognize that disgust reflects matters of taste, Gayle Rubin (1989, 278–79) has long recognized a considerable "fallacy of misplaced scale" when it comes to erotic taste. A more radical theory of sexuality must interrogate this fallacy, its hierarchical valuation of sexual acts, and its domino theory of sexual peril, with a more pluralistic ethic of benign sexual variation (Rubin 1989, 279–83).[22] Rubin highlights: "Most people find it difficult to grasp that whatever they like to do sexually will be thoroughly repulsive to someone else, and that whatever repels them sexually will be the most treasured delight of someone, somewhere" (1989, 283).

From one angle this suggests a kind of indifference to difference: different things disgust different people. This could be one response to the cautions sounded by Ngai, Ahmed, and Brinkema. Both Ahmed and Brinkema consider the futurity of disgust, its apocalyptic promise of things worse than the worst, still to come. If this is how disgust works, and if one cares about those to whom disgust has been attached, and still might be attached and attacked, by its impossibly continuous emissions, then, with Ngai, one could pose that disgust has to be met by more than disgust. This

---

22. In a strange, if brief, connection to biblical studies, Rubin (1989, 278) lays the responsibility for our overwhelming sex negativity that generates these fallacies and hierarchies at the feet of Paul and those who follow him.

cannot just be some liberal "Love Trumps Hate" response. Following one read on Rubin, then, slight spaces in these geographies and temporalities can make more than a slight (in)difference. Did the audiences of Paul's letters recognize that they were supposed to be disgusted? Did they know the figures of disgust circulating in this epistle and the Roman imperial ambiance? Yet, if the wide cultural variety in the objects or subjects that elicit disgust is a feature of the sheer adaptability of disgust, then this variety provides one more geography of disgust: a space between subjects in different subcultures. This spatial difference need not have been too far, too close, or too low ... just ... a little bit distant or different.

This difference may not be as big a deal to auditors of these epistles, audiences then or now. But, slight (in)differences can mean a lot, particularly if the ancient assemblies were zones of contact between people along various intersecting gendered, sexual, cultural, imperial, and ethnoracial trajectories. Given the range of people reflected in the closing greetings of this letter, one quite simple scenario is that some may have disagreed with Paul and his epistle. They may not have been disgusted with him ("with," meaning at the same things as Paul, or "with," meaning at Paul), or just disgusted by different things. They would *get* the argument, but they have not been *feeling* this sort of figuration. One might imagine the letter being read aloud in the workshop or living quarters of Prisca and Aquila, where one assembly among the many assemblies of the gentiles gathered (16:3–5). Such letters were not theological tracts or party manifestos, but on these matters Paul's auditors might hear an overly enthusiastic ally loudly expressing his taste (albeit through the mouth of a messenger acting as a representative of the absent). This type might be familiar to those—like my minister, rabbi, and political organizer friends—laboring in contexts so often dependent upon the efforts of volunteers. You will tolerate the expression of different views or the boisterous outburst of a passionate (if sometimes misguided) member when our overlapping concerns are a priority, requiring the pooling of our collective time and energy. Prisca may need to talk to Paul when he gets here, but for now we can use some of his zeal to get things done besides vilifying the past (or the present) of so many of our members.

From another angle, however, Rubin's radical aim underscores the proximity of disgust and desire. Indeed, Runions reminds us that queerness draws closer, rather than retreats from the disgusting, repulsive, or reviled. This indicates the possibility that the disgusting might be treasured and desired *as* the disgusting, not in spite of or in indifference to it. The disgust

Paul aims to elicit in the letter might be somewhat beside the point then. Disgust is already out there, the epistle does not generate it out of nowhere, the letter's arguments, or its affects, just keep disgust recirculating, sneezing it on Paul's audiences. But, as Ahmed notes, the letter requires the audience, needs them to repeat the disgust in this way, or to make the words mean the way Paul means them. What if one approaches and feels disgust the way some queer thinkers and activists approach and feel shame, by embracing it? Like gay shame—not just the academic conference-cum-collection (Halperin and Traub 2010), but also the more activist collective and affective approach—disgust can be acknowledged and not fled, but sensed and felt and lived, as desired and desirable.[23] This could be something like a preferential option for the disgusting, but pressing further I wonder: what would a community that assembled under, rather than against, the sign and the sensation of the disgusting look and feel like?

The assemblies that received and recirculated these letters and other bodies (and/or as objects) were sites that could elicit disgust, simply by the contact they promoted in their assembling. These would have been spaces and times where such disgust was charged because they presumed that disgust did not prevent contact and collaboration. Did this mean that their allies, or even their opponents, were not objects of disgust? Did they or could we start again with the radically democratizing force of disgust—an earthy recognition and (or just) reaffection that disgust comes for, spews out of, and sticks to all bodies at one point or another? One could object to and project disgust onto (our) Others, as these letters at times appear to do. But, these letters and our encounters with the figures addressed by them can also remind us that we all sweat, spit, excrete, emit, offend, age, fall ill, vomit, expire, and decompose. One cannot get rid of disgust, but one could think and feel again for our common predicament, even as it has differential impacts and affects, tied to histories. If disgust is inevitable, and always just around the corner, perhaps its directionality can be felt, not as a disgust at, but as a way to be in disgust, in a disgusting sympathy, feeling with, and disgusting solidarity, working with and as those to whom it sticks.

Not all dissent necessarily depends upon a difference animated by disgust. Does a politics of solidarity that seeks to stick around and stick

---

23. This approach to disgust in ways like shame might also rhyme some with the approach Virginia Burrus takes to living with shame (2008, 148–53), embracing shame shamelessly (2008, 7–9).

together, with and as those who stick out, to whom the disgust sticks, make such a difference? Does the experience of this form enfleshed, where it meets ours and others' bodies, teach to distrust the lure of disgust in return? Is it possible to embody and organize around a vulnerability tied to proximity and contact, together, instead of trying to distance ourselves from these inevitable qualities, or expel the disgusting from among and inside us?[24] Were the assemblies assemblages of people affected by these affects in their past and present, and opted to assemble together in spite of or even because of disgust, trying to feel something different, or differently, in sticking together? The slight space between epistle and audience, apostle and assembly, allows for and even calls up an unfinished project of solidarity, particularly if occupied by those who were already subjected to, affected by a cultural politics of disgust and debasement, then or now.

Bibliography

Ahmed, Sara. 2004. *The Cultural Politics of Emotion*. New York: Routledge.

Amador, J. David Hester. 1999. *Academic Constraints in Rhetorical Criticism of the New Testament: An Introduction to a Rhetoric of Power*. Sheffield: Sheffield Academic.

Betz, Hans Dieter. 1979. *Galatians: A Commentary on Paul's Letter to the Churches in Galatia*. Hermeneia. Philadelphia: Fortress.

Biles, Jeremy, and Kent L. Brintnall, eds. 2015. *Negative Ecstasies: George Bataille and the Study of Religion*. New York: Fordham University Press.

Blanton, Ward. 2014. *A Materialism for the Masses: Saint Paul and the Philosophy of Undying Life*. New York: Columbia University Press.

Brinkema, Eugenie. 2014. *The Forms of the Affects*. Durham, NC: Duke University Press.

Brooten, Bernadette J. 1996. *Love Between Women: Early Christian Responses to Female Homoeroticism*. Chicago: University of Chicago Press.

Burrus, Virginia. 2008. *Saving Shame: Martyrs, Saints, and Other Abject Subjects*. Philadelphia: University of Pennsylvania Press.

---

24. For related reflections on the performative possibilities of assembling in solidarity through both difference and shared vulnerability, see Butler 2004; 2015.

Butler, Judith. 1990. *Gender Trouble: Feminism and the Subversion of Identity*. New York: Routledge.

———. 2004. *Precarious Life: The Powers of Mourning and Violence*. London: Verso.

———. 2015. *Notes Toward a Performative Theory of Assembly*. Cambridge: Harvard University Press.

Derrida, Jacques. 1981. "Economimesis." Translated by R. Klein. *Diacritics* 11:3–25.

Eastman, Susan. 2013. "Double Participation and the Responsible Self in Romans 5–8." Pages 93–110 in *Apocalyptic Paul: Cosmos and Anthropos in Romans 5–8*. Edited by Beverly Roberts Gaventa. Waco, TX: Baylor University Press.

Eisenbaum, Pamela. 2009. *Paul Was Not a Christian: The Original Message of a Misunderstood Apostle*. New York: HarperOne.

Fisher, Nick. 2017. "Demosthenes and the Use of Disgust." Pages 103–24 in *The Ancient Emotion of Disgust*. Edited by Donald Lateiner and Dimos Spatharas. New York: Oxford University Press.

Gaventa, Beverly Roberts. 2013. "The Shape of the 'I': The Psalter, the Gospel, and the Speaker in Romans 7." Pages 77–91 in *Apocalyptic Paul: Cosmos and Anthropos in Romans 5–8*. Edited by Beverly Roberts Gaventa. Waco, TX: Baylor University Press.

Halperin, David M., and Valerie Traub, eds. 2010. *Gay Shame*. Chicago: University of Chicago Press.

Hartman, Midori E. 2019. "A Little Porneia Leavens the Whole: Queer(ing) Limits of Community in 1 Corinthians 5." Pages 143–63 in *Bodies on the Verge: Queering Pauline Epistles*. Edited by Joseph A. Marchal. SemeiaSt 93. Atlanta: SBL Press.

Hornsby, Teresa J. 2001. "Paul and the Remedies of Idolatry: Reading Romans 1:18–24 with Romans 7." Pages 219–32 in *Postmodern Interpretations of the Bible: A Reader*. Edited by A. K. M. Adam. Saint Louis: Chalice.

Ipsen, Avaren. 2009. *Sex Working and the Bible*. London: Equinox.

Ivarsson, Fredrik. 2007. "Vice Lists and Deviant Masculinity: The Rhetorical Function of 1 Corinthians 5:10–11 and 6:9–10." Pages 163–84 in *Mapping Gender in Ancient Religious Discourses*. Edited by Todd Penner and Caroline Vander Stichele. Leiden: Brill.

Jewett, Robert. 2007. *Romans: A Commentary*. Hermeneia. Minneapolis: Fortress.

Johnson-DeBaufre, Melanie. 2010. "'Gazing Upon the Invisible': Archaeology, Historiography, and the Elusive Wo/men of 1 Thessalonians." Pages 73–108 in *From Roman to Early Christian Thessalonikē*. Edited by Laura Nasrallah, Charalambos Bakirtzis, and Steven J. Friesen. Cambridge: Harvard University Press.

Kahl, Brigitte. 2010. *Galatians Re-imagined: Reading with the Eyes of the Vanquished*. Minneapolis: Fortress.

Keck, Leander. 2001. "*Pathos* in Romans? Mostly Preliminary Remarks." Pages 71–96 in *Paul and* Pathos. Edited by Thomas H. Olbricht and Jerry L. Sumney. SymS 16. Atlanta: Society of Biblical Literature.

Kelly, Daniel R. 2011. *Yuck! The Nature and Moral Significance of Disgust*. Cambridge: MIT Press.

Knust, Jennifer Wright. 2005. *Abandoned to Lust: Sexual Slander and Ancient Christianity*. New York: Columbia University Press.

Korsmeyer, Carolyn. 2011. *Savoring Disgust: The Foul and the Fair in Aesthetics*. Oxford: Oxford University Press.

Kotrosits, Maia. 2011. "The Rhetoric of Intimate Spaces: Affect and Performance in the Corinthian Correspondence." *USQR* 62:3–4:134–51.

———. 2016. "How Things Feel: Biblical Studies, Affect, and the (Im)Personal." *Brill Research Perspectives in Biblical Interpretation* 1:1:1–53.

Lateiner, Donald, and Dimos Spatharas. 2017. "Introduction: Ancient and Modern Modes of Understanding and Manipulating Disgust." Pages 1–42 in *The Ancient Emotion of Disgust*. Edited by Donald Lateiner and Dimos Spatharas. New York: Oxford University Press.

Liew, Tat-siong Benny. 2008. *What Is Asian American Biblical Hermeneutics? Reading the New Testament*. Honolulu: University of Hawai'i Press.

Lopez, Davina C. 2008. *Apostle to the Conquered: Reimagining Paul's Mission*. Minneapolis: Fortress.

Marchal, Joseph A. 2011. "'Making History' Queerly: Touches across Time through a Biblical Behind." *BibInt* 19:373–95.

———. 2014. "Female Masculinity in Corinth? Bodily Citations and the Drag of History." *Neot* 48:1:93–113.

———. 2015a. "The Exceptional Proves Who Rules: Imperial Sexual Exceptionalism in and around Paul's Letters." *Journal of Early Christian History* 5:87–115.

———, ed. 2015b. *The People Beside Paul: The Philippian Assembly and History from Below*. ECL 17. Atlanta: SBL Press.

———. 2019. *Appalling Bodies: Queer Figures before and after Paul's Letters*. New York: Oxford University Press.
Martin, Dale B. 1995. "Heterosexism and the Interpretation of Romans 1:18–32." *BibInt* 3:332–55.
Massumi, Brian. 2002. *Parables for the Virtual: Movement, Affect, Sensation*. Durham, NC: Duke University Press.
Matthews, Shelly. 2015. "A Feminist Analysis of the Veiling Passage (1 Corinthians 11:2–16): Who Really Cares That Paul Was Not a Gender Egalitarian After All?" *lectio difficilior* 2:https://tinyurl.com/SBL0696a.
Menninghaus, Winfried. 2003. *Disgust: Theory and History of a Strong Sensation*. Translated by Howard Eiland and Joel Golb. Albany: State University of New York Press.
Miller, William Ian. 1997. *The Anatomy of Disgust*. Cambridge: Harvard University Press.
Moore, Stephen D. 2014. "Retching on Rome: Vomitous Loathing and Visceral Disgust in Affect Theory and the Apocalypse of John." *BibInt* 22.4–5:503–28.
Nasrallah, Laura S. 2012. "Spatial Perspectives: Space and Archaeology in Roman Philippi." Pages 53–74 in *Studying Paul's Letters: Contemporary Perspectives and Methods*. Edited by Joseph A. Marchal. Minneapolis: Fortress.
Ngai, Sianne. 2007. *Ugly Feelings*. Cambridge: Harvard University Press.
Olbricht, Thomas H. 2001. "*Pathos* as Proof in Greco-Roman Rhetoric." Pages 7–22 in *Paul and* Pathos. Edited by Thomas H. Olbricht and Jerry L. Sumney. SymS 16. Atlanta: Society of Biblical Literature.
Olbricht, Thomas H., and Jerry L. Sumney, eds. 2001. *Paul and* Pathos. SymS 16. Atlanta: Society of Biblical Literature.
Rauhala, Marika. 2017. "*Obscena Galli Praesentia*: Dehumanizing Cybele's Eunuch-Priests through Disgust." Pages 235–52 in *The Ancient Emotion of Disgust*. Edited by Donald Lateiner and Dimos Spatharas. New York: Oxford University Press.
Rubin, Gayle. 1989. "Thinking Sex: Notes for a Radical Theory of the Politics of Sexuality." Pages 267–319 in *Pleasure and Danger: Exploring Female Sexuality*. Edited by Carole S. Vance. London: Pandora.
Runions, Erin. 2011. "From Disgust to Humor: Rahab's Queer Affect." Pages 45–74 in *Bible Trouble: Queer Reading at the Boundaries of Biblical Scholarship*. Edited by Teresa J. Hornsby and Ken Stone. SemeiaSt 67. Atlanta: Society of Biblical Literature.

Schüssler Fiorenza, Elisabeth. 2000. "Paul and the Politics of Interpretation." Pages 40–57 in *Paul and Politics: Ekklesia, Israel, Imperium, Interpretation: Essays in Honor of Krister Stendahl*. Edited by Richard A. Horsley. Harrisburg, PA: Trinity Press International.

———. 2001. *Wisdom Ways: Introducing Feminist Biblical Interpretation*. Maryknoll, NY: Orbis.

Seigworth, Gregory J., and Melissa Gregg. 2010. "Inventory of Shimmers." Pages 1–25 in *The Affect Theory Reader*. Edited by Melissa Gregg and Gregory J. Seigworth. Durham, NC: Duke University Press.

Shantz, Colleen. 2009. *Paul in Ecstasy: The Neurobiology of the Apostle's Life and Thought*. Cambridge: Cambridge University Press.

———. 2013. "Emotion, Cognition, and Social Change: A Consideration of Galatians 3:28." Pages 252–70 in *Mind, Morality, and Magic: Cognitive Science Approaches in Biblical Studies*. Edited by István Czachesz and Risto Uro. Durham: Acumen.

———. 2015. "'I Do Not Understand My Actions': Some Cognitive Bases for Natural Dualisms." Paper presented at the Annual Meeting of the Society of Biblical Literature, Atlanta, GA, 21 November.

Spatharas. Dimos. 2017. "Sex, Politics, and Disgust in Aeschines' *Against Timarchus*." Pages 125–39 in *The Ancient Emotion of Disgust*. Edited by Donald Lateiner and Dimos Spatharas. New York: Oxford University Press.

Stendahl, Krister. 1963. "The Apostle Paul and the Introspective Conscience of the West." HTR 56:119–215.

Stowers, Stanley K. 1994. *A Rereading of Romans: Justice, Jews, and Gentiles*. New Haven: Yale University Press.

———. 1995. "Romans 7.7–25 as a Speech in Character (προσωποπεια)." Pages 180–202 in *Paul In His Hellenistic Context*. Edited by Troels Engberg-Pedersen. Minneapolis: Fortress.

Swancutt, Diana M. 2003. "'The Disease of Effemination': The Charge of Effeminacy and the Verdict of God (Romans 1:18–2:16)." Pages 193–233 in *New Testament Masculinities*. Edited by Stephen D. Moore and Janice Capel Anderson. SemeiaSt 45. Atlanta: Society of Biblical Literature.

Townsley, Gillian. 2006. "*Gender Trouble* in Corinth: Que(e)rying Constructs of Gender in 1 Corinthians 11:2–16." BCT 2.2:17.1–17.14.

Walters, Jonathan. 1997. "Invading the Roman Body: Manliness and Impenetrability in Roman Thought." Pages 29–43 in *Roman Sexuali-*

ties. Edited by Judith P. Hallett and Marilyn B. Skinner. Princeton: Princeton University Press.

"Not Grudgingly, nor under Compulsion":
Love, Labor, Service, and Slavery in Pauline Rhetoric

Robert Paul Seesengood

Although Paul's rhetoric of freedom is drawing increasing interest among contemporary continental Marxist philosophers such as Gorgio Agamben, Paul's central metaphor for Christian life and faith is slavery and servitude. Paul constructs a metaphorical system where followers of Jesus are redeemed ("bought") from sin and now serve their new Lord ("master") with love. The Pauline model merges duty, obligation, and debt with love and (com)passion. Scholarship on the social systems of late capitalism reveals how much aesthetic, spiritual, and affectual encounters are also economic, embodied, and material. Pauline literature advocates late capitalism's emotional labor as it conflates charity and obligation, debt and grace, liberty and compulsion. These systems betray an (often gendered) obsession with (sexual) desire, as well. This essay reviews Paul's rhetoric of community service, fellowship, and reciprocity as a type of emotional labor fusing affects of desire and affection with economics and labor. Love, in Paul, is a labor, a task; service and work, in Paul, should be the result of love. Love is a labor, and labor must be loved (as articulated in Seesengood 2017, 77–94; this essay assumes and expands that argument).

The Biblical Value of Loving Labor

The letters to the Thessalonians reveal a Pauline philosophy of labor, responding to believers who had, apparently, ceased work in anticipation of an impending return of Jesus (1 Thess 4:11–12; for a traditional review, note Malherbe 1987 or Brown 1997, 458–62, 594–96). The idea of remaining productively employed while awaiting Jesus's return is so strongly associated with the advice to the Thessalonians that we find it continues in the Deutero-Pauline 2 Thessalonians as well: "For we hear that some of you are living in idleness, mere busybodies, not doing any work" (2 Thess 3:11).[1] The author's goal in 2 Thess 3:12 is to avoid broad public displeasure (presumably for laggardness) and to keep the community from want. The Thessalonians are instructed to "admonish the idlers" (1 Thess 5:14). The post-Pauline 2 Thessalonians uses a narrative of Paul's behavior to reinforce and illustrate it:

> Keep away from believers who are living in idleness and not according to the tradition that they received from us. For you yourselves know how you ought to imitate us; we were not idle when we were with you, and we did not eat anyone's bread without paying for it; but with toil and labor we worked night and day, so that we might not burden any of you. This was not because we do not have that right, but in order to give you an example to imitate. For even when we were with you, we gave you this command: Anyone unwilling to work should not eat. For we hear that some of you are living in idleness, mere busybodies, not doing any work. Now such persons we command and exhort in the Lord Jesus Christ to do their work quietly and to earn their own living. (3:6–12)

Second Thessalonians is drawing upon a memory of Paul as a self-supporting laborer. The epistle mirrors 1 Cor 9, where Paul asserts that he worked to support himself during his ministry in Corinth, even though he was entitled to a wage (1 Cor 9:9–11). Conventional modern criticism argues that this labor is optional, an illustration of Paul's intellectual independence and autonomy; Paul does not need to work and is entitled to support, but, for larger reasons (centered around the good of the Corinthian believers), he chooses to be covocational (Fee 1987, 397–422).

In the Pauline letters (and in their traditional Protestant interpretation), labor is a virtue, not a forced response to economic reality (see Still 2006). Labor is autonomy, a sign of personal diligence; it facilitates and enables service to God as well as charitable acts. Work, like marriage, child-rearing, or home management, is an expression of service to God (or, among the "worldly," a distraction from God's work if we follow the logic of 1 Cor 7).

Paul's equation of labor with autonomy, on historical consideration, marks conventional social values among the elites. As is evident in works

---

[1]. Biblical translations are from the NRSV.

like Virgil's *Georgics* or Cicero's *Orations*, reasonable effort, thrift, industriousness, and steady employment are patrician virtues in the early Roman Empire. Yet, one wonders how much physical labor any given Roman patrician was obligated to complete. Labor, particularly unskilled labor, in the Roman Empire was normally the purview of the slave, the antithesis of the autonomous. Slavery was endemic, perhaps at its apex in western history (Avalos 2011). Though there are occasions in the Pauline traditions (and also in the gospels) of free, independent labor(ers), in the cultural world of Paul's New Testament, labor, particularly manual or domestic labor, was often slave labor. At the least, to address labor in the New Testament and Roman world is to invoke slavery.

Like labor, slavery is a common metaphor in the Pauline letters for service to God, worship, and missionary teaching.[2] In Romans, often understood as Paul's paean to freedom and grace, Paul self-designates as Jesus's slave and uses the metaphor of slavery in an extended discussion of bondage to sin or to God (Rom 1:1; 6:15–20; see Goodrich 2013). Paul's doctrine of redemption ("you were bought with a price," 1 Cor 6:20; cf. 7:23) is economic and presumes slavery. Paul refers to his own missionary endeavors using labor and agricultural terms (1 Cor 3:6–8), and Paul designates his fellow teachers and missionaries as "fellow workers" (Phil 4:3; Phlm 24). Paul is employing general themes that later appear in traditions of Jesus's own parables and teaching. The agricultural metaphor of missionary work as harvest or gleaning is a fundamentally economic, labor-driven metaphor, as well (Matt 9:37, par. Luke 10:2; John 4:35).

When addressing actual (and not metaphoric) slavery, the Pauline literature compels slaves to serve not just with the obligatory use of their bodies, but also to work affectually; slaves should work as if they *want* to work. Slaves should imitate the patrician attitudes toward work (its elevating aspects, its character reflection), even as they have a different compulsion to work (and, likely, different sorts of tasks). Paul does not need to work, but does so willingly; slaves need to work, but should do so freely and willingly as well. They are called to "obey your earthly masters in everything, not only while being watched and in order to please them, but wholeheartedly" (Col 3:22). Slaves were not at liberty to determine what was done with, by, or to their bodies and could be compelled to do actions

---

2. On slavery and the Bible, see Callahan, Horsley, and Smith 1998; Glancy 2006; Avalos 2011; for works on slavery and Paul, see Byron 2003; 2008; Fantia 2011.

they found immoral. Slaves could be (and often were) considered sexual property of their owners (Marchal 2011). Slaves are admonished to work fully, drawing from an understanding of work and labor that reflects the perspective of the Master.

In Colossians, Paul argues slave obedience to her master is, itself, a form of obedience to God. God is made rhetorically parallel to a slave owner. Colossians 3:24 reminds slaves their true freedom is in God, but this is because they are really slaves of Jesus Christ. In being obedient to their mortal masters, slaves are serving God, and, so, slave obedience becomes piety. Since there are no restraints on the slave owner besides vague admonitions to fairness (Col 4:1), and since the sexual use of slaves was well within acceptable behavior in the Roman context, Colossians can be seen as arguing that submission to violence and rape is (at least potentially) a form of service to God. Colossians is also calling those engaging in forced labor to work as if they enjoy it, are invested in the successful outcome of their labor; in other words, slaves are to work as if they are the slave owners.

This theme is expanded in the Deutero-Pauline letter to the Ephesians. Ephesians returns to the language of Colossians but adds that slaves are to obey "with fear and trembling, in singleness of heart" (Eph 6:5). The linkage of such obedience to service to Jesus is intensified (6:6). Slaves are to "render service with enthusiasm" as if to God (6:7). Slaves are instructed to be "enthusiastic" (lit. "filled with God"). Good obedience will be remediated by God: "we will receive the same again from the Lord, whether we are slaves or free" (6:8). There is no language that suggests compensation to slaves for compulsion to activity against their morals. Ephesians does not even seem to have such a possibility in view (though, without doubt, every household slave, at least occasionally, did).

Labor and slavery are, of course, economic, and the Deutero-Pauline perspective on slaves is consistent with Paul's more general economic statements. Paul's letters explicitly address money management and economic exchange. The central monetary interest in his extant letters was a collection of funds for Jerusalem poor (Gal 2:10; 1 Cor 16:1–4; 2 Cor 8–9; Rom 14:25–27; and probably Phil 4:15–19). The same rhetoric of freely giving one's labor (even if one is compelled, one should act *as if* it were freely given) is used to address giving money to charitable causes. Paul instructs the Corinthians to give "not reluctantly or under compulsion for God loves a cheerful giver" (2 Cor 9:7). The household codes reproduce upper-class attitudes towards these economic virtues and impose them upon the slave class.

Within even later New Testament traditions, 1 Peter calls for believers to disrupt social order as little as possible and to avoid political engagement (1 Pet 2:11-12; 1 and 2 Peter, though not directly within the Pauline tradition(s), are certainly aware of them [cf. 2 Pet 3:14-16]). Slaves are encouraged to "accept the authority of your masters with all deference, not only those who are kind and gentle, but also to those who are harsh" (2:18). First Peter makes it explicit that slaves should even endure physical abuse (2:19), making explicit what is only implied in Colossians and Ephesians. Endurance of a justifiable beating (whatever that might be) is of little credit, but enduring unjust punishment makes the believing slave an imitator of Jesus (2:20-21).

All these various streams—labor, slavery, and affect—are perhaps best seen at work together in Paul's Letter to Philemon. The letter, again and again, equates piety with work and work with emotion. Philemon is praised for his love for the saints, which is demonstrated through service (v. 7). Paul avoids commanding Philemon, but wants (and expects) Philemon's obedience (vv. 9, 14, 21). Paul appeals for Onesimus (who bears a common slave name meaning roughly "Handy"), noting that now Onesimus is a believer and is "useful" (v. 11; on wordplay, see Marchal 2011, 760-62). Historically, Philemon has been read as Paul appealing on behalf of Onesimus, a slave estranged from his master Philemon, making slavery the letter's background and implicit theme. In Philemon, then, we find the capstone, the complete entanglement of Pauline views on embodiment, economics, exchange, emotion, will, desire, and affect.

Paul is emotional. His letters often drip with pathos, anger, and emotional manipulation. His letters seethe with anger at times (Gal 1; 2 Cor 10) and coo with affection at others (Gal 4; 2 Cor 2). Paul is author of the Bible's most soaring tribute to love, 1 Cor 13. Perhaps on a less documentable plane, Pauline scholarship itself often becomes intensely affectual. Paul awakens strong feelings in his readers—even (especially) his academic ones—of loyalty, anger, resistance, admiration, and rage. Paul is, to put it bluntly, begging for an affectual reading.

The Work of Affect: Emotional Labor and Love beyond Reason

Affect and affect criticism have influenced general social science and humanities scholarship of the late twentieth and early twenty-first century (Gregg and Seigworth 2010, 1-9; note, also: Kotrosits 2015, 1-20; 2016; and Koosed and Moore 2014, 381-87). Affect theory provides a way, in humanities scholarship, to bypass debates surrounding essentialism versus constructivism, and the attendant debates about structuralism and emergence of poststructuralism. Affect theory also connects with inquiry into human-animal-technological difference (often, inquiry into the posthuman) and is equally often rooted in queer, gender, and feminist studies—partly because of the emphasis these all placed upon embodiment and partly in response to centuries of argument that emotion was inferior to (masculine) reason and rationality.

Beginning with the work of Silvan Tomkins (1962–1992), especially as his work is adopted by Eve Kosofsky Sedgwick and Adam Frank (Sedgwick and Frank 1995), affect and affect theory focused scholarly attention on feeling and emotional response and the ways these integrate with and enable an array of exchanges and experiences. Tomkins, a psychobiologist, was largely writing about precognitive emotive responses (e.g., interest-excitement, enjoyment-joy, surprise-startle, distress-anguish, anger-rage, fear-terror; Tomkins links affect and emotion but also argues they remain distinct). Affect is responsive, prerational. Quite often, it is beyond one's ability to anticipate or even immediately realize (let alone refine or control); affect would seem to be opposed to elaborate, socially constructed, ideological, cognition and language-driven systems like religion or economics. Yet on closer reflection, one can easily recognize an affective component in/of religion (and define religion, as per Clifford Geertz and others, as a means for systemically organizing that which is prerational; see also Schaefer 2015). Debt and labor, while often compulsory (in a sense), seem, by their tediousness and persistent presence, to be highly conscious, usually rational, activity. Emotion and feeling would seem to be radically immaterial and not subject to economics or labor. What, then, is the role of affect criticism in economics, debt, and labor?

In *The Managed Heart: The Commercialization of Human Feeling*, Arlie Hochschild (1983, 3–9) coined the term *emotional labor* to describe occupations where employees are, as part of the commercial exchange, required to project an emotional connection to clients.[3] Workers in emotional

---

3. Hochschild (1983, 7) specifically defines emotional labor as work that "requires one to induce or suppress feeling in order to sustain the outward countenance that produces the proper state of mind in others—in this case, the sense of being cared for in a convivial and safe space. This kind of labor calls for a coordination of mind and feeling, and it sometimes draws on a source of self that we honor as deep and integral to our being."

labor (waitresses, personal caregivers, clerks) complete service tasks while expected to project and manage positive affects.[4] Sara Ahmed has expanded the concept of emotional labor to include service work that is particularly intimate, often undertaken for affectual motives (nursing and hospice, child care, cooking and housekeeping).[5] Emotional labor becomes the work of making others feel *happy* and cared for. It is disproportionately the labor of women and minorities (see Ahmed 2010, 21–29, 58–60, 121–30), both in the occupations it includes and the workers who engage in it. Standards and productivity expectations of workers often place great affective demands (and stresses) upon these workers even as (because?) these occupations enable and facilitate economic growth and consumption (Ahmed 2010, 128–32). Workers engaged in emotional labor are required to pacify angry customers and (to at least appear) to care deeply about the satisfaction of customer concerns and worries. Workers must not merely be competent and professional—or even courteous (despite often angry and disrespectful clients)—but must also often communicate deep concern for the client's problem. Emotional labor takes a real toll on many workers who are often required to suppress chronic stress and may be professionally evaluated on their ability to manage or even direct the emotional state and felt-satisfaction of customers and clients, even as it seems increasingly unlikely that they can have any real effect on another person's emotions.

As the (highly automated and digitalized) economies of late capitalism increasingly turn toward service industries, a great deal of contemporary labor involves the maintenance of an illusion of affective bonds. Customers must be calmed, in part because doing so increases productivity and efficiency, in part because this affective illusion is much of what customers are paying to receive. Not content with service, consumers report they want workers who embrace their job joyfully; who do more than the bare minimum; who smile, flirt, or flatter and make the transaction happier. Emotional labor is the lubrication of late capitalism and a direct result of increasing income disparity and economic privilege (chapters five and six of Piketty 2014 outline the mechanism and implication of this income inequality), creating the illusion that service workers *want* to make their

---

4. Some careers go further: an actual emotional connection to clients is expected and workers are expected to *actually* care for/love those they serve (teachers, professors, clergy, nursing, childcare providers, etc.).

5. Note, also, the work on emotional labor since Hochschild surveyed in Steinberg and Figart (1999).

clients happy, that they would, really, likely provide their service or pleasure for free. Emotional labor is often the outcome of increasing economic disparity; those served are no longer content with the labor and bodies of their workers, but want their emotions as well. Service workers, in turn, are pleasant often because this affords the minimal disruption and maximizes productivity. Emotional labor is (intentionally) hidden labor. Of course, so is slavery.

The New Testament, as we have seen, makes frequent linkage between service to others (service that is *diakonate*—slavery) and affect (love). New Testament service tends to intimate moments of spiritual weakness and openness; it is performed on and by bodies. In that, it draws from its contemporary models of Roman era slavery: slaves did household and emotional labor, ranging from food provision to cleaning to (in some cases) forced sexual encounter(s). Slaves performed their tasks in a myriad of locations, but most of the heavy labor happened in spaces aloof from leisured classes—cellars, fields, attics, kitchens, latrines, sick rooms, nurseries, and more. Like slavery, emotional labor conceals the work involved, and, even more, hides the laborer. Workers recede into the background of the exchange or *experience*. They foster the illusion that the present exchange arises from some reason other than (compulsory) economic exchange. One might argue, then, that rather than being an outcome of late capitalism, emotional labor is rooted in much older notions of economics and (affective) exchange, perhaps even to norms arising from biblical text and compulsory service of love. If so, one wonders: are we moving toward a system of (at least affective) slavery through late capitalism, where the commodification of emotion results in the minds and affects of workers being *owned* by employers or clients? In modern economic systems, laborers certainly have bodily autonomy undreamt by Roman slaves (or, by corollary, imagined by New Testament writers), but modern service economies that desire emotional, affect-fueled labor require workers to use elements of the *self* that many consider private and core. Workers, though practically free, *feel* owned (Hochschild 1983, 8).

Max Weber argued over a century ago in his seminal volume *Die Protestantische Ethik und der Geist des Kapitalismus*, translated as *The Protestant Ethic and the Spirit of Capitalism* (1930), that religious ideas and values not only reflect our quest for emotional meaning but that they intersect with economics and material culture. Work ethic and systems of good verses bad indebtedness, Weber discovered, were religiously filtered structures. Current readings have explored the affectual nature of economics, as well. Greg Seigworth's essay "Wearing the World Like a Debt Garment" (2016) explores the intersection of culture, ideology, affect, and economics through an affect-critical reading of M. T. Anderson's young adult novel *Feed* (2002). Reading Seigworth leaves, as I suspect he usually intends, more impressions, ideas, and sensations than conventional theses or arguments, a feeling radically in-between comprehension and confusion, between discovering and inventing, always-almost on the edge of a breakthrough. Seigworth's essay enacts the *becomingness* in Deleuzian affect (Deleuze and Guattari 1987, 256: "Affects are becomings"), the moment before the gasp or tear or laugh or *eww*, the precognitive (presentient) discovery before awareness.

Seigworth takes as his essay's focus a plot element of Andersen's science fiction novel, where an array of digital communication systems—ranging from social media to general information to economic data—are digitally encoded and integrated into clothing. Seigworth explores, from this trope, the way that systems of social, technological, and economic interactions become a new sort of *skin*. Identity is *worn*, serving as a barrier to and mediator of the broader world. Seigworth suggests that we *feel* the presence or absence of these interactions as if they were a garment; he goes on to explore clothing, garments, feeling, and integration of debt. More critical for the present argument is his examination of the integration between feeling, affect, and economics. Affect is integral to/in economics.

There is an affectual element, and an emotive response, to economics, debt, and exchange. Indeed, the affective force of debt and indebtedness fuel the desire to labor at tasks which, increasingly, also themselves often require affective engagement. Forced to feelings of insecurity, fear, or anxiety from the affect of debt, workers take on occupations that have affective requirements such as compassion, concern, and pleasure at service. This exchange is, in part, the result of shifts of late capitalism and new modes of labor. Yet it is modeled, indeed perhaps *premiered* or even *precipitated* by idealized views of affectively driven labor and service, which are embedded in biblical texts.

"I tried to touch my credit" (Seigworth 2016, 15; quoting Anderson). How does debt feel? I admit, I have a feeling of dread and liminality as I lay my own debit card upon a countertop, a moment of instability, of fearful commitment, the moment before the rational mind takes over reviewing the numbers and giving me free license to continue, the moment before the longing and the desire to own or consume overrides any concern so mundane as mathematics. The matter becomes particularly acute at a bar, where

"I'll pay for this later" can become an unusually pregnant sentiment. I can't help thinking of the coming revolution in consumption and debt and credit, where smart chips are integrated into my clothing or even, eventually, integrated into my body, a coming mark of systems of (Deleuzian) control, of dominating beasts, without which no one can buy or sell (cf. Rev 13:17). Access to my credit and debt is already integrated into my iPhone, which is, in turn, already becoming an extension of my Self. Weber makes the argument that in contemporary capitalism, good credit is, to many, equal to *moral virtue*. My credit is good, and I am aware of the social privilege that creates—again as per Weber, who argues a certain amount of debt, especially *good debt* (mortgage, business loans, etc.), is what fuels capitalism. Yet, debt, particularly *bad debt* (unsecured debts, credit lines, *wasteful* spending) feels like guilt, fear, and loss of control, even as it also feels like empowerment and access. Debt feels like both sin and redemption. Weber has noted that models and values from religious devotion construct culture and economics, as well (Weber 1930, 184–93). New Testament authors argue that service ought to arise from and be fueled by affect (love). This love is response to the recognition of one's redemption, one's purchase, one's *enslavement* (1 Cor. 6:20). Labor is driven by love; love is fueled by indebtedness. The models for late capitalism's emotional labor lie within biblical text.

Bible and the Commodification of Affect: God, Love and Capitalism

Slavery is the ultimate expression of embodied debt and affective labor. Affect is interstitial. It is the response before cognition, the *knowing* before perception. Like affect, slaves are profoundly interstitial (see Patterson 1985). Slaves have no legal identity or rights, yet they have commercial value. They have a body but it belongs to someone else. Slaves are covered with unique markings, clothing, and piercings that intimately display their identity, but that were never their choice. Slaves use their bodies to perform caretaking, intimate service for someone who owns and confines them. Slavery is a central metaphor in Christian text for the freedom of following Jesus, particularly in Paul. Christian redemption is, in its origins and function, a sacred and ritual action that is fundamentally economic (Grau 2004). Slaves are also the embodiment of the Deleuzian system of dominations (where "Deleuzian system of dominations" is understood as argued in Seigworth and Wise 2000).

Slavery is more present in late capitalism than we may find comfortable. Human trafficking persists in the world and is financially lucrative.

American penal structures look terrifyingly familiar to many previous systems of slave control (Runions 2014, 46–85; 2019). More frequently, systems of emotional labor bind and enforce debt and debt relations in economic indenture (cf. Cherlin 2014; Kunnie 2015) in ways that connect with slave experiences of forced affect. As the economy of the West becomes more service-oriented, employers script emotional exchanges between laborers and consumers that are affective expressions of economic relationships (Hochschild 1983, 122–34).

Debt is quantified (and then embodied) first in labor, then in affect; emotional labor is the *affectification* of debt. Debt and credit in late capitalism establish what services, and what love, we are required to give or entitled to receive. Systems of interobligation and ritual once negotiated via the affect of religiosity are now negotiated by systems of debt and credit. How does debt feel? Like loss? Like potential or power? Is debt the potentiality of the moment that is always between production and consumption, control and enslavement? Is the pain of debt the pain of phantom limbs, of phantom credit? Do threads of debt now bind us, reknit, into garments of slavery, ritual, and religiosity? Are debt, labor, and commerce in some way material expressions of affect, forms of affect?

Affect, from the Latin *affectere* ("to cause, make, produce") is involuntary. It moves another, often before the Other has realized. In affective labor, we see an essential experience in ways that reveal (and revel in) different types of exchange and control. When linked to labor and economics, affect accompanies the exchange of service; affect, then, becomes a quantification, a commodification of desire and the reciprocal response.

Again, these various themes, as we have argued, can be seen intertwined in Paul. In biblical language, forcing affect to accompany service is not merely to render more meaningful or intentional service. The twinned theme of affect and service commands the affect itself, introduces a system where preconscious sensation is regulated, where failure to regulate results in further indebtedness, where affect is mediated to another (in turn, an act of compulsion and control). Emotional labor commodifies feeling and affect; it shifts the conversation from service and compassion to desire and control.

Walter Benjamin reveals how the commodification of desire and affect is linked to sexual desire. Among Benjamin's final works (1999; indeed, it remains incomplete) is a study of the Parisian shopping districts, the arcades. Enabled by new technologies and economies (e.g., changes in steel production), the pedestrian arcades, precursors to the modern shopping mall, were a total transformation of struggling cityscape and retail space (particularly for luxury goods, foods, and services). Benjamin's work on the arcades, like the arcades themselves, idles along as a collection of quotations from various sources interspersed with Benjamin's own reflections. These "rambles" (my dynamic translation of the French) mimic aimless, but pleasant, pedestrian shopping.

Among Benjamin's few structural concepts in *Arcades* is *dreamspace* (on dreamspace and for a general summary review of *Arcades*, see Ferris 2008, 214–27). The arcades (ancestors of the modern megamall) are not really what they seem to be but are idealized fantasies (at times based upon or imitating the real), a problem-free, artificial space often mimicking somewhere exotic, ideal for delight and consumption. Goods, experiences, and commodities become ciphers for desire. Desire, deeply rooted in sexuality and sexual urge, is more pleasurable than satiation. Indeed, since what we desire is desire itself, satiation cannot occur. Benjamin refers to this insatiability, along with its chronic hope for fulfillment, as the "commodity fetish" (see, in general, Ferris 2008, 115–17). Possession, even acquisition, of goods is not, in and of itself, satisfying. Indeed, the need to protect, maintain, repair, insure, et cetera, our goods (and the singularity of any given good or product) often produces anxiety more than satiation.

Following Benjamin, I posit that, in the service-based economies of late capitalism, the hunger for service and social exchange is also a fetish, an unstated, insatiable desire. We seek its resolution in increasingly personal and affectual service. And yet, as with commodities as goods, its *possession* does not satisfy. Instead, we want more and more, craving not just the act of service, but also the affect which it represents or mimics. The result is a complex system of economic exchange that depends upon the sublimation of any other feeling to forced regard and affection. Emotional labor becomes simulated relationship, much as Parisian arcades were simulated space/structure. The affect is both real (it exists) and not real (it is illusory). Though emotional laborers (like, perhaps, slaves) may on occasion or for brief moments actually feel the emotions they portray, though they may create actual brief emotions in the consumer, the exchange is always uneven. One party is required to engage in emotional labor, while the other is not; one is free to feel, the other is not (or at least not free to actualize feeling). In purchasing labor and access to another person's skill, labor, and body, one is also purchasing the other person's (presented) emotional state.

Conclusion
(Or: How *Agape* Isn't as Easily Distinct from *Eros* or *Porneia* as Some Would Like)

In describing emotional labor, we have relied upon description of work for hire which is normally done as a manifestation of care; which is intimate; or where it is integral to the labor that the one providing the service genuinely regard the served, where the *customer* has the sense (s)he is getting something done from affection. Affected labor must also manage and channel emotion and control the feelings and affects of the exchange. Emotional/affected labor has its roots in Pauline metaphors toward service to God and Jesus. Weberian structures would argue that the religious roots, the ideal-type of modern emotional labor, is Pauline Christianity. Emotional labor, we have seen, trades closely on commodification of desire and its feelings, a commodification that Benjamin has argued is inherently sexual. Emotional labor, we have seen, touches on questions of gender and power.

Emotional labor, putting these various threads together, is perhaps most purely embodied in sex work and pornography. The exchange is made more pleasing and less clinical by the appearance of pleasure and emotional attachment. Affective sex work constructs systems of erasure and diminishment, of commodity and exchange. Sex work not only imitates emotional connection and intimacy; doing so is often critical to the satisfaction of the exchange.

The energies inherent in emotional labor and in biblical mandates to love mask capitalism's tendency to construct commodity exchange in the place of relationship. But it also, on investigation, adopts (if not constructs) a more dangerous rhetoric: disproportionate power relationships that commodify emotion. Workers are stripped not only of their labor and bodily independence, but are asked to act in ways that make this exchange appear not only voluntary, but desired. The tension is erasure of the identity and autonomy of the Other. The worker is presumed to feel grateful for the exchange. Mapping this dynamic onto its most brazen example, pornography and sex work, demonstrates the complex ways that affect and emotional labor engage bodies and identities. The essence of pornography (and sex labor), clearly embodied labor, is the performance or display (or artful concealment) of an array of affects such as desire, pleasure, arousal, subordination, admiration, compliance, trust, and in some cases genuine affection. One must not only perform certain acts, but must appear to do so with the appropriate affect (as desired by the client).

This rhetoric of both embodied affect and affect-motivated service and labor—the use of one's body to serve another, and the injunction to do so out of love and regard for the other—appears, of course, often in the Bible. Indeed, one might even argue that the Bible is the root of the cultural ideal of both emotional labor and the emotional entanglements and expectations of sex work. The New Testament, particularly Pauline, equations of affective love and service muddy the waters of labor and command. Believers must serve not just for duty or obedience, or even for love of God (or Jesus). Love must be extended to other people. There is a linkage between biblical commandments to love and sex work and pornography. It is a rhetoric of not only exchange, but also a rhetoric of power, enjoyed or simply obedient.

Bibliography

Ahmed, Sara. 2010. *The Promise of Happiness*. Durham, NC: Duke University Press.

Anderson, M. T. 2002. *Feed*. Cambridge: Candlewick.

Avalos, Hector. 2011. *Slavery, Abolition and the Ethics of Biblical Scholarship*. Sheffield: Sheffield Phoenix.

Benjamin, Walter. 1999. *The Arcades Project*. Translated by Howard Eiland and Kevin McLaughlin. Cambridge: Harvard University Press.

Brown, Raymond E. 1997. *An Introduction to the New Testament*. ABRL. New York: Doubleday.

Byron, John. 2003. *Slavery Metaphor in Early Judaism and Pauline Christianity: A Tradition-Historical and Exegetical Examination*. WUNT 2/162. Tübingen: Mohr Seibeck.

———. 2008. *Recent Research on Paul and Slavery*. Recent Research in Biblical Studies 3. Sheffield: Sheffield Phoenix.

Callahan, Allen D., Richard A. Horsley, and Abraham Smith, eds. 1998. *Slavery in Text and Interpretation*. Semeia 83–84.

Cherlin, Andrew J. 2014. *Labor's Love Lost: The Rise and Fall of the Working-Class Family in America*. New York: Russell Sage Foundation.

Deleuze, Gilles, and Félix Guattari. 1987. *A Thousand Plateaus: Capitalism and Schizophrenia*. Minneapolis: University of Minnesota.

Fantia, Joseph D. 2011. "Recent Research on Paul and Slavery." *BSac* 168:117–19.

Fee, Gordon D. 1987. *The First Epistle to the Corinthians*. NICNT. Grand Rapids: Eerdmans.

Ferris, David. 2008. *The Cambridge Introduction to Walter Benjamin*. Cambridge: Cambridge University Press.
Glancy, Jennifer A. 2006. *Slavery in Early Christianity*. Minneapolis: Fortress.
Goodrich. John K. 2013. "From Slaves of Sin to Slaves of God: Reconsidering the Origin of Paul's Slavery Metaphor in Romans 6." *BBR* 23:509–30.
Grau, Marion. 2004. *Of Divine Economy: Refinancing Redemption*. New York: T&T Clark.
Gregg, Melissa, and Gregory J. Seigworth, eds. 2010. *The Affect Theory Reader*. Durham, NC: Duke University Press.
Hochschild, Arlie Russell. 1983. *The Managed Heart: Commercialization of Human Feeling*. Berkeley: University of California Press.
Koosed, Jennifer L., and Stephen D. Moore, eds. 2014. *Affect Theory and the Bible*. BibInt 22.4–5.
Kotrosits, Maia. 2015. *Rethinking Early Christian Identity: Affect, Violence, and Belonging*. Minneapolis: Fortress.
———. 2016. *How Things Feel: Biblical Studies, Affect Theory, and the (Im)Personal*. Leiden: Brill.
Kunnie, Julian E. 2015. *The Cost of Globalization: Dangers to the Earth and Its People*. Jefferson, NC: McFarland & Company.
Malherbe, Abraham J. 1987. *Paul and the Thessalonians*. Philadelphia: Fortress.
Marchal, Joseph A. 2011. "The Usefulness of Onesimus: The Sexual Use of Slaves and Paul's Letter to Philemon." *JBL* 130:749–70.
Patterson, Orlando. 1985. *Slavery and Social Death: A Comparative Study*. Cambridge: Harvard University Press.
Piketty, Thomas. 2014. *Capital in the Twenty-First Century*. Translated by Arthur Goldhammer. Cambridge: Harvard University Press.
Runions, Erin. 2014. *The Babylon Complex: Theopolitical Fantasies of War, Sex, and Sovereignty*. New York: Fordham University Press.
———. 2019. "Immobile Theologies, Carceral Affects: Interest and Debt in Faith-Based Prison Programs." Pages 55–84 in *Religion, Emotion, Sensation: Affect Theories and Theologies*. Edited by Karen Bray and Stephen D. Moore. New York: Fordham University Press.
Schaefer, Donovan O. 2015. *Religious Affects: Animality, Evolution and Power*. Durham, NC: Duke University Press.
Sedgwick, Eve Kosofsky, and Adam Frank, eds. 1995. *Shame and Its Sisters: A Silvan Tomkins Reader*. Durham, NC: Duke University Press.

Seesengood, Robert Paul. 2017. *Philemon: Imagination, Labor and Love: An Introduction and Study Guide*. T&T Clark Study Guides to the New Testament. New York: Bloomsbury T&T Clark.

Seigworth, Gregory J. 2016. "Wearing the World Like a Debt Garment: Interface, Affect and Gesture." *Ephemera* 16.4:15–31.

Seigworth, Gregory J., and J. Macgregor Wise. 2000. "Introduction: Deleuze and Guattari in Cultural Studies." *Cultural Studies* 14.2:139–46.

Steinberg, Ronnie J., and Deborah M. Figart. 1999. "Emotional Labor since *The Managed Heart*." *The Annals of the American Academy of Political and Social Science* 561.1:8–26.

Still, Todd D. 2006. "Did Paul Loathe Manual Labor? Revisiting the Work of Ronald F. Hock on the Apostle's Tentmaking and Social Class." *JBL* 125:781–95.

Tomkins, Silvan. 1962–1992. *Affect, Imagination, Consciousness*. 4 vols. New York: Springer.

Weber, Max. 1930. *The Protestant Ethic and the Spirit of Capitalism*. Translated by Talcott Parsons. London: Allen & Unwin. [German orig. 1904–1905]

"Though We May Seem to Have Failed": Paul and Failure in Steve Ross's *Blinded*

Jay Twomey

A number of recent literary and cultural appropriations of Paul have tried to humanize the apostle through failure. This is not as common an approach in creative treatments of Jesus, despite the prominence of novels like Nikos Kazantzakis's *Last Temptation of Christ* (1960) and José Saramago's *The Gospel according to Jesus Christ* (1994). Unsurprisingly, as a sign on the highway between Indianapolis and Cincinnati puts it, citing a hymn: "Jesus never fails." But Paul? Well, not according to his own lights, perhaps. Even a text like 2 Cor 13:7—"though we may have seem to have failed [ἀδόκιμοι]"—seems clearly to be a defensive gesture, rather a play for authority than an acknowledgement of deficiency. More typically, as Elizabeth Castelli has noted, failure is entirely on the other side of the equation in Pauline texts. Paul urges his communities to "be perfect" (2 Cor 13:9) in imitating Christ via the model he himself provides (1 Cor 11:1), making failure, *their* failure in this spiritual economy, "inevitable" (Castelli 1991, 13).

Still, Paul's own occasional failure, or even the idea of Paul *as* failure, has been taken up frequently enough in a number of recent texts to hint at a minor trend. Martin Luther King Jr., in a sermon of 1959, refers to Paul's life as "the tragic story of a shattered dream and a blasted hope." He goes on:

> There is hardly anyone here this morning who has not set out for some distant Spain, some momentous goal, some glorious realization, only to find that we had to settle for much less. We were never able to walk as free [people] through the streets of our Rome. Instead, we were forced to live our lives in a little confining cell which circumstances had built around us. (King 2007, 517)

For Paul, that included not just a failed vision for his future western ministry, but also the thorn in his side. He had "prayed fervently for the 'thorn' to be removed from his flesh, but he went to the grave with this desire unfulfilled" (King 2007, 517). King's sermon has a more uplifting message, as you might imagine. Focusing on infinite hope while in straightened, finite circumstances; drawing upon the resources of faith and not acquiescing to a fatalistic complacency—that's the message. Elsewhere on that same spectrum of Paul's turning failure around we find Raenita Wallace's self-help book, *More Than a Conqueror: Biblical Keys to Overcoming Failure*. Because Paul would never have chosen obedience to Christ prior to his experience on the road to Damascus, one might say that he was compelled into a life "repulsive" to his sensibilities (Wallace 2005, 39). Paul is a useful example for Wallace of submission in the face of utterly unexpected divine imperatives, of how detours and "dismal failure[s]" like Paul's can lead to "notable success" (x–xi).[1] Similarly, although in a different register altogether, Robin Yassin-Kassab's 2008 debut novel, *Road from Damascus*, presents a Paul-like figure whose own dismal failures as a student and militant secularist convert him, ultimately, to a more tolerant appreciation of faith.

One finds slightly more complicated versions of this dynamic inversion in William Melvin Kelley's short story "Saint Paul and the Monkeys." A young man named Chig Dunford aspires to something more than a life in a respectable profession. He doesn't know what that something is. But he understands the crisis in his emotional life as a pair of strangely contrasting figurative options. As he tells his fiancée: "I'm living in a dream world of Saint Pauls and baby monkeys" (Kelley 1964, 81). On the one hand, there is the apparently complete conviction of St. Paul's conversion experience, a sense of utter, passionate certainty for one's life choices that

---

1. In a short piece in *The Christian Century*, Heidi Haverkamp (2014, 21) confesses that she is a "recovering perfectionist" who learned to acknowledge her own failures thanks to Rom 7:15–25. "Unlike [Paul]," she writes, who laments his "body of death" and operated in a world of disease and poor hygiene, "we are surrounded by images and examples of perfection," making the inevitable sense of failure so much more acute. Written for an audience of pastors, Haverkamp's essay is but a more narrowly tailored version of Wallace's book, and both would disagree with Castelli that Paul's rhetoric ensures failure. But one wonders if Haverkamp's text doesn't simply misrecognize the source of the perfection impulse; it's not the beautiful vegetables in the contemporary grocery store that serve up a model of *pastoral* effectiveness, obviously, but Paul himself.

he recognizes in his own father's medical career, and that he thinks he ought to feel about his future as a lawyer. On the other hand, there is his memory of watching a baby monkey on television; it had "shivered and whimpered in the corner of a wire cage as lights flashed and the arms of a weird contrivance clawed and battered the air. The monkey had been part of a psychological experiment. Stress had destroyed its mind" (69). On the one hand, serene conviction; on the other, ruinous, abject terror. The stark and comic contrast reflects Chig's own teenage insecurities, but it isn't really a contrast between success and failure. In fact, both Paul and the baby monkey present two unrelated but nevertheless striking models of affective completion. One of them may suggest a greater range of conscious awareness than the other. But in both cases there is no remainder beyond the state (certainty, terror) in question. If Chig imagines failure in terms of the baby monkey, then he misrecognizes failure as a kind of spectacular success since it implies an experience beyond responsibility. And it is precisely responsibility—to himself, first of all, but also to his fiancée and her family as well as his own—that Chig can't quite face. Something Chig probably learns by the end of this short piece is that, even if it is shaped by his dramatic dream imagery, the experience of failure is utterly wakeful and ordinary and fraught with all sorts of complicated obligations.[2]

The differences between Paul in King's speech and Kelley's story are, are I think, interestingly representative of alternative ways of thinking about failure and affect. Failure rendered, in King or Wallace, as a different kind of success, is similar to the way failure is sometimes figured in the anti-normative work of Jack Halberstam, José Esteban Muñoz, and Lee Edelman, among others. Failure is "the always already status of queers and other minoritarian subjects in the dominant social order within which they toil" according to Muñoz (2009, 173). For this reason, it is also a kind of "virtuosity that helps the spectator [the context is performance studies] exit from the stale and static lifeworld dominated by the alienation, exploitation, and drudgery associated with capitalism" (173). Failure is a utopian, even heroic strategy (174), in this view. Halberstam (2011, 11–12) similarly argues that "we might read failure ... as a refusal of mastery, a

---

2. Ninotchka Rosca's "Our Apostle Paul" is another interesting presentation of a Paul figure as a failure in short literary fiction. But this Paul appears to fail only in the petty perspective of his rival. In reality, as the rival eventually discovers, the character he mocks as "our apostle Paul" is really regarded by most others as a hero for standing up to the Marcos regime (1983, 17–31).

critique of intuitive connections within capitalism between success and profit, and as a counterhegemonic discourse of losing." "Heteronormative common sense," Halberstam (89) writes, "leads to the equation of success with advancement, capital accumulation, family, ethical conduct, and hope. Other subordinate, queer, or counterhegemonic modes of common sense lead to the association of failure with nonconformity, anticapitalist practices, nonreproductive lifestyles, negativity, and critique." Obviously, failure is not, in and of itself, a productive good in every alternative critical mode for anti-normative theorists. Halberstam (2011, 92) argues, for example, that the characters in the novel *Trainspotting*, while anticapitalist and counterhegemonic, represent "unqueer failure, failure [as] the rage of the excluded white male, a rage that promises and delivers punishments for women and people of color." Redefinitions of failure need to be aligned carefully with "desired political outcomes" (92). And Halberstam is quite sensitive to the affective experience of even those modes of failure that are most critically productive. Terms in her book *The Queer Art of Failure* that bear synonymous connotations include: loneliness, misery, "confusion … alienation, impossibility, and awkwardness" (97), not to mention the need to deal with "the consequences of homophobia and racism and xenophobia" (99). But there remains the strident optimism that embracing failure in a number of senses can help us to "bring down the winner" (120)—when the winner is understood to be oppressively normative.[3]

In Pauline studies there is, likewise, the occasional sense that failure does not, or does not exactly, entail deficiency. Paula Gooder's *Only the Third Heaven?*, a study of the heavenly ascent in 2 Cor 12, concludes that Paul recounts there a failed ascent. Paul fails to make it beyond the third of seven heavens. "The strange half-telling of the ascent narrative including a lack of a mention of a vision of God—alerts us to the fact that … something is wrong" (Gooder 2006, 201). The thorn in Paul's side further undermines the presentation of this experience as successful. A person

---

3. The critical irony of what we might want to recognize as *success* in the work of Halberstam and others needs to be underscored. The rhetorical aim here is to undo the binary success/failure, not merely to invert the terms. For a different rendering of success and failure as the "affective-effects" of our economic system, see Brian Massumi's *The Power at the End of the Economy* (2015, 16). Macroeconomic failures or successes have microeconomic (perhaps "quantum") origins in "nonconscious," "nonpersonal" (19), and almost entirely unpredictable feelings of distrust or trust, frustration or satisfaction (13).

in Christ was swept into the heavens, but he cannot report on what he learned there; cannot claim to have gotten far; and cannot boast of much of anything beyond an enduring affliction. Except that "this failure was revealed by Christ to Paul as the essence of true discipleship" (210).[4] As a failure that reveals Christ's perfection (2 Cor 12:9), Paul's experience must, in some sense, have been successful. It's not an instance of mastery, to be sure. Indeed, the mastery of the esoteric adept, of the most ostentatious of visionary entrepreneurs—possibly valorized by some in Corinth[5]—is downplayed in favor of a different sort of experience, of weakness and poverty, the disrepute of the "dregs" and "rubbish of the world" (1 Cor 4:13). Paul, as hinted in the first paragraph above, goes on to make rather plain that his valorization of failure is perhaps better characterized as a power play (e.g., 1 Cor 4:21; 2 Cor 13:10). Nevertheless, somewhat like Halberstam, Gooder's Paul might be said to resist a certain normative model of success. Even if the subversive intention doesn't lead to anything like a simplistic inversion of expectations, the revaluation of the value of success is meant to call into question uncritical, most often dominant, cultural tendencies, to destabilize assumptions about what counts as success, even about the whole category of success in itself.

Kelley's story "St. Paul and the Monkeys" suggests something closer to failure as Lauren Berlant discusses it in *Cruel Optimism*. Although failure per se may not be Berlant's focus, the modes of antinormative critique she discusses brings us closer to Chig's middle ground between the only apparently opposed figures of the story's title. For Berlant, the norm may be crushing, but it is also "aspirational" for those who are failures on its terms. A norm is "an evolving and incoherent cluster of hegemonic promises about the present and future experience of social belonging" (Berlant 2011, 167). A norm's temporality is relatively complicated in this view, as is its desirability. In fact, one of the most striking aspects

---

4. One recognizes the same impulse, presented in a more sophisticated critical register and an entirely different context, in Rhiannon Graybill's *Are We Not Men? Unstable Masculinity in the Hebrew Prophets*. The prophetic body, she writes, far from performing hegemonic masculinity and thereby modeling a specific kind of gendered perfection, is more properly understood to be disabled, wounded, afflicted, and transformed—"a body which is vulnerable, necessarily so" (2017, 44).

5. Jerome Murphy-O'Connor (1996, 280) imagines an alliance between those who may have lauded themselves as spiritual or wise in 1 Cor 2–4 and the outsiders whom Paul mocks, in Margaret Mitchell's (2010, 82) words, as "super-duper apostles."

of *Cruel Optimism* is its sympathy for the failure who strives after the norm. Someone like Sara Ahmed, for instance, is also tremendously sympathetic to people caught in the experience of failure. Those who fail to adhere to a norm are unhappy, she says in her book *The Promise of Happiness*, because they cause unhappiness in others—in the parents of a queer child, for instance. "Failure is affective … is an unhappiness-cause"; and we "must learn" from "the translation between causing unhappiness and being described as being unhappy" (Ahmed 2010, 95). We have to learn to recognize the necessity of circumscribing, or short-circuiting, that translation, by thinking differently about how to constitute happiness, or success. Happiness as something other than happiness. Or as Ahmed (222) puts it in her conclusion: "the freedom to be unhappy … include[s] the freedom to be happy in inappropriate ways." But the logic of Berlant's *Cruel Optimism* makes it difficult to imagine a way out. She concludes her book with the reflection that "all of the affective paradoxes of the political in relation to mass demands for social change uttered from the impasse of the present extend from this, cruel optimism's double bind: even with an image of a better good life available to sustain your optimism, it is awkward and it is threatening to detach from what is already not working" (Berlant 2011, 263).

This double bind suspends William Melvin Kelley's character Chig between Saint Paul and the monkeys. At some level Chig probably recognizes that one is simply the inverse of the other and that awareness leaves him, it seems, with no options. Berlant's realism is not so pessimistic, though. What is required of Chig, she would say, is a different fantasy, "a surrealistic affectsphere to counter the one that already exists" (263).

In contrast with my examples above—narratives setting Paul in opposition to failure, or treating Pauline failure as a path to success, or at least to a better life—Paul himself can also be imagined productively both as a sign of normative aspirations and as a character in need of a different trajectory thanks to those punishing norms; he both pursues and represents "negating rhythms of self-continuity" (Berlant 2011, 113) and is himself a kind of affective impasse. I focus here, from among several examples of such reimagined Pauls, on a 2008 graphic novel by Steve Ross called *Blinded*. Not entirely unlike Pier Paolo Pasolini's sketch for a film about Paul, *Blinded* progresses through a historically palimpsestic reading of the political relevance of Acts and the epistles. Unlike Pasolini's *Saint Paul* (2014), though, *Blinded* is sort of a mess of political intuitions or aims. Right before his conversion, for example, Ross's Paul is a jaded agent for an overzealous homeland security-like organization.⁶ While such a move might have been intended to encourage US Christians, especially conservatives, to cast themselves as the Muslim victims of repressive state policing after 9/11, it also aligns the biblical Paul's Judaism with the most pernicious forms of military authority. At one point, Ronald Reagan and Louis XIV join together as Festus and Agrippa and visit Paul in prison. Reagan/Festus declares that the "flesh eaters hate our freedom"—but why Reagan (who considered the predecessors of the Taliban and their allies to be freedom fighters) rather than George W. Bush? (Ross 2008, VIII/130).⁷ The slave-holding American South is populated by Christians, but they are Paul's own allies. In fact, Paul quells a slave insurrection by converting the slaves, so that they can continue to serve their Christian masters (V/80). This mass conversion is most likely a critical comment on Onesimus's ambiguous status in Philemon, and more generally on the role Pauline texts have played in supporting slavery and, later, segregation in the American South. But why does *Blinded* still use what seems perilously close to racist caricature of the excessively plump lips of its African-American characters—even a character like Timothy, whom Ross seems to favor more positively as a character than he does Paul?

But despite the oddly marred expressions of Ross's progressive politics, *Blinded* is compelling especially in the way it wants to emphasize the failure of Paul's visions. The book begins with an image that gets repeated, with variations, throughout: the earth's demise in a planetary Armageddon, an urban landscape in ruins, and a hand reaching from the rubble, seeking salvation. We learn that Paul had always suffered from "terrifying visions of the end of the world" and that his terror was only amplified by the knowledge that he "alone had the key to preventing it." So he struck a childhood deal with God: in exchange for perfect obedience, God would "deliver [him] from [his] nightly visits to hell" (I/25). The fact that the first images in the book are clearly a dream sequence from Paul's precon-

---

6. For convenience I refer to this character, also known as Saul or even Tarsus (his boss's nickname for him), as Paul.

7. This substitution is all the more perplexing in light of an image later in the novel that is meant to evoke the (potentially staged) toppling of a statue of Saddam Hussein in Baghdad's Firdos Square in 2003. No sooner does the Hussein statue come down than a nearly identical one, but this time in the likeness of Reagan, takes its place (X/162). My citations from the unpaginated *Blinded* give section and then page number (counting the first section marker of the book as page 1).

Ross 2008, II/28. © 2008 Church Publishing Incorporated, New York. Used by permission.

version *adulthood* suggest that either God or Paul did not quite hold up their end of the bargain. What's more, these visions become Paul's reality when Philippi is bombed by Rome. By this point, of course, Paul is now working for the other side, in support of "the flesh eaters." He's been imprisoned in Philippi for having freed a young woman called "the Oracle." She is something of a cross between the fortune-telling slave girl from Acts 16:16 and *Minority Report*'s "precogs," deployed by Rome as an intelligence tool (IV/54). But in an act of rebellion against her masters, before her encounter with Paul, she provides bogus coordinates for Roman airstrikes in Philippi. "The official story was an earthquake," Paul notes as we see a hand, likely that of his jailor, straining out of the rubble for help; but in fact the prison complex and other military installations throughout the city had been hit with friendly fire. Nevertheless, in Paul's view Rome was only the proximate cause. In reality, "it was the beginning of the end of the world" (IV/68).

Later, and especially after believers have started dying (à la 1 Thess 4:13), Paul starts to wonder if the end of the world had been postponed (VII/120). Or maybe he'd simply misunderstood all along? In a strange subsequent sequence, he transmits his horrifying apocalyptic vision to the Reagan/Louis XIV duo but explains to them that what they're seeing is not the world's future end, now, but rather the revelation of its true current state, which "the Kingdom of Heaven is going to undo" (X/167). Eschatological literalism quickly becomes allegory. But before he witnesses the divine restoration, Paul himself is executed by firing squad. We see Paul shot, tumbling into a pit, and then, against the backdrop of space, falling endlessly into nothingness. Ross's montage over the next few pages is quite striking. Juxtaposed panels showing a version of the Ravenna Paul mosaic and a construction vehicle leaving a mass burial site are followed by a full-page image of eyeglasses tumbling and shattering on the ground. The accompanying text reads: "For every Alpha … an Omega; for every glorious martyr ... hundreds of nameless bodies in an unmarked grave; for every vision ... a blind spot" (X/233–34). Paul reappears, alive, in the closing pages of the novel. He's an old man now in a blighted landscape, without a community, and apparently bereft of hope. He reflects bitterly that he's "become something of a legend in these parts. The creepy old blind guy sitting alone year after year, waiting" (Epilogue/226–27). Then, suddenly, against a black background, a hand reaches up once more; and counter to every other instance of this motif, another hand finally reaches down to help. Priscilla has returned to collect Paul, who soon finds himself a child again on the deck of a ship sailing off into the sunset.

Certainly the concluding images seems to be working along the lines of the model of failure with which this essay opened. That is, if Ross isn't simply imagining Paul going to his heavenly reward, Paul's failed and broken visions, possibly emblematic of the ordinary failures of the rest of us, are the basis for, or in some sense support, eventuate in, a kind of success: sailing away into the wild blue yonder of some perfect Spanish afterlife. And note the way this whole scene plays itself out. The youthful Paul races Priscilla along the deck of a ship, with no adults in sight, as they might in an animated feature of the sort that Halberstam discusses in *The Queer Art of Failure*.

For Halberstam, "failure is what allows us to escape the punishing norms that discipline behavior and manage human development with the goal of delivering us from unruly childhoods to orderly and predictable adulthoods. Failure preserves some of the wondrous anarchy of childhood and disturbs the supposedly clean boundaries between adults and children, winners and losers." She goes on to say in the same passage that the "negative affects" that accompany failure help us "to poke holes in the toxic positivity of contemporary life" (Halberstam 2011, 3). For Ann Cvetkovich (e.g., 2012, 5, 110), failure can itself be a negative feeling. Thinking of depression and its cultural roots in acedia (sloth, apathy, laziness), the failure of a monk "to keep his spiritual mission" (88), Cvetkovich brings us even closer to Ross's Paul. Not that early monasticism is an entirely apt frame of reference for reading the Paul of *Blinded*. Still, Cvetkovich is particularly interested in understanding physical activity as a cure for acedia, and she cites John Cassian on the late-third–early-fourth-century Abbot Paul's daily ritual of collecting palm leaves simply as a way of staying occupied (Cvetkovich 2012, 112). "Acedia ... has lessons to offer [both] about contemporary depression that takes the form of a breakdown in functionality" (113) and about the "somatic therapies" to which one might turn in

Ross 2008, Epilogue/232-3. © 2008 Church Publishing Incorporated, New York. Used by permission.

"Though We May Seem to Have Failed" 167

Ross 2008, Epilogue/231. © 2008 Church Publishing Incorporated, New York. Used by permission.

search of healing (114). The arc of Paul's narrative, in *Blinded*, from his early promise of total devotion to his late, morosely passive tarrying on a bench in the dark, evokes, in a figure of failure, feelings that are the inverse of (in this case, apocalyptic) fervor. Devoid of purpose, plan, and activity, almost entirely nonfunctional, Paul seems genuinely depressed and depressing in his old age.

Ross 2008, Epilogue/227. © 2008 Church Publishing Incorporated, New York. Used by permission.

Despite the escapist tenor of the last pages of Ross's book, especially when compared to the adult Paul's concluding panels, the open-ended sea journey amounts to a rejection of both the rigidly structured, militaristic, statist powers that be, on the one hand, and Paul's own apocalyptic visions on the other. Both ultimately amount to the same thing: dreams of mastery, fantasies of control. Here, by contrast, as the text has it, night succumbs to day, rules to exceptions, and laws to miracles (Ross 2008, Epilogue/231). At the same time, though, the heavy-handed, clichéd affirmation of childhood as a time of limitless possibility is itself a highly defensive controlling mechanism of its own. Whose childhood? What sorts of exclusions are required for this vision to be effective? The apparently disabled, quite possibly homeless Paul of the panels from the epilogue must undergo a radical makeover, must become cute, youthful, vaguely Aryan. He's got to leave his darkness behind, his dour pessimism, his realism; the Paul who knows something (just *what* might be open to debate, but *something*) about degradation (XIII/140), mourning (VI/108), sexual desire (VI/96–97)—that Paul is gone, cast off in the darkness below decks (Epilogue/230).

Yet *Blinded* also proposes an intriguing fantasy to counter the cultural logic yoking Paul to dialectics of failure and success in the first place. In the novel's penultimate panel Ross cites 1 Cor 13:11 ("when I was a child …"), but only to reject it: the maturation of Pauline vision, the giving up of childish ways, turns out to have been "the problem all along" (Epilogue/231). As I note above, Paul's failed visions throughout the book lead from one kind of rationalization to another. Tracing developments in early Christian eschatology as though Paul himself were undergoing those interpretive changes from city to city, year to year can produce interesting insights. But here Ross arguably calls into question not only Paul's visions, but the entirety of Paul's ministry and gospel … his presence in the New Testament. From a practical perspective it's difficult to understand how Paul's return to childhood can resolve anything. We saw earlier that Paul's childhood visions were so terrifying that he asked God for a deal in order to spare himself the emotional trauma they caused. Giving up maturity and returning to childish ways would simply return Paul to those earliest visions again. And yet the end of the book is obviously a departure—and it's depicted as such: a voyage away from any recognizable Paulinism. This is Paul without Paul, or Saul for that matter. Accepting the failure at the heart of Paul's project seems *not* to lead into a successful detour from or renewal of that project, but to its undoing. These are happy kids on a boat, with no responsibilities, no interest in theology, no commitment to churches.

Gore Vidal's *Live from Golgotha* (1993) does something vaguely similar by imagining, quaintly, that the tapes on which the New Testament's texts were recorded are being erased by a diabolical hacker. But Vidal's purpose is not at all the same as Ross's. Probably, it is safe to say that nothing would really have pleased Vidal more than the unwriting of Christian history. Ross wants something different: a fresh start, a different path.

Yet *Blinded* also reveals the cruelty at the heart of a kind of (Christian) optimism that is essentially a double bind. Embedded within the Paul of *Blinded*'s vision of the open horizon of possibility, after all, is his own annihilation. And even if the last panel doesn't invite us to read the book's concluding image as deeply ironic, other moments in *Blinded* more than suggest that it is an unstable, unsustainable fantasy. Over and over again, characters in the graphic novel risk everything, leaving behind what isn't working for something that promises a better good life, only to find themselves worse off than before. I discuss here only one such scene; a bizarre little commentary on two Pauline texts regarding circumcision: Gal 5:12, in which Paul advocates castration for those preaching circumcision; and Acts 16:3, according to which Paul had Timothy circumcised to make him acceptable as a missionary companion. Ross has a character present himself to Paul after a rather extreme self-circumcision. Paul points out his error ("you just have to cut the foreskin"), but before he can reassure the man that "it's just a technicality" and that the castration won't affect the man's ability to join with Paul's movement (II/35–37), the magnitude of what he's done in his uninformed enthusiasm becomes overwhelming and the man jumps to his death. Since Ross also gives Pauline references to slavery and glossolalia (VII/116) a similar treatment, consistently transforming promise into usually permanent failure,[8] I can't see why the optimism with which the graphic novel ends should be anything but a ruse.

Ross also wrote a graphic novel about the gospel of Mark, called *Marked* (2005), which has much of the same over-the-top, pop-cultural extravagance and deeply sarcastic mockery to be found in *Blinded*: both books cast the early church, especially its evangelical ministry, as a circus sideshow scam. Ross is a member of Saint Bartholomew's Episcopal Church in New York City; according to the church's web site (http://

---

8. The more enthusiastic of Christians not only speak in tongues but levitate as they do so. Paul (not quite as in 1 Cor 14:18) outdoes the others so surprisingly that one levitating Christian falls to the floor and breaks his neck. And this, in turn, becomes the first Christian death.

stbarts.org/), he has produced artwork for church events and has led, with his wife Julie, the Youth at the Center program at Saint Bartholomew's. The church is progressive and, if its mission statement is a reliable indication of the community's ethos, welcomes the gadfly and the pious alike. In both of his books, Ross acknowledges the Reverend William Tully, who was at the time the rector at Saint Bartholomew's. Tully even wrote a short note introducing *Marked*, in which he attests to Ross's "deep faith, his Christian practice ... and his own faithful reflection on the gospel—as it is read, preached, and reflected upon [in] his own parish." But Tully also warns: "let the reader beware" (Ross 2005, "Introduction"). There is most definitely something strange at work in these texts.

In an interview published just before the publication of *Cruel Optimism*, Berlant remembers discovering that American students would often think that the study of American literature taught them "something ontological about the United States—so I had to alienate the object, show it in its complexity as a magnet both of practices and fantasies" (McCabe 2011). Perhaps that is what Ross is essentially up to here as well: picturing the magnetic tug of an American Paul in such extreme caricature as to effect the same alienation. And he seems to do so, considering the contemporary geopolitical contextualization of the book, in order to undermine (US Christian) political fantasies of self-possession, security, and restoration. The last two situations in *Blinded*—represented by images of an old frail failure dying alone on a park bench, and a young boy and girl on a fantastic voyage—are really depictions of the same moment of Pauline undoing. By holding them in tension, *Blinded* may be presenting a portrait of the evangelical demographic that supported but was ultimately betrayed by the George W. Bush administration (and/or by its own failures), in the hopes that a jarring self-recognition might lead to a radically different, and ultimately healthier, set of affective investments.

Bibliography

Ahmed, Sara. 2010. *The Promise of Happiness*. Durham, NC: Duke University Press.

Berlant, Lauren. 2011. *Cruel Optimism*. Durham, NC: Duke University Press.

Castelli, Elizabeth A. 1991. *Imitating Paul: A Discourse of Power*. Louisville: Westminster John Knox.

Cvetkovich, Ann. 2012. *Depression: A Public Feeling.* Durham, NC: Duke University Press.

Gooder, Paula. 2006. *Only the Third Heaven? 2 Corinthians 12.1–10 and Heavenly Ascents.* New York: Continuum.

Graybill, Rhiannon. 2017. *Are We Not Men? Unstable Masculinity in the Hebrew Prophets.* New York: Oxford University Press.

Halberstam, Judith [Jack]. 2011. *The Queer Art of Failure.* Durham, NC: Duke University Press.

Haverkamp, Heidi. 2014. "Living by the Word." *The Christian Century.* June 25:20–21.

Kazantzakis, Nikos. 1960. *The Last Temptation of Christ.* Translated by P. A. Bien. New York: Simon & Schuster.

Kelley, William Melvin. 1964. *Dancers on the Shore.* New York: Doubleday.

King, Martin Luther, Jr. 2007. "Shattered Dreams." Pages 514–25 in *Advocate of the Social Gospel, September 1948–March 1963.* Vol. 6 of *The Papers of Martin Luther King, Jr.* Edited by Clayborne Carson et al. Berkeley: University of California Press.

Massumi, Brian. 2015. *The Power at the End of the Economy.* Durham, NC: Duke University Press.

McCabe, Earl. 2011. "Depressive Realism: An Interview with Lauren Berlant." *Hypocrite Reader.* http://hypocritereader.com/5/depressive-realism.

Mitchell, Margaret M. 2010. *Paul, the Corinthians, and the Birth of Christian Hermeneutics.* New York: Cambridge University Press.

Muñoz, José Esteban. 2009. *Cruising Utopia: The Then and There of Queer Futurity.* New York: New York University Press.

Murphy-O'Connor, Jerome. 1996. *Paul: A Critical Life.* New York: Oxford University Press.

Pasolini, Pier Paolo. 2014. *Saint Paul: A Screenplay.* Translated by Elizabeth Castelli. London: Verso.

Rosca, Ninotchka. 1983. *The Monsoon Collection.* Saint Lucia, Australia: University of Queensland Press.

Ross, Steve. 2005. *Marked.* New York: Seabury.

———. 2008. *Blinded: The Story of Paul the Apostle.* New York: Seabury.

Saramago, José. 1994. *The Gospel according to Jesus Christ.* Translated by Giovanni Pontiero. New York: Harcourt Brace.

Vidal, Gore. 1993. *Live from Golgotha.* New York: Penguin.

Wallace, Raenita. 2005. *More Than a Conqueror: Biblical Keys to Overcoming Failure.* Lincoln, NE: iUniverse.

Yassin-Kassab, Robin. 2008. *The Road from Damascus*. London: Hamish Hamilton.

Responses

Palpable Traumas, Tactile Texts, and the Powerful Reach of Scripture

Erin Runions

Biblical texts touch and press—on bodies and communities. They circulate through the social, and through materialities (human and nonhuman). For many people (women, LGBT folks, and minority populations), biblical texts circulate in toxic, traumatic, and limiting ways. Yet even then the text can still be taken up for solace. As much as the biblical texts are read for justification of political ideologies and actions, they are read by many for comfort and healing. Affect theory provides a way to address the conflicting emotional impacts in/of the texts and to show how they are tied to structures of power, as they affect bodies, subjectivity, and social formations.

The essays in this collection follow biblical texts' power and traumas—mostly their traumas, although sometimes also their delights—as they circulate socially, through human and nonhuman animal bodies, objects, emotions, and desires. They draw on the influential feminist, queer, and antiracist elaborations of affect theory to trace anger, sadness, disgust, failure, exclusion, desire, love, trust, security, and everyday practices. These essays take seriously the damage and (sometimes) the healing effected by the biblical text, unpacking how the operations of power behind the texts propel themselves into new dynamics in the present. Rather than flatten out, denigrate, or dismiss the emotions in the texts and their reception, they acknowledge the affective tensions and complications. The authors' use of affect theory allows them to bring together the historical, the political, the personal, the literary, and the structural aspects of texts and power.

This achievement is made possible by the fact that the authors are grounded in the intersectional feminist and queer strand of affect theory that has grown out of an insistence on analyzing the histories and effects of traumas. The authors draw on theorists such as Sara Ahmed (2010; 2015), Lauren Berlant (2011), Ann Cvetkovich (2003; 2012), Judith Halberstam (2011), Donna Haraway (2003; 2016), Jasbir Puar (2007), Denise Riley (2005), Donovan Schaefer (2015), Eve Sedgwick (2003), and Kathleen Stewart (2007). I can't emphasize enough how important the insights of this lineage are—including those of Mel Chen (2012), Anne Anlin Cheng (2001), David Eng and Shinee Han (2019), Roderick Ferguson (2004), Paul Gilroy (2005), Heather Love (2007), Sianne Ngai (2005), and others. This genealogy of work is formative not only for this volume but in the humanities and to the study of religion. The work teaches cultural historians, critics, and textual interpreters always to reckon with power; to attend to the growing pile of detritus caused by colonial, racist, sexually-othering, imperialist, and humanist history; to feel traumas and work against repeating them; and to look for sites of reclamation and healing.

Feminist and queer affect studies has come into the field of biblical studies largely through the work of Maia Kotrosits, whose first book, *Rethinking Early Christian Identity: Affect, Violence, and Belonging* (2015), was the first monograph to use affect studies in biblical studies. Kotrosits thinks about the affect of the Judean traumas of colonization and destruction that deeply influence the development and narratives of the new sect of Judaism that becomes Christianity. She has since written an excellent introduction to affect studies in the field (2016). Several volumes of collected essays have also helped to inaugurate affect-oriented biblical studies, including the special themed issue of *Biblical Interpretation* edited by Jennifer Koosed and Stephen Moore (2014a), and *Sexual Disorientations: Queer Temporalities, Affects, Theologies*, edited by Kent Brintnall, Joseph Marchal, and Stephen Moore (2018).

Joining this intellectual project, the authors in this volume show how bodily movements and emotions are tied to the damages caused by processes of domination. Rather than skim over or diminish the negative affects that produce and circulate through Scripture, these essays sit with them, honor them, and work through them. They read negative scriptural affects as telling us something important about the impossible and punishing demands and norms of the social order, historically and in the present moment. They value those who do not accede to these demands and are hurt by them, and they try to imagine how texts might be read differently, more justly, to reduce trauma.

Beyond Personalized Emotion

As affect theorists have often insisted, affect goes beyond human emotion. The essays by Ken Stone and Rhiannon Graybill are insistent on this point. They look at the ways humans become affectively attached to animals, plants, and objects. They show how affect flows between humans, creatures, plants, and objects.

Although the essays are ordered by the place of their object of inquiry in the canon, Stone's opening essay sets the stage beautifully for the entire volume, moving from personalized emotion to socially and structurally produced affect. Stone rereads the story of King David's response to Nathan's parable of the poor man's lamb. He argues that it is inadequate to read this text on solely personal and emotional terms, as many authors have done. He shows how affective relations between humans and animals are used to express gender and power.

David's reactions are not merely about inner states, Stone argues. The king's reaction is not an unbalanced sentimental response to a lamb, as some might have it. Rather, the king responds to having his prerogative curtailed—as a man, and as a king—to collect and exchange women and animals. Drawing on Ahmed and Schaefer, Stone reveals how affect follows circuits of domination in an economy where the king-as-shepherd's affection, connection, and even kinship with sheep would be understood. Original audiences would know that sheep will follow a human leader because of the way they form their own social networks, becoming close with their human. The disruption of the pastoral order in Nathan's parable is an affront. David recognizes the rich man's usurpation of the poor man's human-sheep relationship and is enraged—but he is unable to recognize it as a critique of his own patriarchal actions until Nathan spells it out.

Stone does not explicitly highlight the queer aspects of this reading, but it clearly follows in his enormously important subfield-making work on queer hermeneutics and his more recent turn to animal studies (e.g., 2005; 2018). Tracing the circulation of affect destabilizes norms of masculinity. Further, Nathan's story queers the human-animal divide, it troubles contemporary readers' notions of kinship, and shows how David's reaction is one of dismay to God upending the hierarchies of gender and kingship.

Likewise, critical of merely personalized readings of emotion, Graybill's essay shows the inadequacy of frequent readings of the prophet Jonah's actions as petulant and petty. Readings grounded in personalized understandings may not adequately take into account contexts of conquest and demands for assimilation. Graybill's reading is provocative and compelling (as is the norm for her work; see 2016; 2017), arguing that the book of Jonah is not, in fact, offering a universalizing appeal to Yahweh's justice and mercy. Rather the text raises questions about that notion (or compulsion, as Graybill calls it). Jonah, she implies, drawing on Ahmed's discussion of immigrants, is forced to assimilate to a universalizing Yahwism.

Like other essays in the volume, Graybill's takes up Ahmed and Berlant to show that affect circulates through objects. Desire and pleasure attach to objects that act as containers for an often unattainable cluster of promises. In a stroke of genius, Graybill connects John Locke's unfulfilling grapes to Jonah's disappointment in his plant: "Grapes? Or, we might ask with Jonah … *A castor bean plant?*"

Thinking through Jonah's unhappiness, Graybill explores the textual and readerly assumptions that turn Jonah into what Ahmed calls an "affect alien." Jonah's anger at the loss of his plant is melancholic, Graybill suggests, an internalization of another ungrieved loss. The demand to forgive Assyria/Nineveh, many years later at the time of the text's writing, must surely stand in for another demand to excuse the powerful. Although she does not go this far, this melancholia might also incorporate the Tanakh's less-grieved loss of Samaria to Assyria. The essay brings to mind Rey Chow's argument about the racial and ethnic specificities, and the harms, that get lost in the universalizing and assimilationist demand for forgiveness (2009). We could read assimilation as the end goal of the text; or we could read Jonah's unhappiness—including his transit through the nonhuman animal body of the whale, that leviathan—as a resistance to a universalizing polity's demands. As in Stone's essay, resistance is signified through animals.

Touching across Time

Affect also allows consideration of how texts touch readers across time, to borrow an idea from Joseph A. Marchal (2011a) and Carolyn Dinshaw (1999), on whom he draws. Both Marchal and Amy C. Cottrill explore how affect touches across historical and contemporary moments.

Marchal takes up this theme in this volume to show how the disgust produced in Pauline texts projects backward and forward at the same time—retroactively creating disgust for readers and apocalyptically imagining the worst for the future. Indeed, disgust takes on its force over time and in the face of time, as it sticks to people and intensifies, as Ahmed argues. Disgust negatively and traumatically positions people within social orders and imagined futures.

Disgust is a powerful but unstable tool for Paul. He creates disgust in his letters to the gentiles, by using ethnocultural stereotypes about gentiles themselves. He abjects his audience. Through the stickiness of affect, this tactic has produced disgust in many readers about the bodies and behaviors Paul so describes. And yet the hold of disgust is not as fixed in maintaining borders as we might imagine, Marchal shows, as he develops a persuasive and innovative rereading of the disgust toward same-sex practices produced by Rom 1. Given the connection between disgust and desire, as Marchal outlines, there is no real higher ground for disgust; the disgusted are always implicated, always desiring the thing that they reject and rejecting the thing that they desire. Recognizing this dynamic can undercut the production of disgust in Paul's writings.

Marchal contends with the othering of disgust in another way as well. Cleverly turning Paul upside down, as is his want (see also Marchal 2019), he asks, might we embrace disgust? All bodies are disgusting in some way. Disgust is "a common predicament." Marchal queers disgust by asking whether we empathetically consider and even identify with the way in which the gentile converts may have been disgusting to the dominant culture. Here the touch across time requires imagining just what innovation in the early church produced disgust because of its difference. Thus imagined, Marchal suggests that we could appreciate, rather than condemn, the gentiles that Paul others.

Cottrill's essay helpfully focuses on the way that feeling is *made* by Ps 109 and therefore by the world that structures the language of the text. While sensitive to the histories and cultures that produce the lament psalms, she is also interested in how they circulate and make meaning for readers precisely through feeling. She gestures toward affect-oriented performance criticism, which deals with the fleetingness of performance, as a strategy for thinking about the absence of concrete historical background for the psalms.

Readers' affects are tied to the poem's conflicting rhetorical strategies, Cottrill points out, for instance between the psalmist's subservience and supplication toward God, but aggressiveness and violence toward his enemies. For readers who invariably try to inhabit the "I" of the poem, the shifts between threat and aggression can create a split subjectivity, Cotrill suggests. Her ideas draw to mind Jay Twomey's invocation of Berlant: at some level, the psalm "negat[es] rhythms of self-continuity." Perhaps in destabilizing the subject position of a reader, the text creates a space for alternate identifications or affects that can shift ideological positioning (Runions 2001)—either for someone who is traumatized or someone who assumes the right to aggress.

Cottrill importantly asks how the aggressive language in Ps 109 might impact "those who know and experience fear and threat on a personal and social level." This question is regrettably deferred to a later date. But it resonates with Marchal's attention to the way that texts can negatively impact readers through their affect. The question further pushes us to consider whether the traumatized are encouraged by the text to become violent, as Black asks (in this volume), or whether they are caught, as Twomey says of Pauline optimism (in this volume), in a double bind between giving voice to the oppressed and authorizing oppression.

Biblical Circulations through Capital

Biblical affect also generates, supports, and circulates through capitalist social formations, as Robert Paul Sessengood and Twomey illustrate. Both show the ambiguity of Pauline texts' circulation in capital, doing harm even while ostensibly providing the solace to heal that harm.

Seesengood astutely looks at the way that Pauline affect is positively focused on labor in ways that continue to influence the shape and demands of labor in the twenty-first century. Like the demand for Jonah to be a happy prophet, a demand is made on workers to be happy and to make others happy. Capitalism is the universalizing system that demands love and fealty, no matter what traumas it imposes.

Work for the apostle Paul, Seesengood shows, is allied with love; it is imagined as an expression of love. Paul's approach to labor situates it as a virtue, not a necessity; and yet in reality, much work in Paul's time would be forced, done by slaves. Indeed, Paul diminishes the harsh reality of slavery by using it as metaphor for himself and by demanding the obedience of slaves to their masters. Here Seesengood cites the excellent work by Jennifer Glancy (2006) and Marchal (2011b) on Paul and slavery as well as drawing on his own (e.g., 2010; 2017).

The Pauline demand for a positive approach to (forced) labor presages and subtends the late-stage capitalist demand for low-wage work, emotional labor, desire for commodities (following Walter Benjamin's analysis of the play of sexual desire and commodity fetishism), and also debt. Seesengood points to the traumatic inner workings of Paul's teaching on redemption: the redeemed are indebted to God, but must also love God. The crucial insight here is that Paul's imbrication of love and debt lays the groundwork for the proliferation of emotional labor and the normalization of debt. These demands mask the power relations at the heart of capital—that is, the requirement for some people to be subservient to others, for some to feel precarity and want more than others, even while forcing a smile. Drawing on Gregory Seigworth (2016) and Max Weber (2012 [1904]), Seesengood draws out the way that the feeling of credit-and-debt is both a feeling of mobility and power and of the precarity that generates hard labor (for this point in relation to prisons, see Runions 2019).

Twomey's essay provides deft critique of this capitalist Pauline trajectory, in a perceptive meditation on Pauline failure. In his reading of *Blinded*, a graphic novel about the apostle by Steve Ross, Twomey provides a critique of Paul's demands as they have played out in US capitalist and hegemonic Christian "political fantasies of self-possession, security, and restoration." Twomey draws on scholars of Paul, especially Elizabeth Castelli (1991), who have pointed to Paul's contradictory demand for perfection and failure. He turns to Halberstam, Ahmed, and Cvetkovich to think about the negative affects evoked by Paul's own demand for positive affect (for instance, happiness, or as Seesengood has shown, love and redemption). As in other of his theoretically sophisticated readings, Twomey shows how Paul's rhetoric generates powerful affects (2011; 2013).

The critical edge of the essay comes from Berlant's notion of cruel optimism, which Paul's writings and their afterlives seem to make manifest. The tension between (apocalyptic) perfection and (sinful) failure in Paul presents a double bind of the kind Berlant discusses. The norms that Paul sets forward can never meet their promises. Indeed, this failure structures the Christian message. A redemptive/sacrificial/violent sacrifice is always needed.

Throughout the novel and particularly in its ending, Ross stages these self-perpetuating demands of perfection and failure. In the hands of Twomey, Ross's novel is an illustration of the false hopes of restoration and self-possession within late stage capitalism. And yet the graphic novel itself fails in its critique, Twomey argues, by not interrogating the racial politics that it depicts and the way race has always been the constitutive outside to such political fantasies.

Turning Things Around—Healing Trauma

Power so often produces trauma, and trauma produces literature that transmits feeling. The essays by Fiona C. Black and Jennifer L. Koosed follow Kotrosits in turning to the work of Cvetkovich. They illustrate how Hebrew lament and Jewish liturgy work through the political traumas of colonization and exile. Cvetkovich insists that affect, including depression, is political and that it finds its way into literature and art, making a tangible and material archive. Both essays are concerned to do more than voice trauma, though; they show how the imagery and materiality of the text can help work through trauma.

Black takes up Cvetkovich's work to suggest how the lament psalms might be such an archive of depression, both public and personal. Black explores the emotions that come with depression as they appear in the laments, including alienation, fear, sadness, and pain, which threaten to undercut the subjectivity of the speaker. The lament psalms are personalized to be sure, and like Cottrill, Black notes that the psalms are therefore frequently read devotionally as reflecting personal states, even if scholars recognize their social formation. Taking this insight further, Black turns to Ahmed to read the pain of the psalmist as indicating and blurring the border between individual and collective.

Black perceptively highlights just how much the laments look like depression, and, as part of the archive of depression, may even provide vocabulary for contemporary iterations. Yet it is not strictly personal, because depression is not simply an individual medical condition; it can result from traumas that are socially and, often, colonially produced, as Cvetkovich argues (2012). What, Black asks, if we take the lament psalms as giving voice to the politically caused depression of the exile and its traumas? Resonating with Graybill's essay, Black beautifully draws attention to the way everyday objects are layered with emotion, as for instance the harp in Ps 137, or the powerful image that might otherwise go unnoticed in Ps 102:8 of the psalmist lying awake as a bird on the roof (see also Black 2015).

Rather than read for the resolution of angst in the final expressions of trust in the lament psalms, as is so often done, Black insists that we stay with the pain a little to see how it can move toward action. Black sees the lament psalms as a starting place for "pry[ing] apart the biblical colonial narrative." She urges us to consider how the voice of the psalmist can speak back to the power that causes pain. She expresses the need for what

Love (2007, 151) has called "turning grief into grievance—to address the larger social structures, the regimes of domination that are at the root of such pain."

Koosed lyrically argues that the traumas to which the Tanak responds (the Assyrian conquest, the Babylonian destruction of Jerusalem and exile, and the persecutions of Hellenization) have everything to do with the affects of the text in its afterlives. She attends particularly to the book of Lamentations and the Jewish liturgy and prayer book as archives of that trauma, again following Cvetkovich (2003). Trauma produces literature and liturgy and their material, bodily effects on Jewish communities. More than that, the Jewish prayer book is "an act of collective recovery" that builds community from past to present, from Jerusalem to diasporic communities.

Koosed's essay elegantly highlights the ambiguity of the text and its affects (see also 2014). She explores how trauma and healing stand in tension with one another and coexist in Jewish liturgy. Koosed reveals the complexities of the opening phrase of the first morning prayer in the siddur, the *Modeh ani*. Taken from Lamentations' famous and perplexing avowal of faith in the middle of destruction and pain, the citation becomes in Koosed's reading of the siddur, a rich reflection on the relation between death, exile, sleep, waking, and return, whether physical or spiritual. The prayer balances trauma and life, insecurity and trust. The use of Lam 3 in this morning prayer—as well as the placement of Lam 5 in the Torah service—Koosed suggests, allows the faithful a space to voice doubt, worry, and anxiety, along with a sense of assurance. Trauma produces new liturgical archives that allows for complicated affective expression, as well as "new forms of community and culture."

Koosed further reflects on the materiality of Scripture and its mediation of trauma. Showing the physicality of religious experience (see also Koosed and Moore 2014b), she writes: "Traumatized animal bodies become books; traumatized animal bodies write books." The prayer book and the animal skin scrolls are carried, touched, kissed. They are tactile reminders of the tension between sleep and waking, trauma and healing. In this everyday materiality the faithful find consolation in the text.

Conclusion

This is a rich and engaging volume that shows us how biblical texts affectively press on bodies, subjectivities, objects, and epochs. They express harm, create harm, and heal harm. Their affects flow through historical contexts and readers, animals and objects, and above all relations of power. The essays in this volume offer readings to reduce harm, to side with the powerless and disaffected, and to imagine how the text could turn grief into grievance and the feeling of precarity into a sense of security.

Bibliography

Ahmed, Sara. 2010. *The Promise of Happiness*. Durham, NC: Duke University Press.

———. 2015. *The Cultural Politics of Emotion*. New York: Routledge.

Berlant, Lauren. 2011. *Cruel Optimism*. Durham, NC: Duke University Press.

Black, Fiona C. 2015. "A Bird on the Roof: Trauma and Affect in Psalm 102." Pages 89–106 in *Poets, Prophets, and Texts in Play: Studies in Biblical Poetry and Prophecy in Honour of Francis Landy*. Edited by Ehud Ben Zvi, Claudia V. Camp, David M. Gunn, and Aaron W. Hughes. LHBOTS 272. New York: Bloomsbury.

Brintnall, Kent L., Joseph A. Marchal, and Stephen D. Moore, eds. 2018. *Sexual Disorientations: Queer Temporalities, Affects, Theologies*. New York: Fordham University Press.

Castelli, Elizabeth A. 1991. *Imitating Paul: A Discourse of Power*. Louisville: Westminster John Knox.

Chen, Mel Y. 2012. *Animacies: Biopolitics, Racial Mattering, and Queer Affect*. Durham, NC: Duke University Press.

Cheng, Anne Anlin. 2001. *The Melancholy of Race*. Race and American Culture. Oxford: Oxford University Press.

Chow, Rey. 2009. "'I Insist on the Christian Dimension': On Forgiveness … and the Outside of the Human." *differences* 20.2–3:224–49.

Cvetkovich, Ann. 2003. *An Archive of Feelings: Trauma, Sexuality, and Lesbian Public Cultures*. Durham, NC: Duke University Press.

———. 2012. *Depression: A Public Feeling*. Durham, NC: Duke University Press.

Dinshaw, Carolyn. 1999. *Getting Medieval: Sexualities and Communities, Pre- and Postmodern*. Durham, NC: Duke University Press.

Eng, David L, and Shinhee Han. 2019. *Racial Melancholia, Racial Dissociation: On the Social and Psychic Lives of Asian Americans*. Durham, NC: Duke University Press.

Ferguson, Roderick A. 2004. *Aberrations in Black: Toward a Queer of Color Critique*. Minneapolis: University of Minnesota Press.
Gilroy, Paul. 2005. *Postcolonial Melancholia*. New York: Columbia University Press.
Glancy, Jennifer A. 2006. *Slavery in Early Christianity*. Minneapolis: Fortress.
Graybill, Rhiannon. 2016. *Are We Not Men? Unstable Masculinity in the Hebrew Prophets*. New York: Oxford University Press.
———. 2017. "Yahweh As Maternal Vampire in Second Isaiah: Reading from Violence to Fluid Possibility with Luce Irigaray." *JFSR* 33.1:9–25.
Halberstam, Judith. 2011. *The Queer Art of Failure*. Durham, NC: Duke University Press.
Haraway, Donna. 2003. *The Companion Species Manifesto: Dogs, People, and Significant Otherness*. Chicago: Prickly Paradigm Press.
———. 2016. *Staying with the Trouble: Making Kin in the Chthulucene*. Durham, NC: Duke University Press.
Koosed, Jennifer L. 2014. "Moses: The Face of Fear." *BibInt* 22.4–5:414–29
Koosed, Jennifer L., and Stephen D. Moore, eds. 2014a. *Affect Theory and the Bible*. *BibInt* 22.4–5.
Koosed, Jennifer L., and Stephen D. Moore. 2014b. "Introduction: From Affect to Exegesis." *Affect Theory and the Bible*. *BibInt* 22.4–5:381–87.
Kotrosits, Maia. 2015. *Rethinking Early Christian Identity: Affect, Violence, and Belonging*. Minneapolis: Fortress.
———. 2016. *How Things Feel: Biblical Studies, Affect Theory, and the (Im) Personal*. Leiden: Brill.
Love, Heather. 2007. *Feeling Backward: Loss and the Politics of Queer History*. Cambridge: Harvard University Press.
Marchal, Joseph A. 2011. "'Making History' Queerly: Touches across Time through a Biblical Behind." *BibInt* 19:373–95.
———. 2011b. "The Usefulness of Onesimus: The Sexual Use of Slaves and Paul's Letter to Philemon." *JBL* 130:749–70.
———. 2019. *Appalling Bodies: Queer Figures before and after Paul's*. Oxford: Oxford University Press.
Ngai, Sianne. 2005. *Ugly Feelings*. Cambridge: Harvard University Press.
Puar, Jasbir K. 2007. *Terrorist Assemblages: Homonationalism in Queer Times*. Durham, NC: Duke University Press.
Riley, Denise. 2005. *Impersonal Passion, Language as Affect*. Durham, NC: Duke University Press.

Runions, Erin. 2001. *Changing Subjects: Gender, Nation and Future in Micah*. London: Sheffield Academic.

———. 2019. "Immobile Theologies, Carceral Affects: Interest and Debt in Faith-Based Prison Programs." Pages 55–84 in *Religion, Emotion, Sensation: Affect Theories and Theologies*. Edited by Karen Bray and Stephen A. Moore. New York: Fordham University Press.

Schaefer, Donovan O. 2015. *Religious Affects: Animality, Evolution and Power*. Durham, NC: Duke University Press.

Sedgwick, Eve Kosofsky. 2003. *Touching Feelings: Affect, Pedagogy and Performativity*. Durham, NC: Duke University Press.

Seesengood, Robert Paul. 2010. *Paul: A Brief History*. Blackwell Brief Histories of Religion. Chichester: Wiley-Blackwell.

———. 2017. *Philemon: Imagination, Labor and Love: An Introduction and Study Guide*. T&T Clark Study Guides to the New Testament. New York: Bloomsbury T&T Clark.

Seigworth, Gregory J. 2016. "Wearing the World Like a Debt Garment: Interface, Affect and Gesture." *Ephemera* 16.4:15–31.

Stewart, Kathleen. 2007. *Ordinary Affects*. Durham, NC: Duke University Press.

Stone, Ken. 2005. *Practicing Safer Texts: Food, Sex and Bible in Queer Perspective*. London: T&T Clark.

———. 2018. *Reading the Hebrew Bible with Animal Studies*. Stanford, CA: Stanford University Press.

Twomey, Jay. 2011. "The Biblical Man in Black: Paul in Johnny Cash/Johnny Cash in Paul." *BibInt* 19:223–52.

———. 2013. *2 Corinthians: Crisis and Conflict*. Phoenix Guides to the New Testament 8. Sheffield: Sheffield Phoenix.

Weber, Max. 2012. *The Protestant Ethic and the Spirit of Capitalism*. Translated by Stephen Kalberg. New York: Routledge. [Orig. 1904]

The Rage for Method and the Joy of Anachronism: When Biblical Scholars Do Affect Theory

Stephen D. Moore

> There is, quite simply, not a culture, community, or endeavor on earth in which affect isn't implicated, and yet, it is not and never can be universalized, because its circulations and manifestations are always tied to the specific cultural milieu of a particular individual, or group of beings, at a particular place and time.
>
> — Atkinson, "Hashtag #Affect"

What is affect theory becoming in biblical studies? "Another method of biblical criticism" would appear to be the foreordained answer. Exegesis is the flesh that confers mass on the body of biblical scholarship, after all, and method is the skeletal structure that confers acceptable shape on that mass. Yet method—at least in the standard biblical-scholarly sense of the term, which is to say a repeatable, quasi-formulaic protocol or tactic for interpretation—is not something to which any of the contributors to the present collection, save one, seem to aspire: the question of method is explicitly articulated only in Amy C. Cottrill's essay.[1] In this the majority of the contributors show themselves to be true children of the theoretical times; for contemporary theory—at least the more influential forms of it that find expression in literary and cultural studies, including affect theory—is postmethodological through and through.[2] Most of the essays in the present collection, then, are not methodological exercises in the traditional biblical-scholarly mode—which is not to say, however, that the

---

1. Otherwise, and rather remarkably for a biblical studies volume, the term *method* appears only once in its main essays (see Koosed).
2. As I have argued elsewhere; see most recently Moore 2017a, 21–24, specifically with reference to affect theory.

question of method is irrelevant to the volume as a whole. Far from it, as we shall see.

First, some broad descriptive strokes. What are the affects with which these essays engage, and who are the affect theorists recruited to assist with engaging them? Affect theorists have a reputation for hanging out in the grimmer, grittier end of the affective spectrum—the end clouded by shame and paranoia (Sedgwick 2003); pain, hate, fear, and disgust (Ahmed 2004; Brinkema 2014); loneliness, guilt, and the "Why me?" response to personal disaster (Riley 2005); illusory happiness, trauma, depression, and psychosomatic disorders (Ahmed 2010b; Cvetkovich 2003; 2012; Brennan 2004); deluded optimism (Berlant 2011); and ugly feelings in general (Ngai 2005)—and most of the essayists do not disappoint in that regard. The affects into which they descend include *ineradicable unhappiness* (Rhiannon Graybill); *feelings of failure* (Jay Twomey); *utter disgust* (Joseph A. Marchal); *grief, isolation, despair, and fear* (Fiona C. Black); *anguish and aggression* (Amy C. Cottrill); *anguish, anxiety, anger, and dejection* (Jennifer L. Koosed); and *commodified emotion* caught up in exploitative economic exchange (Robert Paul Seesengood); although they also include *cross-species affection* redolent with eco-positive valence (Ken Stone).[3]

What of the affect theorists accorded speaking roles or walk-on parts in the essays? In particular, do many or all of the essays fall decisively on either side of the great epistemic divide customarily ascribed to affect theory: on one side, the version of affect theory said to originate in the psychobiology of Silvan Tomkins as channeled and refined by queer theorist Eve Kosofsky Sedgwick; on the other side, the version said to originate in the Spinozan philosophy of Gilles Deleuze as channeled and refined by post-poststructuralist theorist Brian Massumi?[4]

---

3. Buoyant emotions feature more prominently in the list of affects that the comparable collection, *Mixed Feelings and Vexed Passions: Exploring Emotions in Biblical Literature* (Spencer 2017b), tackles: "Anger, fear, sadness (grief), disgust, joy, happiness, surprise (awe/wonder), pride, shame, insatiable desire, compassion, and faith/trust" (Spencer 2017a, 30). Affect theory is peripheral to the *Mixed Feelings* volume, however, as we shall see.

4. This two-trajectory depiction of affect theory found its most influential expression in Seigworth and Gregg 2010, 5–6. Jennifer Koosed and I adopted it in our own introduction to affect theory (2014). The model has frequently been called into question, however (including by Karen Bray and myself in yet another introduction to affect theory [2019]).

Tomkins is mentioned only once in the present volume (Seesengood), and Sedgwick only twice (Seesengood; Stone). But Deleuze scarcely features more prominently in it (Seesengood), nor does Massumi (Cottrill; Marchal; Twomey). Sara Ahmed—who herself rejects the affect-emotion distinction that subtends the epistemic divide (more on which below)—is the most frequently adduced affect theorist in the volume. Her work is fundamental to three of the essays—those of Graybill, Marchal, and Stone—and is mined or referenced in all the remaining essays. Which other affect theorists are important for the contributors? Ann Cvetkovich fundamentally informs Black's and Koosed's essays. Denise Riley and Kathleen Stewart also feature in Black's essay. Lauren Berlant is a significant theoretical resource for Twomey's essay, although far from his sole resource. Gregory Seigworth plays a comparable role in Seesengood's essay. Eugenie Brinkema and Sianne Ngai both play prominent roles in Marchal's essay.

A caveat: I confess to distributing my attention rather unevenly among the essays in what follows, according more of it to Cottrill's essay than the others. No lack of interest in the other essays is thereby signaled. But rather than drum up an evenly divided laundry list of critical quibbles with the individual essays, I have opted instead to frame the entire set of essays with certain overarching questions and reflections.

Reader Emotional-Response Criticism?

Let's turn back to the question of method. What in methodological terms does affect theory in biblical studies look like? Cottrill's essay models one rigorous answer to that question—rigorous because she refuses to oversimplify affect theory, even though that refusal eventually causes her methodology to run aground. As it happens, the question of affect and method has also been raised outside biblical studies, and from an unexpected quarter. "An Inventory of Shimmers," Gregory Seigworth and Melissa Gregg's intoxicating introduction to *The Affect Theory Reader* (2010), has nothing explicit to say about method, literary criticism, or even literature. (And why should we be surprised? As Stone astutely observes in the present volume, turning to affect theory for tools to read literary texts is an ironic exercise given affect theory's own insistence "that we have placed too much emphasis on language and symbols.") Biblical scholars seeking sturdy handholds of the methodological kind in *The Affect Theory Reader* will find only precarious toeholds at best.[5] More recently, however, introducing the first issue of the first affect theory journal, *Capacious*, Seigworth waxes not just methodological but metamethodological. "Different disciplines and angles of academic inquiry will take affect (and affects) up in subtle and often dramatically different ways," he muses. "Ultimately, the point is not to dissolve tensions by imagining that affect study will somehow magically turn into some kind of overarching über-discipline … or, even more basically, into a single multi-discipline-straddling methodology" (2017, i). Seigworth (2017, ii) then asks:

> How might any specifically-angled engagement with "affect" precipitate a re-imagining of the thresholds and continually shifting weight-bearing presuppositions/procedures/objects/relations that give unique texture, shape and rhythm to any discipline's sense of capaciousness? How far might a given set of knowledge-practices and theories stretch at their boundaries and yet remain recognizably, albeit elastically, "within the true" of their own singular historically-derived sets of practices and problematics?

Nothing yet to disturb the tranquil dreams of the traditionally minded biblical scholar; that comes only in Seigworth's (ii) next paragraph:

> The study of affect is not only perceived, for some, as an unwelcome blurring of certain disciplinary boundaries and procedures but, more so, as an outright rejection or negation of such world-making fundamentals as "consciousness," "intentionality," "cognitive," the "discursive," the "individual," the "linguistic," the "social," the "representational," the "human," the "personal" etc. etc.—after all, studies of affect have been known to attach a "non-" and/or a "pre-" prefix to these terms. With the affixing of the dash (-) of the non-/pre-, some have heard the opening of a gap: a rupture, a tear, a spacing, a kind of chasm.

Seigworth himself proceeds to de-negate and de-nihilize the non- and the pre-; but the specter, once conjured up in the chasm, is not easily exor-

---

5. This is not to imply that there have been no significant engagements with literature from within affect theory. See, in particular, the series Palgrave Studies in Affect Theory and Literary Criticism, eight volumes of which have appeared at the time of writing, together with the 883-page companion tome *The Palgrave Handbook of Affect Studies and Textual Criticism* (Wehrs and Blake 2017).

cised. Again, what might affect theory of this—or any—ilk yield in the way of method?

Cottrill prompts me to pose the question. Her essay boldly takes the methodological bull by the horns, purporting to "describe a methodology," to offer "methodological guidance," for enabling critical purchase on such slippery matters as how the language of the first-person psalms of lament "create an affective experience in the one who inhabits the subject position of the speaker" and how that experience might become "politically relevant." This affective experience is not, for Cottrill, limited to the historically situated positionality of the psalmist, but bleeds over into the experiences of individuals and communities who appropriate and reactivate the psalm. "What happens to one's body when one performs these words as prayer?," Cottrill asks. "What happens between and among bodies standing together praying these words? How do those feelings and bodily sensations ... become socially, ideologically, and politically persuasive in certain times and places?"

The exploration of such questions in relation to the psalms and other biblical material Cottrill terms *affect criticism*.[6] When I first encountered that term in her essay—it appears already on her first page—I confess that my reaction was somewhat supercilious. After all, Yvonne Sherwood and I had argued at wearying length in *The Invention of the Biblical Scholar* (2011, see esp. 31–41) that method is our madness in biblical studies and methodolatry our religion, methodology being what is supposed to keep our professional discourse on the Bible from being subjective, devotional, or homiletical. Or *affective*, which is partly to say the same thing.[7] My immediate suspicion, indeed, on reading Cottrill's opening-page sentence, "I discuss aspects of affect criticism that provide foundation for engaging the lament psalms of the individual," was that this was the first time that the words "affect" and "criticism" had been conjoined. I was wrong—mortifyingly so, as it turned out. Cottrill goes on to cite a statement Jennifer Koosed and I had made in our introduction to a thematic issue of *Biblical Interpretation* on affect theory. Pondering the task of translating affect

---

6. Seesengood also uses the term, albeit in passing: "When, then, is the role of affect criticism in economics, debt and labor?"

7. Note, for example, Walter Wink's (2010, 4, emphasis added) critique of classic historical criticism's "ideology of objectivism": "Objectivism as used here refers to the academic ideal of detached observation of phenomena without interference by *emotions*, will, interests, or bias."

theory—which up to that point had shown little interest in literary criticism—into biblical exegesis, Jennifer and I wondered aloud: "What might affect theory look like transmuted into affect criticism?" (2014, 386, referenced in Cottrill). What, indeed? The challenges are considerable, as Cottrill's own essay illustrates.

One prominent challenge concerns the endlessly debated question of whether or how to distinguish affect from emotion. Cottrill appears at first to lean into the Deleuzian-Massumian concept of affect, which differentiates it from emotion.[8] She writes: "Affect theory asks about what is happening in our preconscious, prelinguistic responses ... often sound[ing] more like poetry than argument-based scholarship, referring to the shimmers, intensities, forces, rhythms, sensations, resonances, movements, and vibrations that are part of ... preconscious experience." Earlier she had asked how "feelings and bodily sensations evoked by ... the laments, *not yet taken up by the conscious mind and categorized into emotions*, become ... persuasive" (her emphasis).[9] Affect, feeling, and sensation, understood as synonyms, pulsate on one side of the conceptual divide evoked by Cottrill, while emotion throbs on the other side.[10]

When Cottrill begins to home in on her methodology, however, emotion slips surreptitiously to center stage. Cottrill has recourse to the reading strategies of medievalist Sarah McNamer. Unlike Cottrill, McNamer uses the terms *emotion* and *feeling* synonymously, a difference Cottrill neglects to note. More substantially, McNamer resurrects Stanley Fish's *affective*

---

8. As mediated by Seigworth and Gregg 2010, 1, whom Cottrill quoted.

9. Compare Massumi 2002, 28, the canonical formulation of the affect-emotion distinction: "Emotion is qualified intensity ['intensity,' for Massumi, is a synonym for 'affect'], the conventional, consensual point of insertion of intensity into semantically and semiotically formed progressions, into narrativizable action-reaction circuits, into function and meaning.... It is crucial to theorize the difference between affect and emotion." See also Massumi 2015, 5: "An emotion is a very partial expression of affect."

10. Other contributors also construe affect along Deleuzian-Massumian lines, at least in passing; see, for example, Koosed: "Affect theory probes the body and all that which resists representation"; Seesengood: "To command the affect itself, to introduce a system where pre-conscious sensation is regulated"; and Marchal: "When imagined as those 'visceral forces beneath, alongside, or generally *other than* conscious knowing, vital forces insisting beyond emotion,' affect problematizes the (imagined) comforts of a divide between reason and emotion." Marchal is quoting Seigworth and Gregg (2010, 1), who themselves are channeling Deleuze. Black references and riffs on the same passage from Seigworth and Gregg.

stylistics, his term for his seminal version of reader-response criticism (Fish 1970), retooling it so that it better lives up to its name: if Fish and other reader-response critics were primarily concerned with the question of how texts make *meanings*, McNamer and Cottrill are more interested in how texts make *feelings* (McNamer 2007, 247–48; cited in Cottrill).

The question Cottrill implicitly raises about affect criticism's relationship to reader-response criticism is thought-provoking.[11] In the heyday of biblical reader-response criticism, the reader-responses that critics claimed to find scripted, encoded, or implied in biblical texts came in two kinds: *cognitive* and *emotional*. The implied reader wrestled intellectually with the knotty cerebral problems thrown up by, say, Mark's cryptic parable theory or his enigmatic nonending, but the implied reader also emoted appropriately at each prescribed moment in Mark's affect-laden narrative.[12] Reader emotional-response criticism?[13]

Cottrill comes closest to resurrecting reader-response critical sensibilities when she describes the psalms of lament as "offer[ing] the speaker an emotional script." The problem with old-school reader-response criticism was that the presumed script, whether cognitive or emotional, was excessively prescriptive: the implied reader was the creation—indeed, the creature—of the implied author, and both were creations of the reader-response critic in turn. Reader-response criticism in its formalist biblical-scholarly manifestations allowed no role for the unscripted messiness, the ineluctable subjectivity, of *real* reading. Cottrill, to her credit, is cognizant of the formalist pitfall. "There is nothing determinative about

---

11. Michal Beth Dinkler (2017, 265–66) also provokes reflection on this relationship: "I am concerned with the ways that ancient narratives—qua narrative—shape the emotional repertoires of their intended audiences, partly by representing emotional experiences like joy within the story itself and partly by engendering experiences of emotion like joy in their implied audiences." Indeed, Dinkler "adopt[s] the approach of narrative and reader-response critics" for her study of joy in Luke-Acts (266 n. 4).

12. As does the implied audience in Michael Whitenton's "moment-by-moment account of emotions at the end of Mark," to cite the subtitle of his 2016 article, a fusion of reader-response criticism, performance criticism, and cognitive studies of emotion.

13. Tellingly, Robert Fowler's *Let the Reader Understand*, the consummate product of biblical reader-response criticism, contains a section titled "Emotions." Fowler (2001, 123, emphasis original) writes: "I take the predominance of [certain] emotions in the [Markan] story as a token of what the narrator hopes to achieve through his discourse. If these emotions are regularly elicited *in* the story, most likely the narrator feels that they would be appropriate responses by the reader *to* the story."

affect," she insists. "I do not argue that an individual who allows himself or herself to be represented by the 'I' of this lament [Ps 109] will necessarily feel or respond to the language in a particular way. Affect is unpredictable." Indeed, Cottrill raises the bar dauntingly high in her affect-attuned analysis of the psalm. She wants to know not just how the psalm elicits *feeling* (in the sense of emotion, à la McNamer), but also how it elicits *sensation* (in the sense of affect, à la Deleuze and Massumi).

Ultimately, however, Cottrill sails under the bar rather than over it. She discovers a maelstrom of warring affects in the psalm: "Subject positions of submission and frailty and then violent aggression oscillate and move, creating instability. How does that disharmony and tension ... combine in the sensory registers of the speaker? How does the volatility of this psalm both reflect and create a bodily experience for the speaker?" Cottrill leaves these perplexing questions unanswered for now: "That physical experience of volatility and movement undermines static interpretive attempts." Arguably, however, the most obvious strategy for tackling such questions, for edging past the impasse, would be to write out of one's own sensory registers, one's own bodily experience of the psalm. In other words, just as Cottrill's essay reads to me like reader-response criticism resurrected and reclothed on the other side of the affective turn in theory—which is to say, no longer as structuralist spinoff nor even as poststructuralist production, but as post-poststructuralist performance—the conundrum that brings the essay to an abrupt halt is comparable to that which eventually compelled some biblical reader-response critics to take the plunge into autobiographical criticism, declaring a moratorium on talking about what the text was doing to an imagined implied reader in order to talk about what it was doing to them.[14]

As it happens, Marchal hints at how affect criticism in an autobiographical or personal register might look,[15] and right from his opening lines:

---

14. Jeffrey Staley's *Reading with a Passion* (1995) was the most ambitious example of this critical shift. Staley (114) confessed: "When you've been hiding behind implied and encoded readers as long as I have, it's not easy to slip into something more comfortable, curl up in a chair, and tell a stranger who you are." But this is precisely what Staley undertook to do in this book, and with considerable theoretical finesse.

15. Maia Kotrosits more than hints at it in her extended introduction to affect theory in biblical studies. She prefaces that dimension of her article with statements such as the following: "Affect's relationship to psychoanalysis and the somatic reminds us that the 'facts' or most relevant details of any intellectual history not only exceed what gets committed to paper, but actually might reside elsewhere as well: the indef-

Nose twitches, eyebrows shoot up (or sometimes just cinch), lips curl, as a mouth spits out: "Ugh. How could you study that?" Sometimes I am the object of disgust, "how could *you* study that?" What makes a pervert like you qualified to say anything of value about such sacred texts? Yet, often times, such texts—and especially Paul's letters—are what instigate such reactions, "how could you study *that*?"

But Paul is not only a potential object of disgust; he is also a vehicle of disgust, as Marchal later demonstrates. Paul wallows in "ancient stereotypes about gentile bodies," conjuring up a veritable parade of "vilified figures": "castrated bodies," "viceful bodies," "androgynous bodies".... "After only a few ... initial encounters with affect theory," Marchal admits, "I now realize that the subjects of my own attention have recurrently been such objects of disgust for Paul. I may have been preoccupied with disgust for over a decade now, without even knowing it!"

Yet articulating what a text is doing to one affectively is undoubtedly harder, not easier, after affect theory. One of the lessons of affect theory, indeed, is that "my feelings are not my own"; rather, they are "culturally scripted" (Jensen and Wallace 2015b, 1252; see also Brennan 2004, 1–3; Ahmed 2014, 1–2). We learn to feel appropriately, normatively, by being socialized into emotions "through family, school, work, religious institutions, and other 'ideological state apparatuses,'" extending to television and other yet more omnipresent media. "Because certain emotions are required in certain contexts," ranging from intimate relationships to patriotic rituals, we "learn to perform them" even when we do not feel them (Jensen and Wallace 2015b, 1252). The emotional script is always a pre-script, and in both senses of the term.

Emotions Are Hard to Talk About

Most of the contributors to the present collection are squirmy about emotions, in any case (Koosed being the exception that proves the rule; she seems comfortable talking about emotions, to the extent that the word punctuates almost every page of her essay). Tellingly, Graybill manages

---

inite electricity of interpersonal moments; the temperature or mood of any given room; the hyper-particular situation in which something is said or the way in which something unfolds; the historical and cultural force fields and unconscious desires that coalesce people, give ideas traction, or sweep possibilities away" (2016, 2).

to write an entire essay on unhappiness that uses the word *emotion* or its derivatives only once, and, even then, in a quotation. In Twomey's essay on failure, the word emotion appears only twice, also in passing. Seesengood's essay is openly and centrally about emotion; but the kind of emotion with which he wrestles is frequently formulaic and often impersonal. Seesengood describes "emotional labor," his theme, as "the lubrication of late capitalism," although he also finds it present in embryo in the Pauline letters. Black is also attuned to the manufactured quality of emotion, even though emotion is not only that for her. Still, "[the] passage between what is felt [by the individual] and what is produced for the collective is barely traceable *as a passage*; instead, the two conflate" (her emphasis). Interiority is the first casualty of this conflation. The (heavily qualified) depression that Black claims to find in the psalms of lament "could never be thought of uniquely as an interior, personal affliction." Rather, "depression's affects" in these psalms "work via the outside, not on the inside." Stone likewise problematizes emotional interiority, taking previous interpreters of 2 Sam 12 to task for "replicat[ing] a widespread understanding of emotions as psychological phenomena existing inside individuals who may express them externally." Rather than attempting to reconstruct the "inner states" of David or other characters, Stone proposes "to reconsider 2 Sam 12 in terms of what we might call, borrowing from Sara Ahmed, 'the sociality of emotions,'" whereby emotions circulate by attaching or "sticking" to objects that themselves are in motion (cf. Ahmed 2014, 8–11). Stone is also intent on posthumanizing emotion, on dislodging it from its presumed privileged association with, or attachment to, human beings. For Stone, 2 Sam 12 concerns "the affective relations that can flow between humans and sheep,"[16] and not just one way, since sheep are also subjects of "emotional intelligence." By implication, then, emotion is both less and more than human.

For the most part in this collection, as is evident from these examples, emotion is a queried category when it is not an object of conspicuous omission. There is also much ambivalence around emotions in this volume; for even when contributors seem squeamish about using the word(s) *emotion(s)* or *emotional*, easily identified emotions are the foci of their essays anyway, as we noted earlier: unhappiness, feelings of failure, and so on.

---

16. As Meera Atkinson (2018, iii) remarks, "Affect is … a living, breathing membrane between the human and the nonhuman…. Affect animates the diversity of individual beings referred to as 'animals.'"

Perhaps we should not give up too hastily on emotions, in any case—or so we're told, and on good authority. Ahmed, in particular, has some biting things to say about the theoretical elevation of affect over emotion in the Deleuzian-Massumian brand of affect theory: "A contrast between a mobile impersonal affect and a contained personal emotion suggests that the affect/emotion distinction can operate as a gendered distinction," she contends. "It might even be that the very use of this distinction performs the evacuation of certain styles of thought (we might think of these as 'touchy feely' styles of thought, including feminist and queer thought) from affect studies" (2014, 205–6).[17] Could the issue be articulated any more acerbically than that? Apparently, it could; listen to Megan Boler (2015, 1491):

> Shunned, silenced, and excluded, refused entry into the hallowed halls, emotions have been on the margins of academe for hundreds of years,[18] while the cherished son—reason—has had pride of place and free rein in the master's house, awarded crowns while the lowly sisters shiver in disrepute.... In this long, gendered history, only in the recent blink of an eye have emotions gained a place at the master's table—thanks to the tireless political force of the second wave of feminism, from the late 1960s to the 1980s.[19]

In the oppressive shadow of this *longue durée*, the hierarchical opposition elevating affect over emotion—forcibly and manfully (re)pressing

---

17. Ann Cvetkovich (2012, 8) also resists the affect/emotion dichotomy, in part because she wishes to remain true to a tradition of feminist scholarship that long preceded the so-called affective turn in theory (cf. Clough 2007): "Feelings were ... at the heart of this theoretically informed [feminist] scholarship, including projects on emotional genres, such as the gothic, the sentimental, the sensational, and the melodramatic, and sophisticated accounts of the history of emotions, the relation between private and public spheres, and the construction of interiority, subjectivity, embodiment, and intimate life."

18. Or much longer; only consider the place of the passions in ancient Greek philosophical thought.

19. Katrin Pahl (2015, 1457) goes even farther: "I ... prefer the ugliness of the word *emotionality* and its pejorative connotations [to the word *emotions*]. It is time to reclaim this attribute, which has been used as an insult to exclude voices from the public sphere. When women, queers, and racialized or culturally othered peoples have been called emotional, this has always meant too emotional.... To combat this mechanism of exclusion, we must refuse to other the emotional."

emotion under the bar once more, just as it has finally succeeded in raising its head above it—acquires sinister significance, indeed.

But does the choice between affect and emotion in the biblical studies context carry the same political weight or freight as the choice between affect and emotion in the literary and cultural studies context? As we are about to see, an affect/emotion split does also operate in biblical scholarship responsive to "the emotional turn in the humanities and social sciences";[20] but it is not a split that predominantly positions feminist- and/or queer-identified scholars on the emotional side of the divide. Who, then, is unapologetically "doing" emotions in biblical studies?

"Emotions are in full bloom in biblical scholarship." So begins Françoise Mirguet and Dominika Kurek-Chomycz's (2016, 435) introduction to a recent thematic issue of *Biblical Interpretation* on emotions. So profuse is this emotional blossoming in biblical scholarship, indeed, that the footnotes needed to testify to it occupy almost the entire first two pages of their introduction. Much of this scholarship on emotions is German. Most of it is cognitive in thrust. Almost all of it is historicist in intent. And almost none of it engages with affect theory.[21]

But the essays in the present collection do not reference this burgeoning body of work on biblical emotions either or the extrabiblical social-scientific work on emotions that underpins most of it. This lack of dialogue is hardly surprising. Affect theory at full post-poststructuralist gallop (Massumi's *Parables for the Virtual* [2002] immediately comes to mind) is a different animal from the cognitive or social constructivist studies of emotion that inform the typical paper presented in the Society of Biblical Literature's Bible and Emotion unit or the European Association of Biblical Studies' Emotions and the Biblical World unit. One could probably not mistake a page even of Ahmed's *The Cultural Politics of*

---

20. The title of a recent essay (Lemmings and Brooks 2014).

21. A handful of exceptions may be noted. Mirguet and Kurek-Chomcyz (2016, 437–38) briefly discuss affect theory in their introduction to the thematic issue, and Mirguet refers to it further in her "What Is an 'Emotion' in the Hebrew Bible?" (2016, 444, 464–65), one of the main articles in the issue, as well as in her subsequent monograph on ancient Jewish compassion (2017, 10–11, 13–14). Affect theory plays a less peripheral role in *Mixed Feelings and Vexed Passions: Exploring Emotions in Biblical Literature* (Spencer 2017b). While central to my own contribution to that collection (Moore 2017b), it also features in Scott Spencer's (2017a, 25–28) introduction to the volume, and in Juliana Claassens's (2017, 79, 81–82, 87) and Michal Beth Dinkler's (2017, 272, 278–79, 283, 284–85) essays for it.

Emotion (2004)—notwithstanding Ahmed's own lack of enthusiasm for affect theory in the Massumian mode—for a page of, say, Anna Wierzbicka's *Emotions across Languages and Cultures* (1999); nor could one easily mistake Eugenie Brinkema's discussion of emotion in ancient Greek philosophy in her *The Forms of the Affects* (2014, 2–5) for any portion of David Konstan's *The Emotions of the Ancient Greeks* (2006). The theoretical and critical idiom is markedly different, as is the driving sense of what matters most (in Ahmed's case, for example, race, gender, and sexuality).

What Ahmed *does* have in common with Wierzbicka, of course, as with Konstan, is a central focus on emotions; for even in literary and cultural studies, as I note above, emotions (or feelings, as in the case of Cvetkovich) are often the preferred focus of analysis rather than affects (in the elaborately torqued Deleuzian sense of the term). For a further example of this preference, consider the thematic issue that the affective turn in literary and cultural studies belatedly prompted in *PMLA*, the flagship journal in those fields. The issue is titled *Emotions* rather than *Affects* (Jensen and Wallace 2015a). The editors explain their choice: "Historically, [the] psycho-physiological category [to which the issue is devoted] has been designated *passions, sentiment, sensibility*, and, most recently, *affect*. Yet we chose the messier term *emotions* for this issue because it is a recognizable, modern, everyday word rather than a historically or theoretically specific one" (Jensen and Wallace 2015b, 1255).

Of course, it is precisely the familiarity, the contemporaneity, of the term *emotions* that causes so many of the historians of ancient emotions to squirm uncomfortably—more uncomfortably, indeed, than any of the contributors to the present volume. If, in general, the academic study of emotions makes discussion of emotions harder rather than easier, such difficulty increases exponentially when the analyst of emotions happens also to be an historian of ancient Israel, ancient Judaism, or early Christianity. Introducing the aforementioned thematic journal issue, *Emotions in Ancient Jewish Literature*, all of whose articles emerged from the European Association of Biblical Studies program unit Emotions and the Biblical World, Mirguet and Kurek-Chomycz (2016, 439) note: "What 'we' (a convenient way to refer to contemporary speakers, mainly of Western languages) call emotions [is] a category that is diversely problematized throughout this special issue." The problematization begins with Mirguet's own article for the issue:

> Talking about "emotions" in Biblical Hebrew … is problematic at different levels. First, … Biblical Hebrew words that are usually translated

> by emotional terms, such as love or fear, exceed our emotional realm, as they also include actions, ritual gestures, and physical sensations.... Biblical Hebrew does not organize human experience by delimiting a strictly emotional dimension comparable to ours. The absence of a "meta-description" for both our noun "emotion" and our verb "to feel" makes difficult a more precise statement; this absence, however, is meaningful in itself, not least hinting that such a realm of experience is not conceptualized as such. (Mirguet 2016, 463)

And it is not just in the Hebrew Bible that emotion *sous rature* (emotion that is simultaneously nonemotion) is experienced but not conceptualized. For the most part, this is also true of the Greek Bible (the Septuagint and the New Testament), as Scott Spencer observes in his introduction to another recent collection on biblical emotions, *Mixed Feelings and Vexed Passions* (Spencer 2017b), this one a product of the Society of Biblical Literature program unit Bible and Emotion. Even if we take the optimistic step of translating the ancient Greek word *pathos* as "emotion," we discover that of the sixty-seven occurrences of *pathos* in the Greek Bible, only five occur outside of 4 Maccabees, and all three of the New Testament occurrences (Rom 1:26; Col 3:5; 1 Thess 4:5) refer specifically to sexual lust rather than a general category of emotion in our sense of the term.[22]

A certain ineffability, then, regularly attends the category and concept of emotion in recent biblical-scholarly work on emotion, scholars writing on ancient emotion without quite believing in ancient emotion ("I will make [the claim] that 'emotion' does not exist as a category in the Hebrew Bible," David Lambert [2017, 140] asserts in his contribution to the Spencer collection),[23] attempting to express the inexpressible in the manner of apophatic theologians—or, for that matter, of affect theorists pronouncing on affect (albeit through the medium of an entirely different discursive apparatus). For such biblical scholars, all our taken-for-granted assumptions about emotions need to be thoroughly deconstructed and

---

22. My loose paraphrase of Spencer 2017a, 6–9.

23. In her monograph on compassion in Hellenistic Judaism, Mirguet (2017, 9, emphasis original) at one point inquires: "Is the history of emotions ... truly a history of *emotions*? Is it not rather a history of discourses, constructions, and norms? Are emotions, per se, social constructs?"—although she then proceeds to soften this strong constructivist perspective. For an affect theorist like Massumi, meanwhile, that which exceeds both discourses on emotions and emotions themselves is, precisely, affect.

defamiliarized before we can begin to understand "emotions" (now ringed about with shrieking scare quotes) in biblical and other ancient texts. One might, indeed, be forgiven for concluding that such scholars need a term other than *emotion* for their declared object of study—perhaps a term like *affect*, which is more amenable to apophatic approaches. The paradox, in any case, is that biblical affect critics seem to have more to say about emotion than affect, if the present volume is any indication, whereas when biblical historical critics set out to write about emotion, they often end up evoking something more akin to affect.

A Presentist Revolt against Pastist Rule?

Implicit in the preceding paragraphs is a matter all but unnamed in the essays that constitute the present volume, yet crucial to their significance, namely, the problem of anachronism. The final article in the *Biblical Interpretation* issue on ancient emotions, Anke Inselmann's "Emotions and Passions in the New Testament," has much to say about this matter, a highly fraught and heavily freighted one for many biblical scholars. Inselmann (2016, 538, 546, her emphasis) details eight challenges to the project of "interpreting passions from a different *age*" (*passions* being her preferred term for Greco-Roman *emotions*), according an emphatic final position to the following challenge:

> Lastly but importantly, the suspicion of *anachronism* always remains a factor. There is no denying that there is a danger when interpreting texts from a time long since past and from a different local and cultural environment. We will always remain children of our time. When dealing with passions, many interpretations risk the danger of drawing conclusions that result from one's *own emotional experience* in one's own contemporary culture. It seems to be natural and tempting to mistake our everyday emotional experience as a stable human constant, as a universal phenomenon. But this underlying and basic assumption is risky

—and so on. And a little later: "Some scholars claim it would be anachronistic to superimpose a modern psychological pattern on biblical texts. On the other hand, we have to tackle the danger of anachronism due to an everyday, non-critical psychology" (547).

Suspicion, danger, risk, temptation—all phenomena calculated to set hearts pounding and pulses racing. Inselmann conjures up an affect-suffused scholarly existence. And why not? Even "scholarly life is full of visceral experiences," as Melissa Gregg notes. Gregg's (2006, 6–7) examples include "the fear and adrenaline that come with presenting work in public, the ferocity with which disciplinary ideologues stake out their turf, the indignant soliloquies of aging colleagues faced with one more bureaucratic imposition, or the consuming doubt that can descend on even the most gifted writers." But these are all transdisciplinary academic affects. There is a further affect that might be said to be defining or determinative of biblical scholarship as an academic discipline, namely, *the fear of anachronism*.

Not coincidentally, the article in the *Biblical Interpretation* issue on emotions that conjures up the specter of anachronism most vividly (it haunts the entire issue, and also rattles its chains in the *Mixed Feelings and Vexed Passions* collection[24]) is also the article that worries most audibly about method: "What is … astonishing when investigating passions in New Testament literature is the fact that no methodology has yet been established" (Inselmann 2016, 537). Methodology's primary purpose in biblical scholarship, since the inception of the discipline, has been to hold anachronism at bay.[25] Methodology has been our main bulwark against the fear of anachronism.

Inselmann's combined remarks, which both articulate and epitomize the enabling assumptions and affective energies of mainstream bibli-

---

24. See, for example, Spencer 2017a, 31: "Dealing with biblical languages and cultures far removed from south Texas [the author's birthplace, as he has just divulged] undoubtedly places a heavier burden on resisting anachronistic and ethnocentric transfers of emotional interpretation." (Is exegetical anachronism inevitably ethnocentric? I don't think so; otherwise it would be impossible to, say, deliver a biblically-inspired sermon uninformed by historical criticism that condemned xenophobia or urged hospitality toward refugees.) Similarly, Dennis Olson (2017, 163) summarizes and apparently accepts Lambert's argument "that we often wrongly impose anachronistic expectations or concepts on alleged Hebrew Bible repentance texts"; David E. Fredrickson (2017, 324, emphasis original) refers to certain ancient acts and passions that "some scholars today anachronistically call *homosexuality* or *homosexual behavior*"; and Katherine M. Hockey (335 n. 20) explains: "I have elected to use the word *emotion* for the ancient concepts of *pathos* (and *animi motus/affectus*), knowing that there are anachronistic difficulties."

25. The invention and develop of anachronism as a concept, indeed, was coextensive with the invention and development of critical biblical scholarship. "The word anachronism … was first used in the seventeenth century," as Judith Pollmann (2017, 48–49) notes, and gradually evolved into a historiographic "habit of thought" postulated on the past's radical difference from the present.

cal scholarship, beg to be contrasted with the enabling assumptions and affective energies of the contributors to the present collection. But both sets of assumptions and affects ought first to be reframed in relation to a cross-disciplinary debate about historical method that has been raging for decades in the humanities and social sciences in fields ranging from medieval studies and literary studies to the history of science, the history of sexuality, and the field of history in general, namely, the debate about *presentism*, its synonyms, and its antonyms.

"Presentism is widely understood to mean the practice of representing, interpreting, and, more importantly, evaluating the past according to the values, standards, ambitions, and anxieties of a later 'present,'" as medievalist Louise D'Arcens explains (2014, 181). Presentism is also called *continuism* (although the latter term is sometimes colored by subtle shades of difference from the former term). In an essay on lesbian historiography, Valerie Traub (2007, 124) notes: "Scholars whose historical accounts take a continuist form have tended to emphasize a similarity between past and present concepts of sexual understanding; those who instead highlight historical difference or alterity (as it is termed by literary scholars) have tended to emphasize problems of anachronism." *Alteritists*, then, is another name for scholars for whom anachronism is a source of anxiety. Such scholars are also dubbed *pastists*, however, as a more symmetrical antonym for *presentists*. D'Arcens (2014, 181), for example, writes of the "camps of pastists and presentists" within medieval studies. "Pastism regards the past and the present as bounded temporal objects that cannot come into contact for fear of scholarly contamination" (181). Yet more fear, then. Scholarship is dangerous work, it seems.

Most of the contributors to the present volume dance blithely through the pastist minefield. Their scholarly predilections are conspicuously continuist, if a desire to bridge past and present, to demonstrate the continuing relevance of the past, even the remote past, for understanding and also transforming the present are to be taken as the hallmarks of continuism. Several of the contributors also have a penchant for large claims,[26] some of which are continuist claims. Seesengood, in particular, argues that modern emotional labor, across a broad spectrum of activities extending from child care to sex work, "has its roots in Pauline metaphors toward

---

26. Large claims are often thought-provoking. Consider, for example, Graybill's assertion that "prophecy is a practice of unhappiness," or Koosed's assertion that the siddur "may be the most underexplored site of the greatest affective archive in Judaism."

service to God and Jesus," while Black contends that the psalms of lament may be productively situated in the history of depression: "Even biblical poets can be depression's public intellectuals."

That the presentism debate is scarcely ever referenced in biblical studies is hard to fathom; so many of the conflicts within our field patently arise from pastist-presentist tensions. Consider, for example, the following remarks from historian Alexandra Walsham's introduction to a special section of the journal *Past and Present* on presentism. Their applicability to many of the assumptions—but also many of the fears—that fuel biblical historical criticism hardly needs belaboring:

> The *Oxford English Dictionary* dates the first use of the word [presentism] to 1916, and its subsequent examples are all derogatory in tone and character. They reflect anxiety about the distorting effects and dangers of approaching the past from the perspective of the present.... They are closely linked with the opinion that anachronism is the most heinous sin of the historian. The instinctive suspicion of presentism that prevails among many historians is also a legacy of the lofty ideal of objectivity that we have inherited from the positivists who placed the discipline of history on a professional footing in the nineteenth century. It is a function of the conviction that we should study the past for its own sake and not in order to advance other agendas. (Walsham 2017, 213)

On this account, anachronism is not only a source of danger and a cause of anxiety, but also—and aptly for the biblical studies context—an occasion of sin. The other agendas that, in recent decades, have seduced many biblical scholars from the professional study of the biblical past "for its own sake" include political agendas of various kinds (feminist, anti-racist, queer, postcolonial, etc.), but also a desire to open biblical studies up to major intellectual currents in the humanities and social sciences, most recently the affective turn. The biblical scholars whom Mirguet and Kurek-Chomycz (2016, 435) mainly have in mind when they write that "emotions are in full bloom in biblical scholarship" have been seduced by the affective turn, broadly conceived; but they prefer, for the most part, to pursue it through pastist modes of scholarship, whereas the contributors to the present volume prefer, for the most part, to pursue it through presentist modes of scholarship.

Consider Black's essay, for example. "There is a large body of literature on lamentation in the Hebrew Bible," she notes; "its scholars might be troubled at seeing [lamentation] used interchangeably with depression."

Too bad, because that is what Black proceeds to do.[27] Seesengood, for his part, begins his essay conventionally enough with a meticulous explication of the rhetorical function of the concept of labor, extending to slave labor, in the Pauline letters. But precisely where a *Journal of Biblical Literature* article, say, would then lead us off on a learned (de)tour through philosophies and ideologies of labor in ancient Greek and Latin sources, Seesengood takes us instead on an equally (but differently) erudite (de)tour through modern concepts of emotional labor and eventually to some incisive reflections on Walter Benjamin's rambling ruminations on the Parisian protoshopping malls known as the arcades. In contrast, Marchal's essay doesn't begin conventionally at all, and the stomach-unsettling tour of disgust on which he takes us—his own (de)tour section with coguides Ahmed, Brinkema, and Ngai—does not once allude, rather remarkably, to ancient concepts of disgust or ancient objects of disgust, even the *kinaidos* or the *tribas*, those queer ancient figures of disgust whom Marchal engages elsewhere.[28] Twomey, for his part, opens his essay with a veritable volley of modern or contemporary texts—Jesus novels, a highway billboard, a Martin Luther King Jr. sermon, a Christian self-help book, a novel on Paul, a short story on Paul—that cumulatively ensure that his piece could not possibly be imagined between the covers of a long and illustrious list of biblical studies journals, beginning with the *Journal of Biblical Literature* and *New Testament Studies*. But Twomey is only getting started; the bulk of his essay provides a close, critical analysis, not of the letters of Paul, but of a graphic novel on Paul. Paul's self-representation(s) in his letters play second fiddle in Twomey's essay to contemporary cultural representations of Paul. This, of course, makes the essay an exercise in cultural studies. But it also makes it a notable instance of exegetical anachronism, untethered and floating free not just from pastist historiographic presumptions, but also from methodology in the conventional biblical-scholarly sense of the term.

Most of the essays in this collection, indeed—to return to my opening observation—are not methodological exercises in the traditional

---

27. And does so with considerable nuance, it should be said. But Black is also capable of statements such as the following: "The idea of the mutability of depression [in response] to external stimuli ... is very much depression's bailiwick, from psalm to Prozac, and beyond."

28. Ancient sexual "scare figures" (Marchal's term) do, however, crop up in his Paul section.

biblical-critical mode, or even the traditional biblical-literary-critical mode. That is, they are not seeking to superimpose upon a biblical text a preexisting interpretive protocol extracted from a work of literary or cultural theory, even a work of affect theory. To differing degrees, none of the essays (even Cottrill's in the final analysis) entails the precise application of a methodological grid to a biblical text. Their enabling gesture is not overlaying so much as juxtaposing, not superimposing so much as setting side by side. Ahmed's *The Cultural Politics of Emotion* is set adjacent to 2 Sam 12 in Stone's essay, and Ahmed's *The Promise of Happiness* is set adjacent to the book of Jonah in Graybill's essay. In Koosed's essay, Cvetkovich's *An Archive of Feelings* is juxtaposed with the book of Lamentations and the siddur. In Black's essay, Cvetkovich's *Depression*, Ahmed's *The Cultural Politics of Emotion* and "Happy Objects" (2010a), Riley's *Impersonal Passions*, and Stewart's *Ordinary Affects* (2007) are read side-by-side with the psalms of lament. In Twomey's essay, Halberstam's *The Queer Art of Failure* and Berlant's *Cruel Optimism*, together with Steve Ross's *Blinded* (2008), cozy up to the apostle Paul. In Marchal's essay, Ahmed's *The Cultural Politics of Emotion*, Brinkema's *The Forms of the Affects*, and Ngai's *Ugly Feelings* all rub shoulders with Paul's letters. In Seesengood's essay, texts by authors from the affect theory canon, together with texts by affect theorists *avant la lettre*, are also placed in contiguity with Paul's letters. At base, these essays are all exercises in, or performances of, intertextuality at its least formulaic and most creative—intertextuality more audacious, indeed, than any generally found even outside the field of biblical studies. For what, after all, does Ahmed's *The Promise of Happiness* have to do with the book of Jonah? Absolutely nothing, needless to say. And yet much in every way, as Graybill succeeds in showing.[29]

Perhaps *interaffectivity* would be the better term for the particular confluences these innovative essays stage,[30] inchoate but intensely felt affects swirling between

---

29. And not by spending her entire essay skulking in the "Melancholic Migrants" chapter of Ahmed's book either. Rather, Graybill insists that the bewildered Jonah also hang out in the "Feminist Killjoys" and "Unhappy Queers" chapters of the book.

30. I naively imagined I had just invented this term, but on Googling it to be certain I learned it already existed, "Intercorporeality and Interaffectivity" being the title of a recent essay (Fuchs 2017). The spin on interaffectivity that follows, however, is entirely my own.

(1) *the biblical texts*, sodden with something *like* emotion that is *not yet* emotion, and as such is all but unnamable;
(2) *the texts of affect theory*, by turns effulgently illuminating, maddeningly opaque, and affectingly personal; and
(3) *the affect-challenged biblical scholar*, for centuries fearful of feelings, but now determined (let us imagine), not just to feel hitherto unfelt things about the numbingly overfamiliar biblical texts, but even to write about these fleeting feelings—and if not that, then at least to write about someone else's feelings for the texts, or, failing even that, to write about the feelings *in* the texts.

What, then, is the principal affect that pervades the present collection? Not the *fear* of anachronism, certainly; if anything, it is the *joy* of anachronism.

Bibliography

Ahmed, Sara. 2004. *The Cultural Politics of Emotion*. New York: Routledge.
———. 2010a. "Happy Objects." Pages 29–51 in *The Affect Theory Reader*. Edited by Melissa Gregg and Gregory J. Seigworth. Durham, NC: Duke University Press.
———. 2010b. *The Promise of Happiness*. Durham, NC: Duke University Press.
———. 2014. *The Cultural Politics of Emotion*. 2nd ed. with afterword. New York: Routledge.
Atkinson, Meera. 2018. "Hashtag #Affect." *Capacious: Journal for Emerging Affect Inquiry* 1.2: i–vi.
Berlant, Lauren. 2011. *Cruel Optimism*. Durham, NC: Duke University Press.
Boler, Megan. 2015. "Feminist Politics of Emotions and Critical Digital Pedagogies: A Call to Action." *PMLA: Publications of the Modern Language Association of America* 130.5:1489–96.
Bray, Karen, and Stephen D. Moore. 2019. "Introduction: Mappings and Crossings." Pages 1–18 in *Religion, Emotion, Sensation: Affect Theories and Theologies*. Edited by Karen Bray and Stephen D. Moore. Transdisciplinary Theological Colloquia. New York: Fordham University Press.
Brennan, Teresa. 2004. *The Transmission of Affect*. Ithaca, NY: Cornell University Press.

Brinkema, Eugenie. 2014. *The Forms of the Affects*. Durham, NC: Duke University Press.

Claassens, L. Juliana. 2017. "From Fear's Narcissism to Participatory Imagination: Disrupting Disgust and Overcoming the Fear of Israel's *Hērem* Laws." Pages 77–96 in *Mixed Feelings and Vexed Passions: Exploring Emotions in Biblical Literature*. Edited by F. Scott Spencer. RBS 90. Atlanta: SBL Press.

Clough, Patricia Ticineto, with Jean Halley, eds. 2007. *The Affective Turn: Theorizing the Social*. Durham, NC: Duke University Press.

Cvetkovich, Ann. 2003. *An Archive of Feelings: Trauma, Sexuality, and Lesbian Public Cultures*. Series Q. Durham, NC: Duke University Press.

———. 2012. *Depression: A Public Feeling*. Durham, NC: Duke University Press.

D'Arcens, Louise. 2014. "Presentism." Pages 181–88 in *Medievalism: Key Critical Terms*. Edited by Elizabeth Emery and Richard Utz. Cambridge: D. S. Brewer.

Dinkler, Michal Beth. 2017. "Reflexivity and Emotion in Narratological Perspective: Reading Joy in the Lukan Narrative." Pages 265–86 in *Mixed Feelings and Vexed Passions: Exploring Emotions in Biblical Literature*. Edited by F. Scott Spencer. RBS 90. Atlanta: SBL Press.

Fish, Stanley E. 1970. "Literature in the Reader: Affective Stylistics." *New Lit. Hist.* 2.1:123–62.

Fowler, Robert M. 2001. *Let the Reader Understand: Reader-Response Criticism and the Gospel of Mark*. 2nd ed. Harrisburg, PA: Trinity Press International.

Fredrickson, David E. 2017. "When Enough Is Never Enough: Philosophers, Poets, Peter, and Paul on Insatiable Desire." Pages 311–30 in *Mixed Feelings and Vexed Passions: Exploring Emotions in Biblical Literature*. Edited by F. Scott Spencer. RBS 90. Atlanta: SBL Press.

Fuchs, Thomas. 2017. "Intercorporeality and Interaffectivity." Pages 3–24 in *Intercorporeality: Emerging Socialities in Interaction*. Edited by Christian Meyer, Jürgen Streeck, and J. Scott Jordan. Oxford: Oxford University Press.

Gregg, Melissa. 2006. *Cultural Studies' Affective Voices*. New York: Palgrave Macmillan.

Halberstam, Judith. 2011. *The Queer Art of Failure*. Durham, NC: Duke University Press.

Hockey, Katherine M. 2017. "The Missing Emotion: The Absence of Anger and the Promotion of Nonretaliation in 1 Peter." Pages 331–53 in

Mixed Feelings and Vexed Passions: Exploring Emotions in Biblical Literature. Edited by F. Scott Spencer. RBS 90. Atlanta: SBL Press.

Inselmann, Anke. 2016. "Emotions and Passions in the New Testament: Methodological Issues." *BibInt* 24.4–5:536–54.

Jensen, Katharine Ann, and Miriam L. Wallace, eds. 2015a. *Emotions. PMLA: Publications of the Modern Language Association of America* 130.5.

———. 2015b. "Introduction—Facing Emotions." *PMLA: Publications of the Modern Language Association of America* 130.5:1249–68.

Konstan, David. 2006. *The Emotions of the Ancient Greeks: Studies in Aristotle and Classical Literature*. Robson Classical Lectures. Toronto: University of Toronto Press.

Koosed, Jennifer L., and Stephen D. Moore. 2014. "Introduction: From Affect to Exegesis." *BibInt* 22.4–5:381–87.

Kotrosits, Maia. 2016. "How Things Feel: Biblical Studies, Affect Theory, and the (Im)personal." *Brill Research Perspectives in Biblical Interpretation* 1:1–53.

Lambert, David A. 2017. "Mourning over Sin/Affliction and the Problem of 'Emotion' as a Category in the Hebrew Bible." Pages 139–60 in *Mixed Feelings and Vexed Passions: Exploring Emotions in Biblical Literature*. Edited by F. Scott Spencer. RBS 90. Atlanta: SBL Press.

Lemmings, David, and Ann Brooks. 2014. "The Emotional Turn in the Humanities and Social Sciences." Pages 3–18 in *Emotions and Social Change: Historical and Sociological Perspectives*. Edited by David Lemmings and Ann Brooks. New York: Routledge.

Massumi, Brian. 2002. *Parables for the Virtual: Movement, Affect, Sensation*. Post-contemporary Interventions. Durham, NC: Duke University Press.

———. *Politics of Affect*. 2015. Cambridge: Polity Press.

McNamer, Sarah. 2007. "Feeling." Pages 241–57 in *Oxford Twenty-First Century Approaches to Literature: Middle English*. Edited by Paul Strohm. Oxford: Oxford University Press.

Mirguet, Françoise. 2016. "What Is an 'Emotion' in the Hebrew Bible? An Experience That Exceeds Most Contemporary Concepts." *BibInt* 24.4–5:442–65.

———. 2017. *An Early History of Compassion: Emotion and Imagination in Hellenistic Judaism*. Cambridge: Cambridge University Press.

Mirguet, Françoise, and Dominika Kurek-Chomycz. 2016. "Introduction: Emotions in Ancient Jewish Literature." *BibInt* 24.4–5:435–41.

Moore, Stephen D. 2017a. *Gospel Jesuses and Other Nonhumans: Biblical Criticism Post-poststructuralism*. SemeiaSt 89. Atlanta: SBL Press.

———. 2017b. "Why the Johannine Jesus Weeps at the Tomb of Lazarus." Pages 287–309 in *Mixed Feelings and Vexed Passions: Exploring Emotions in Biblical Literature*. Edited by F. Scott Spencer. RBS 90. Atlanta: SBL Press.

Moore, Stephen D., and Yvonne Sherwood. 2011. *The Invention of the Biblical Scholar: A Critical Manifesto*. Minneapolis: Fortress.

Ngai, Sianne. 2005. *Ugly Feelings*. Cambridge: Harvard University Press.

Olson, Dennis. 2017. "Emotion, Repentance, and the Question of the 'Inner Life' of Biblical Israelites: A Case Study in Hosea 6:1–3." Pages 161–76 in *Mixed Feelings and Vexed Passions: Exploring Emotions in Biblical Literature*. Edited by F. Scott Spencer. RBS 90. Atlanta: SBL Press.

Pahl, Katrin. 2015. "The Logic of Emotionality." *PMLA: Publications of the Modern Language Association of America* 130.5:1457–66.

Pollmann, Judith. 2017. *Memory in Early Modern Europe, 1500–1800*. Oxford: Oxford University Press.

Riley, Denise. 2005. *Impersonal Passion: Language as Affect*. Durham, NC: Duke University Press.

Ross, Steve. 2008. *Blinded: The Story of Paul the Apostle*. New York: Seabury.

Sedgwick, Eve Kosofsky. 2003. *Touching Feeling: Affect, Pedagogy, Performativity*. Series Q. Durham, NC: Duke University Press.

Seigworth, Gregory J. 2017. "Capaciousness." *Capacious: Journal for Emerging Affect Inquiry* 1.1:i–v.

Seigworth, Gregory J., and Melissa Gregg. 2010. "An Inventory of Shimmers." Pages 1–25 in *The Affect Theory Reader*. Edited by Melissa Gregg and Gregory J. Seigworth. Durham, NC: Duke University Press.

Spencer, F. Scott. 2017a. "Getting a Feel for the 'Mixed' and 'Vexed' Study of Emotions in Biblical Literature." Pages 1–41 in *Mixed Feelings and Vexed Passions: Exploring Emotions in Biblical Literature*. Edited by F. Scott Spencer. RBS 90. Atlanta: SBL Press.

———, ed. 2017b. *Mixed Feelings and Vexed Passions: Exploring Emotions in Biblical Literature*. Edited by F. Scott Spencer. RBS 90. Atlanta: SBL Press.

Staley, Jeffrey L. 1995. *Reading with a Passion: Rhetoric, Autobiography, and the American West in the Gospel of John*. New York: Continuum.

Stewart, Kathleen. 2007. *Ordinary Affects*. Durham, NC: Duke University Press.

Traub, Valerie. 2007. "The Present Future of Lesbian Historiography." Pages 124–45 in *A Companion to Lesbian, Gay, Bisexual, Transgender, and Queer Studies*. Edited by George E. Haggerty and Molly McGarry. Oxford: Blackwell.

Walsham, Alexandra. 2017. "Introduction: Past and ... Presentism." *Past and Present* 234.1:213–17.

Wehrs, Donald R., and Thomas Blake, eds. 2017. *The Palgrave Handbook of Affect Studies and Textual Criticism*. New York: Palgrave Macmillan.

Whitenton, Michael R. 2016. "Feeling the Silence: A Moment-by-Moment Account of Emotions at the End of Mark (16:1–8)." *CBQ* 78:272–89.

Wierzbicka, Anna. 1999. *Emotions across Languages and Cultures: Diversity and Universals*. Cambridge: Cambridge University Press.

Wink, Walter. 2010. *The Bible in Human Transformation: Toward a New Paradigm for Biblical Study*. 2nd ed. Minneapolis: Fortress.

Contributors

Fiona C. Black is Walter B. Cowan Professor of Religious Studies at Mount Allison University in Sackville, NB, Canada. She researches and publishes in a number of different areas: gender, sexuality, and the body in poetic Hebrew Bible texts such as Song of Songs and Psalms; reception history of the Bible; affect and sense criticisms; and postcolonial Caribbean identities and the Bible. She has written widely on the Song of Songs especially and is the author of *The Artifice of Love: Grotesque Bodies and the Song of Songs* (T&T Clark, 2009).

Amy C. Cottrill is the Denson N. Franklin Associate Professor of Religion at Birmingham-Southern College in Birmingham, AL. She is the author of *Language, Power, and Identity in the Lament Psalms of the Individual* (T&T Clark, 2008), as well as numerous articles related to the lament psalms, violence and trauma, and affect theory. She currently serves as the cochair of the Bible and Emotion section of the Society of Biblical Literature.

Jennifer L. Koosed is professor of religious studies at Albright College in Reading, PA. She is the author of *(Per)mutations of Qohelet: Reading the Body in the Book* (Continuum, 2006); *Jesse's Lineage: The Legendary Lives of David, Jesus, and Jesse James* (with Robert Paul Seesengood; Continuum, 2013), *Gleaning Ruth: A Biblical Heroine and Her Afterlives* (University of South Carolina, 2011), and *Reading the Bible as a Feminist* (Brill, 2017). She is the editor of *The Bible and Posthumanism* (SBL Press, 2014) and *Affect Theory and the Bible* (with Stephen D. Moore; thematic issue of *Biblical Interpretation*, 2014).

Joseph A. Marchal is professor of religious studies (and affiliate faculty in women's and gender studies) at Ball State University. Marchal is the author and editor of several works, most recently *The People Beside Paul: The Philippian Assembly and History from Below* (SBL Press, 2015), *Philippians:*

Historical Problems, Hierarchical Visions, Hysterical Anxieties (Sheffield Phoenix, 2017), *Sexual Disorientations: Queer Temporalities, Affects, Theologies* (with Kent L. Brintnall and Stephen D. Moore; Fordham University Press, 2018), *Bodies on the Verge: Queering Pauline Epistles* (SBL Press, 2019), and *Appalling Bodies: Queer Figures before and after Paul's Letters* (Oxford University Press, 2019).

Stephen D. Moore is Edmund S. Janes Professor of New Testament Studies at the Theological School, Drew University. He is author or editor, coauthor or coeditor, of more than two dozen books. His most recent monograph is *Gospel Jesuses and Other Nonhumans: Biblical Criticism Post-poststructuralism* (SBL Press, 2017). With Jennifer L. Koosed, he coedited *Affect Theory and the Bible* (thematic issue of *Biblical Interpretation*, 2014); with Kent L. Brintnall and Joseph A. Marchal he coedited *Sexual Disorientations: Queer Temporalities, Affects, Theologies* (Fordham University Press, 2018); and with Karen Bray he coedited *Religion, Emotion, Sensation: Affect Theories and Theologies* (Fordham University Press, 2019).

Erin Runions is professor in the Department of Religious Studies at Pomona College. She explores how biblical teaching and citation shapes political subjectivity, gender, sexuality, US national sovereignty, and biopolitics. Her most recent book is *The Babylon Complex: Theopolitical Fantasies of War, Sex and Sovereignty* (Fordham University Press, 2014). Her next book will be on the influence of biblical interpretation on the prison industrial complex.

Robert Paul Seesengood (Ph.D., Drew University) is Associate Dean of First-Year and General Education, and professor of religious studies and classics at Albright College in Reading, PA. He is the author and coauthor of several articles and four books, most recently *Philemon: Imagination, Labor and Love* (Bloomsbury, 2017).

Ken Stone is professor of Bible, culture, and hermeneutics at Chicago Theological Seminary. He is the author of several books, including *Reading the Hebrew Bible with Animal Studies* (Stanford University Press, 2017) and *Practicing Safer Texts: Food, Sex, and Bible in Queer Perspective* (T&T Clark, 2005), and coeditor with Teresa Hornsby of *Bible Trouble: Queer Reading at the Boundaries of Biblical Scholarship* (Society of Biblical Literature, 2011).

Jay Twomey is an associate professor of English at the University of Cincinnati. He is the author of *The Pastoral Epistles through the Centuries* (Wiley-Blackwell, 2009) and *2 Corinthians: Crisis and Conflict* (T&T Clark, 2013), as well as numerous essays on the reception of Paul. He coedited the volume *Borges and the Bible* (Sheffield Phoenix, 2015) and edited a special issue of *Postscripts* on messianism in literature, pop culture, and theory (2010).

Ancient Sources Index

Hebrew Bible/Old Testament		Numbers	
		10:36	47
Genesis		11:12	20, 109
12	41		
16:5	19	Deuteronomy	
29:9	28	5:21	27
29:11	28	7:14	30
29:13–14	28		
29:20	28	Judges	
29:30	28	11:35	30
29:31	28		
30:25–30	28	Ruth	
30:32	28	4:16	20
30:37–42	28		
30:43	28	1 Samuel	
31	28	10:10	31
31:41	28	16:11	23, 25
32:14–15	29	16:14–23	31
33:4	29	16:19	23, 25
33:13	29	17:15	23, 25
34	27	17:20	23, 25
34:2	27	17:28	23, 25
34:3	27	17:34-37	23, 25
34:4	27	18:10–11	31
34:16–17	27	19:20–24	31
34:21–23	27	28:24	24
Exodus		2 Samuel	
13:2	30	6:13	31
13:12–13	30	6:14	31
34:19–20	30	6:16	31
20:17	27	6:17–19	31
22:29–30 (Heb 22:28–29)	30	6:20–23	31
		11	15
		11:3	26

2 Samuel (cont.)

11:26	15
11:27	15
12	7, 14–15, 17, 19, 23, 26, 30, 177, 196, 206
12:1–12	15–16
12:2	26
12:3	19–21, 26
12:4	26
12:5	17, 20–21
12:8	19, 26, 29
12:8–11	26
12:11	29
12:14–23	29
12:16–17	16
12:18	16
12:20	16
12:22	17, 29
12:24	17
13	26
13:14	27

1 Kings

3	20
3:20	20
17	110
17:19	20

Psalms

22	78–79, 87
22:10	84
22:13–14	87
22:14	84
22:15	87
22:16	87
22:17	78, 87
22:17–18	87
22:18	87
22:21–22	87
31	78
88	78, 79
90–100	77
91	71, 77, 80, 90
91:1	91
91:5–6	77, 79
93 (92)	31
102	79
102:3	84
102:4	84
102:8	77, 182
109	8, 56, 62–64, 66–67, 179–80, 194
109:1	56
109:1–2	64
109:6–20	65
109:8	65
109:12	56
109:13	65
109:21	64
109:21–31	65
109:22	65
109:23	56
109:24	65
109:26	64
132	47
137	82–83, 85, 88, 91, 182
137:1–2	84
137:2	86
137:5–6	83
137:9	91

Proverbs

3:17	48
3:18	48

Isaiah

6:9–10	110
29:11–12	110

Jeremiah

12–20	109
20:7	110

Lamentations

1–3	52
2	20
2:12	20
2:20–21	46
3	52, 183
3:1	44
3:2–3	44

3:4	44	New Testament	
3:8	44		
3:13	44	Matthew	
3:14	44	9:37	143
3:16	44	27:46	87
3:21–23	44		
3:23	44	Mark	
5	52, 183	15:34	87
5:20–22	49		
5:21	49, 50	Luke	
		10:2	143
Ezekiel			
2:7	110	John	
		4:35	143
Daniel			
6:27 (Eng 6:26)	45	Acts of the Apostles	
		16:3	169
Jonah		16:16	164
1	101		
1–2	97	Romans	
1:12	97	1	126–27, 179
1:12–16	109	1:1	143
2	97	1:18–31	127
3	97, 102, 107	1:18–32	125
3–4	107	1:19–23	127
3:4	99, 102	1:21	126
3:5–9	99	1:24–27	126
3:7–8	97	1:26	200
3:10	97	1:27	131
4	97, 99, 105, 108–9	1:29–31	126
4:5	99, 101	1:32	126
4:6	99, 102	2:1	127
4:7	99	2:1–6	127
4:7–11	99	6:15–20	143
4:8	99	6:17–22	125
4:9–11	107	7	127–28, 130–31
4:11	99	7:5	128, 132
		7:7	127–28
Apocryphal/Deuterocanonical Books		7:7–25	127
		7:9	128
Ben Sira		7:15	128
24	48	7:15–20	132
		7:15–25	158
		7:18–19	128
		7:20	128

Romans (cont.)
7:23	128, 132
14:25–27	144
16:1–16	132
16:3–5	133

1 Corinthians
2–4	161
3:6–8	143
4:13	161
4:21	161
5	126
5:1	125
5:6–8	125
5:11	125
6	126
6:11	125
6:12–18	125
6:15–20	115
6:20	143, 150
7	142
7:23	143
9:9–11	142
11:1	157
13	145
13:9	157
13:11	168
14:18	169
16:1–4	144

2 Corinthians
2	145
8–9	144
9:7	144
10	145
12	160–61
12:19	161
13:7	157
13:10	161

Galatians
1	145
2:10	144
2:15	125
3:23	125
4	145
4:3	125
5:12	169
8–11	125

Ephesians
6:5	144
6:6	144
6:7	144
6:8	144

Philippians
4:3	143
4:15–19	144

Colossians
3:5	200
3:22	143
3:24	144
4:1	144

1 Thessalonians
4:5	200
4:11–12	141
4:13	164
5:14	142

2 Thessalonians
3:6–12	142
3:11	142

Philemon
7	145
9	145
11	145
14	145
21	145
24	143

1 Peter
2:11–12	145
2:18	145
2:19	145
2:20–21	145

2 Peter
    3:14–16   145

Revelation
    13:17   150

Greco-Roman Literature

Aristotle, *Nicomachean Ethics*   104

Cicero, *Orations*   143

Virgil, *Georgics*   143

Modern Authors Index

Ahmed, Sara   2–3, 8–10, 15, 17–19, 24, 26–31, 51, 53, 58, 67, 78–81, 85–88, 91–92, 96–111, 114–22, 132, 134–35, 147, 154, 162, 170, 176–79, 181–82, 184, 188–89, 195–99, 205–7
Agamben, Gorgio   141
Ahn, John   82, 92
Amador, J. David Hester   124, 135
Anderson, A. A.   74, 92
Anderson, M.T.   149, 154
Armstrong, Philip   26, 31
Atkinson, Meera   187, 196, 207
Austern, Linda Phyllis   60, 67
Avalos, Hector   143, 154
Bar-Efrat, Shimon   17, 31
Bataille, George   127
Beal, Lissa Wray   60, 68
Bechtel, Lyn   27, 31
Benjamin, Walter   151–54, 180–81 , 205
Berlant, Lauren   9–10, 102, 111, 161–62, 170, 176, 178–81, 184, 188–89, 206–7
Betz, Hans Dieter   124, 135
Biles, Jeremy   127, 135
Black, Fiona C.   6, 10, 74, 76, 78, 90, 92, 182, 184
Blake, Thomas   190, 211
Blanton, Ward   130, 135
Boase, Elizabeth   38–39, 42, 52–53
Boer, Roland   23, 26, 31
Boler, Megan   197, 207
Borowski, Oded   23–24, 32
Bourdieu, Pierre   103, 111
Bosworth, David   82, 92
Bray, Karen   6, 10, 188, 207
Breed, Brennan   90–92
Brennan, Teresa   2–3, 10, 74, 77, 92, 188, 195, 207
Brinkema, Eugenie   8, 10, 114–24, 127, 132, 135, 188–89, 199, 205–6, 208
Brintnall, Kent L.   6, 10, 127, 135, 176, 184
Brooks, Ann   198, 209
Brooten, Bernadette J.   126, 135
Brown, Raymond E.   141, 154
Broyles, Craig   71, 78, 92
Brueggemann, Walter   81, 92
Burrus, Virginia   5, 10, 134–35
Butler, Judith   111, 121–22, 135–36
Byron, John   143, 154
Calarco, Matthew   14, 32
Callahan, Allen D.   143, 154
Carr, David   38, 53
Certeau, Michel de   76, 92
Castelli, Elizabeth   157–58, 170, 181, 184
Chen, Mel   176, 184
Cheng, Anlin   176, 184
Cherlin, Andrew J.   151, 154
Chez, Keridiana   14, 32
Chow, Rey   178, 184
Christenson, Randall   72, 92
Claassens, L. Juliana   198, 208
Clough, Patricia Tincineto   197, 208
Clutton-Brock, Juliet   23, 25–26, 32
Coats, George W.   20, 32
Cottrill, Amy C.   56–57, 60, 62–63, 65, 68
Colman, Felicity J.   4, 10
Craigie, Peter C.   95, 111
Croft, Stephen L.   73, 92
Culley, Robert C.   71, 74–75, 78, 93

Cvetkovich, Ann   3, 7–10, 38–39, 41–42, 50, 52–53, 71–77, 80, 82–84, 86, 88, 90–93, 165, 171, 176, 181–84, 188–89, 197, 199, 206, 208
D'Arcens, Louise   203, 208
Davis, Simon J. M.   25, 32
Deleuze, Gilles   3–5, 10, 149–50, 154, 188–89, 192, 194, 197, 199
Derrida, Jacques   19, 32, 118, 136
Dinkler, Michal Beth   193, 198, 208
Dinshaw, Carolyn   178, 184
Duhm, Bernard   102, 112
Düring, Bleda   25–26, 34
Eastman, Susan   128, 136
Edelman, Lee   159
Eisenbaum, Pamela   128–29, 136
Elbogen, Ismar   41, 53
Eng, David   176, 184
Fantia, Joseph D.   143, 154
Fee, Gordon D.   142, 154
Ferguson, Roderick   176, 185
Ferris, David   152, 155
Fewell, Danna Nolan   19, 32
Figart, Deborah M.   147, 156
Fish, Stanley E.   61, 68, 192–93, 208
Fisher, Nick   124, 136
Fowler, Robert M.   193, 208
Frank, Adam   3–5, 12, 146, 155
Franklin, Sarah   26, 32
Franko, Mark   62, 68
Frechette, Christopher G.   39, 42, 53
Fredrickson, David E.   202, 208
Frolov, Serge   95, 112
Freud, Sigmund   108, 112
Fuchs, Thomas   206, 208
Gaventa, Beverly Roberts   128, 136
Geertz, Clifford   146
Glancy, Jennifer A.   143, 155, 180, 185
Goodall, Jane   14, 32
Gooder, Paula   160–61, 171
Goodrich, John K.   143, 155
Gottwald, Norman K.   95, 112
Grau, Marion   150, 155
Graybill, Rhiannon   102, 112, 161, 171, 178, 185

Greenberg, Gary   73, 93
Gregg, Melissa   2–5, 12, 20, 35, 57–58, 69, 84, 94, 115, 139, 145, 155, 188–89, 192, 202, 208, 210
Gross, Aaron   14, 32
Guattari, Félix   3–5, 10, 149, 154
Gunkel, Hermann   25, 32, 71, 74, 93
Gunn, David M.   19, 32
Guthrie, Stewart   14, 32
Halberstam, Judith [Jack]   9, 11, 159–61, 165, 171, 176, 181, 185, 206, 208
Halperin, David   134, 136
Halpern, Baruch   25, 33
Han, Shinee   176, 184
Haraway, Donna   22–23, 25, 33, 176, 185
Harrod, James B.   14, 33
Hartman, Midori E.   125, 136
Haverkamp, Heidi   158, 171
Hesse, Brian   23, 25, 33, 36
Hochschild, Arlie Russell   146–48, 151, 155
Hockey, Katherine M.   202, 208–9
Horn, Dara   37, 53
Hornsby, Teresa J.   127, 136
Horsley, Richard A.   143, 154
Inselmann, Anke   201, 202–3, 209
Ipsen, Avaren   115, 136
Ivarsson, Fredrik   124–25, 136
Jensen, Katharine Ann   195, 199, 209
Jewett, Robert   128, 136
Johnson, Mark   58, 68
Johnson-Debaufre, Melanie   126, 137
Kahl, Brigitte   130, 137
Kaltner, John   102, 112
Kazantzakis, Nikos   157, 171
Keck, Leander   127, 137
Kelley, William Melvin   158–59, 161–62, 171
Kelly, Daniel R.   114, 116, 122, 137
King, Martin Luther, Jr.   157–59, 171, 205
King, Philip J.   23–24, 33
Knight, George A. F.   74, 93
Knust, Jennifer Wright   57, 68, 124, 137
Koenig, Sara   26, 33

Konstan, David 199, 209
Koosed, Jennifer L. 1, 3, 5–7, 11, 15, 33, 39, 53, 57–58, 61, 68, 145, 155, 176, 183, 185, 188, 191–92, 209
Korsmeyer, Carolyn 116, 137
Kotrosits, Maia 3–6, 11, 15, 33, 39–40, 53, 57–58, 62, 68, 116, 130, 137, 145, 155, 176, 182, 185, 194–95, 209
Kunnie, Julian E. 151, 155
Kurek-Chomycz, Dominika 198–99, 204, 209
Lacan, Jacques 130
Lakoff, George 58, 68
Lambert, David 200, 202, 209
Landy, Francis 6, 11
Langer, Ruth 48–50, 54
Lateiner, Donald 114, 116, 137
Lasine, Stuart 17, 20–22, 33
Lemmings, David 198, 209
Levenson, Jon D. 30, 34
Liew, Tat-siong Benny 130, 137
Lindström, Fredrik 86, 93
Locke, John 98, 178
Lohfink, Norbert 102, 112
Lopez, Davina C. 130, 137
Lorde, Audre 101, 112
Love, Heather 176, 183, 185
MacDonald, Nathan 23, 34
McCabe, Earl 170–71
McCarter, P. Kyle, Jr. 19, 34
McKay, Megan 78, 93
McKenzie, Steven L. 102, 112
McNamer, Sarah 8, 11, 61–62, 68, 192–94, 209
Malherbe, Abraham J. 141, 155
Marchal, Joseph A. 6, 10, 115, 125–27, 137–38, 144–45, 155, 176, 178–80, 184–85
Martin, Dale B. 126, 138
Marx, Dalia 52, 54
Massumi, Brian 3, 8, 11, 59, 68, 131, 138, 160, 171, 188–89, 192, 194, 197–200, 209
Matthews, Shelly 125, 138
Menninghaus, Winfried 117, 127, 138

Miller, Patrick D. 71, 75, 78, 93
Miller, William Ian 118, 121–22, 138
Mirguet, Françoise 198–200, 204, 209
Mitchell, Margaret M. 161, 171
Moore, Stephen D. 1, 3, 5–7, 10–11, 15, 33–34, 39, 53, 57–58, 61, 68–69, 115–16, 138, 145, 155, 176, 183–85, 187–88, 191–92, 198, 207, 209–10
Morey, Darcy F. 25, 34
Mowinckel, Sigmund 74, 93
Muñoz, José Esteban 159, 171
Murphy-O'Connor, Jerome 161, 171
Nasrallah, Laura S. 126, 138
Nasuti, Harry P. 74, 93
Newsom, Carol 60, 69
Ngai, Sianne 8, 11, 95, 112, 114–15, 118, 121–22, 132, 138, 176, 185, 188–89, 205–6, 210
Nietzsche, Friedrich 101, 112
Olbricht, Thomas 114, 124, 138
Olson, Dennis 202, 210
Pahl, Katrin 197, 210
Pasolini, Pier Paola 162, 171
Patterson, Orlando 150, 155
Paul, Elizabeth 21, 35
Piketty, Thomas 147, 155
Pollmann, Judith 202, 210
Prince, Catheryn J. 42, 54
Prinsloo, Gert T. M. 100–101, 112
Puar, Jasbir 106, 112, 176, 185
Rauhala, Marika 124, 138
Richards, Annette 62, 68
Riley, Denise 8, 11, 59–60, 69, 78, 80–81, 91, 93, 176, 185, 188–89, 206, 210
Rosca, Ninotchka 159, 171
Ross, Steve 9, 162–67, 168–71, 181, 206, 210
Rowell, Thelma 25, 34
Rowell, C. A. 25, 34
Rowell, T. E. 25, 34
Rubin, Gayle 26, 29, 34, 50, 132, 133, 138
Rudy, Kathy 22, 34

Modern Authors Index

Runions, Erin 5, 12, 15, 34, 57, 69, 90, 93–94, 115, 131, 133, 138, 151, 155, 180–81, 186
Russell, Nerissa 25–26, 34
Saramago, José 157, 171
Sasson, Aharon 23, 34
Schaefer, Donovan 3–4, 7, 12–15, 19, 28–31, 34, 146, 155, 176–77, 186
Schipper, Jeremy 17, 20, 35
Schonfield, Jeremy 40–43, 45, 47, 49, 52, 54
Schüssler Fiorenza, Elisabeth 114, 120, 139
Schwartz, Regina M. 26, 35
Sedgwick, Eve Kosofsky 3–5, 12–13, 35, 146, 155, 176, 186, 188–89, 210
Seesengood, Robert Paul 141, 156, 180, 186
Seigworth, Gregory J. 2–5, 12, 20, 35, 57–58, 69, 84, 94, 115, 139, 145, 149–50, 155–56, 181, 186, 188–90, 192, 210
Serpell, James A. 21–22, 35
Shantz, Colleen 6, 12, 114, 125, 128, 139
Sherwood, Yvonne M. 95, 112, 191, 210
Singer, Simeon 51, 54
Smith, Abraham 143, 154
Snediker, Michael D. 12–13, 35
Spatharas, Dimos 114, 116, 124, 137, 139
Spencer, F. Scott 6, 12, 188, 198, 200, 202, 210
Spinoza, Benedict 57, 69
Stager, Lawrence E. 23–25, 33, 35
Staley, Jeffrey 194, 210
Stavrakopoulou, Francesca 30, 35
Steinberg, Ronnie J. 147, 156
Stendahl, Krister 129, 139
Stewart, Kathleen 2, 12, 83–85, 94, 176, 186, 189, 206, 211
Still, Todd D. 142, 156
Stone, Ken 14–15, 19, 23, 26, 30, 35, 177, 186
Stowers, Stanley K. 126, 128, 139
Sumney, Jerry L. 114, 138
Swancutt, Diana M. 127, 139

Tate, Marvin E. 77, 94
Taussig, Hal 6, 11
Tchernov, Eitan 25, 35
Tomkins, Silvan 3–5, 146, 156, 188–89
Townsley, Gillian 125, 139
Traub, Valerie 134, 136, 203, 211
Trill, Suzanne 60, 69
Tuan, Yi-Fu 30–31, 36
Tully, William 170
Twomey, Jay 181, 186
Valla, François R. 25, 32, 35
Vasquez, Manuel A. 13, 36
Vidal, Gore 169, 171
Villanueva, F. 74, 94
Wallace, Miriam L. 195, 199, 209
Wallace, Raenita 158–59, 171
Waller, Alexis G. 57, 69
Walsham, Alexandra 204, 211
Walters, Jonathan 126, 139
Wapnish, Paula 23, 25, 33, 36
Watters, Ethan 73, 89–90, 94
Weber, Max 148, 150, 153, 156, 181, 186
Wehrs, Donald R. 190, 211
Weiser, Artur 77, 94
Wesselius, J. W. 26, 36
Whitenton, Michael R. 193, 211
Wierzbicka, Anna 199, 211
Williamson, H. G. M. 74–75, 94
Wilson, Elizabeth 73, 82, 94
Wink, Walter 191, 211
Winckler, H. 102, 112
Wise, J. Macgregor 150, 156
Yassin-Kassab, Robin 158, 172
Youngblood, Kevin J. 107, 112
Zeder, Melinda 23, 36

www.ingramcontent.com/pod-product-compliance
Lightning Source LLC
Chambersburg PA
CBHW030825230426
43667CB00008B/1386